D0179857

HOLLYWOOD
TALKS TURKEY

HOLLYWOOD
TALKS TURKEY
The Screen's Greatest Flops

Doug McClelland

Faber and Faber   Boston and London

All rights reserved under International and Pan-American Copyright conventions, including the right of reproduction in whole or in part in any form. Published in the United States by Faber and Faber, Inc., 50 Cross Street, Winchester, MA 01890 and in Great Britain by Faber and Faber, Ltd., 3 Queen Square, London WC1N 3AU.

Cover Photo: Lucille Ball and Desi Arnaz in *Forever Darling* (1956)

Copyright © 1989 by Doug McClelland

Library of Congress Cataloging-in-Publication Data
McClelland, Doug.
    Hollywood talks turkey : the screen's greatest flops / by Doug McClelland.
        p.   cm.
    ISBN 0-571-12901-3 : $14.95
    1. Motion pictures—California—Los Angeles—History.   I. Title.
PN1993.5.U65M38   1990
791.43′0979494—dc20   89-48363
                                                              CIP

Cover design by Nancy Dutting
Printed in the United States of America

Books by Doug McClelland

THE UNKINDEST CUTS
The Scissors and the Cinema

SUSAN HAYWARD
The Divine Bitch

DOWN THE YELLOW BRICK ROAD:
The Making of The Wizard of Oz

THE GOLDEN AGE OF "B" MOVIES

HOLLYWOOD ON RONALD REAGAN
Friends and Enemies Discuss Our President, The Actor

HOLLYWOOD ON HOLLYWOOD
Tinsel Town Talks

STARSPEAK
Hollywood on Everything

BLACKFACE TO BLACKLIST:
Al Jolson, Larry Parks and "The Jolson Story"

ELEANOR PARKER:
Woman of a Thousand Faces

Contents

Introduction

"If people won't go to the boxoffice, you can't stop 'em."

Thus spake legendary Hollywood producer (and even more legendary language mangler) Samuel Goldwyn, who, like almost everyone else in the movie business, knew from flops.

In Hollywood, a film can be hailed by critics as a masterpiece, but if it doesn't "have legs"—read: make money—it is written off as a failure. These are the films dealt with in this book. The flops . . . bombs . . . lemons . . . disasters . . . duds . . . turkeys. Many rotten films have still gone on to turn a profit, sometimes very handsome ones. *Hollywood Talks Turkey* is not concerned with such films. It deals only with productions—good, bad and indifferent —that failed at the boxoffice, which is the only kind of turkey the Southern California film factories have ever recognized. And, by way of exclusive interviews and existing comments collected here, the saga of Tinsel Town turkeys is presented in the words of Hollywood itself. The roll call includes stars, supporting players, directors, studio heads, producers, writers, cameramen, composers, choreographers, costume designers and publicity people, going as far back as the ingénue Lillian Gish and as far forward as Kevin Costner.

If anyone should wonder *why* such a book, the answer is—why not? Failures have played a prominent role in the history of Hollywood, a city whose primary export, celluloid, has enriched, entertained and even educated the world for decades. There is heartbreak and drama in the personal recollections of these turkeys, but more often than not there is the heightened humor of the professional entertainer who belongs to a resilient and prevailing citizenry.

In addition, a turkey has often simply been more fun to discuss—read: tear apart—than a hit (unless, of course, one happened to have worked in or on it). Certainly the worst of turkeys has always brought out the best in critics: they traditionally have been able to wax far more eloquent when panning a film than when praising one. Reviewer Judith Crist was made when her 1963 critique of Elizabeth Taylor's most notorious, $34,000,000 vehicle appeared in the *New York Herald Tribune*. Its classic headline: "*Cleopatra* a Monumental Mouse." How many reviews of films that won Academy Awards stay in the memory?

Perhaps some explanation concerning the word "turkey" is in order. Research has provided three main reasons for the use of "turkey" to label a show business failure. One source claims that it fell into usage after some long-forgotten Broadway play opened and closed on the same Thanksgiving Day. Another proffers that a wealthy if improvident stage producer (likewise lost to the decades), who was determined to have his show seen despite poor reviews and attendance, began giving free performances of his production on Thanksgiving.

Yet another more obvious reason for the word's double meaning is that the bird's physical unattractiveness and premature demise on Thanksgiving caused it to become synonymous with an ill-fated show business venture. Could one have called *Heaven's Gate* a swan?

Whatever the actual derivation, Hollywood discovered the meaning of turkey very early. In the bustling second decade of this century, as silent films were gaining public acceptance and the techniques of filmmaking were being invented, the most resounding flop was a film called *Intolerance*, produced and directed by "the father of film," D. W. Griffith. A complicated spectacle, its failure at the boxoffice just about broke Griffith's heart—and pocketbook. (Much later, it was recognized as a masterwork of moviemaking.)

The 1920s brought a woolly golden age of Hollywood creativity. Although films were still silent, cinematography in particular had reached a level of exquisite sophistication, bestowing an artistic patina on even the most banal of plots and exaggerated pantomime. Movie stars (a designation coined in the previous decade) had grown increasingly popular, and probably the most beloved of all female stars then was "America's Sweetheart," Mary Pickford. But when she attempted to change her girlish image and play more worldly roles, as in *Rosita*, even she could experience the disinterest of the movie-going populace. Another Hollywood actress, the struggling Louise Brooks, went to Germany to shoot a silent called *Pandora's Box*, but by the time it opened in America a revolution had occurred that rendered it obsolete (until another era when, like *Intolerance*, it was lauded by film historians).

In 1927, Warner Brothers' *The Jazz Singer*, starring Al Jolson, ushered in the talking picture, and movies went on to reach their true potential, combining the visual element with sound—the sound of music, the sound of dialogue, the sound of coins in tills.

Garbo talked in 1930's *Anna Christie*; so did money. Despite the Depression (or maybe because of it), people flocked to movies in greater number than ever before, and somehow the stars seemed more glittering than in previous decades, too. Ginger Rogers and Fred Astaire whirled, Clark Gable and Joan Crawford clinched, William Powell and Myrna Loy sleuthed, Jeanette MacDonald and Nelson Eddy duetted, Claudette Colbert and Cary Grant charmed (oddly, never together), Irene Dunne frolicked, Shirley Temple effervesced, Ronald Colman spoke, Paul Muni emoted, Bette Davis suffered, Gary Cooper "yepped" and James Cagney did everything.

The loyalty of fans then notwithstanding, even these luminaries could come a cropper once in a while. For instance, all his life Gable bore the onus of the biographical turkey called *Parnell*, while almost from her deathbed Joan Crawford was still disowning *Ice Follies of 1939*.

And the 1940s commenced with Shirley Temple's expensive, career-damaging failure, *The Blue Bird*. Still, the forties became the movies' last great decade, though one of tremendous change. World War II began in 1941, and for the next four years the film capital was dedicated as never before to turning out glossy, escapist entertainments frequently with musical stars Judy Garland, maturing into one of the screen's most dazzling talents, and Betty Grable, "The Queen of Technicolor." Everyone went to the movies—Grandma, Grandpa, Mom, Dad (if he wasn't wearing khaki) and the kids. And almost everything made money. The big exception was the mammoth 20th Century-Fox biography of our 28th President titled *Wilson*, studio chief Darryl F. Zanuck's labor of love and lucre that became the costliest boxoffice failure of the war years.

After the war, Hollywood product turned more serious and socially conscious. Releases that didn't spotlight modern, timely themes usually got short shrift, and several productions today recognized as classics, such as James Stewart's Christmassy *It's a Wonderful Life*, Orson Welles' melodramatic *The Lady from Shanghai* and Joan Fontaine's *Letter from an Unknown Woman*, were little seen then. *That Hagen Girl*, incongruously pairing ex-serviceman Ronald Reagan and a teenage Shirley Temple, had a particularly quick death at the boxoffice; but even the male lead's later illustrious change of occupation couldn't resuscitate this one for re-evaluation.

Furthermore, by the late forties politics was rearing its controversial head on the film front, and it was said that Charlie Chaplin's unpopular statements in that area foredoomed what would still become his favorite vehicle, *Monsieur Verdoux*.

As if more problems were needed, the studios were forced by the government to relinquish their ownership of movie theaters, while that new menace, television, was keeping picture patrons home in alarming numbers.

As the 1950s began, the film companies realized something had to be done quickly to draw audiences back into theaters. Marilyn Monroe and teen alienation themes helped, as did CinemaScope, VistaVision, Todd-AO and other wide screen gimmicks that nevertheless were best suited, as heretical cinematographer Joseph Ruttenberg pointed out, to photographing snakes.

Withal, boxoffice turkeys continued to taint the Hollywood bill of fare —*The Red Badge of Courage, Sincerely Yours, The Prodigal, The Spirit of St. Louis, Saint Joan, A Farewell to Arms* and *The Story of Mankind*, among many losers. Lucille Ball and Desi Arnaz, at their peaks on fifties television, hoped the millions of *I Love Lucy* fans would turn out for their theater feature, *Forever Darling*. Viewers preferred to watch them on TV. It proved an irreversible trend: the fifties saw about one third of the nation's movie theaters shut down.

During the sixties, intermissions were effected to make the decade's desperately overinflated spectacles seem special, but they only made them more of a trial. Notable celluloid catastrophes then were Marlon Brando's *Mutiny on the Bounty*, Elizabeth Taylor's *Cleopatra*, Julie Andrews' *Star!*, Peter O'Toole's *Goodbye, Mr. Chips* and Barbra Streisand's *Hello, Dolly!* My personal memories of this epoch at the movies are mainly of walking out on almost everything, or at least not returning after the intermission.

Ever in pursuit of innovation, in the seventies Hollywood did away with intermissions but still the lavish bombs were whistling toward their ever-dwindling targets, the nation's theaters. They fell in perhaps greater blitzkrieg than ever before—*Darling Lili, Man of La Mancha, Lost Horizon, Mame, At Long Last Love, Won Ton Ton, The Dog Who Saved Hollywood, The Blue Bird, Gable and Lombard, New York New York, The Wiz, 1941*, etc.

The 1980s saw its share of flops, too, and although it hardly seemed possible, film budgets continued to escalate. Things began with a whimper: the extravagant *Heaven's Gate*, the failure of which caused the sale of United Artists to Metro-Goldwyn-Mayer. The cortège was soon joined by *Pennies from Heaven, The Razor's Edge, The Cotton Club, Howard the Duck, A Chorus Line, Leonard Part 6* and maybe the most notorious gobbler of all, *Ishtar*, starring Warren Beatty and Dustin Hoffman, a multi-million-dollar indulgence whose title has become practically synonymous with turkey. By now, as admission prices scaled new peaks, the moviegoing public had pretty much been whittled down to teenagers and very young adults. Older people were content to stay home and watch television and (after they had figured out how to work it) that new technological sensation, the VCR. In a recent trend, some theater duds like the decade's *Harry and the Hendersons* were going on to enjoy a modicum of success on home video.

Since a number of earlier films that failed in their time earned acclaim when the smog cleared, perhaps even *Ishtar* stands a chance of being recognized someday as a comedy classic. For the time being, though, when Dustin Hoffman says of that fiasco, "I like the movie," he stands more alone than the executive who first enthused, "We'll star Liberace, give him two beautiful girlfriends and call the picture *Sincerely Yours*."

◻

Hollywood Talks Turkey has not been an easy book to do. If there is anything Hollywood hates almost as much as having flop pictures, it's talking about them. I found this out when I started approaching denizens of movieland for this book on flop movies through the decades.

Many of the more realistic, down-to-earth film people responded positively to my requests for interviews or comments. A real coup was getting the alluringly graceful but elusive Lucille Bremer, in my opinion Fred Astaire's finest post-Ginger Rogers dancing partner in the forties films *Ziegfeld Follies* and the lush turkey *Yolanda and the Thief.* This may have been Miss Bremer's first interview since her retirement four decades ago. In probably his last interview, dashing 1940s–50s leading man Cornel Wilde talked to me about his spectacular flop *Forever Amber* on, I learned later, the eve of his hospitalization for leukemia. He died a few weeks later on October 16, 1989. Over the phone, it became obvious that he was not the young athlete anymore, but he never mentioned being ill nor did he give any indication that his time was running out so rapidly.

Some prospective interviewees, however, backed off; some tried to.

One wide-eyed female star from the forties and fifties who appeared in almost 50 films but had only two real hits, said, "But I can't think of any flops I've been in." I refreshed her memory and got the interview.

A comic actor from the same period told me he had never been in "a money loser," then proceeded to tell me the story behind a film that was one of the bigger bombs of the early fifties.

Of course, the spring, summer and fall of 1989 were not the best of times for a stranger—even one with nine published books—to approach the Hollywood elite. Tabloid headlines were at their most lurid. Stab victim actress Theresa Saldana was crusading to keep her assailant in prison. An intruder on the *Dallas* television lot killed himself. A man showed up at Universal Studios allegedly to kill actor Michael Landon. A woman sent five thousand menacing letters to actor Michael J. Fox. A fan threatened singer Tiffany while two others stalked actresses Justine Bateman and Kelly LeBrock. A woman was regularly arrested for breaking into TV star David Letterman's home. A confessed ax killer threatened 50 Hollywood actresses. A fan shot and killed actress Rebecca Schaeffer.

Shortly after Miss Schaeffer's death, her former television co-star Pam Dawber was asked if she was now more careful about fans. Her answer: "Of course. We don't open any mail that comes to our house that we don't recognize."

Clearly, it was not a period in which film folks were very interested in talking to people they didn't know—and about flops, yet.

When the veteran actor Don Ameche, famous for inventing the telephone in the non-flop, *The Story of Alexander Graham Bell*, was appearing in an off-Broadway play, I wrote him requesting an interview for the book. A couple of weeks later, my self-addressed, stamped envelope returned. I opened it —and out fell a lined index card with "Don Ameche" hand-written on it. Nothing else. He had sent me his autograph! Instead of writing, maybe I should have called him on "the Ameche," as the phone was once known.

On to Madeline Kahn, whom I wanted to interview about her fabled (if by no means final) flop, *At Long Last Love*. Squeezed in at the bottom of my very warm and complimentary letter to her, in her own scrawl, were the words "I never discuss failure. End of topic. M. Kahn." So much for the actress whose fame has been predicated on a noteworthy sense of humor.

Next, the legendary Ginger Rogers, whom I wrote at her ranch in Oregon specifying the subject on which I hoped she would discourse. Practically by return mail I received a sizeable packet of literature from Miss Rogers' secretary including a form letter bestowing blessings on me for being Miss Rogers' "fan"; a card offering Ginger Rogers photos for sale, with prices; a biographical sketch of the star and a listing of her films. There was no reply to my request to Miss Rogers for information on her *The First Traveling Saleslady*, a calamitous flop.

My favorite "turndown(s)", however, came from Jeanne Crain.

I had interviewed this today inactive but once major star a few years ago for my book *Hollywood on Hollywood*, finding her not only thoroughly cooperative but as charming as I had remembered from forties films. Now, I hoped to talk about a rare turkey from her heyday, *The Fan*.

The first time I phoned her home and asked for Jeanne Crain, I immediately recognized the voice at the other end as hers. And except for her husband, ex-actor Paul Brinkman, father of her seven children, who would know better than I? My constant VCR showings of Miss Crain's enchantingly cheerful 1945 musical, *State Fair*, have driven family, friends and even felines from my house.

"Oh, this is the maid," an indisputable, dulcet-toned Jeanne Crain fibbed to me. "They're all traveling now."

Very strange.

Remembering what a delightful chat we had had for my earlier book, several weeks later I called again. I got the same "maid," obviously still Miss Crain: "Oh, they're in Europe now." The title of an old Rex Reed book about Hollywood kept spinning in my mind: *People Are Crazy Here*.

I was mystified (Miss Crain had been so pleasant and talkative during our previous interview) but determined. Hadn't I grown up seeing several versions of the old Hecht-MacArthur play *The Front Page*? Not for nothing had I once been a reporter on a daily newspaper myself. "Get the story!" was the fourth estate's battle cry in those years; maybe it still is.

A month and a half later, I embarked on a different ploy: I wrote her a letter, explaining that I was the author she had given an interview for *Hollywood on Hollywood* and stated specifically what I wanted this time. I said I would phone the following week, and did. This time, I decided that immediately I heard her voice I would launch into my appeal, without asking for Jeanne Crain—which could give her "maid" a chance to say she wasn't there. Well, she was ready for me. When I quickly said, "Hello-Miss Crain-this-is-Doug McClelland-would-you-have-a-few-minutes-this-afternoon-to-talk-about-*The Fan*?", she answered in her slow-sweet, almost musical manner, "Oh, no, I wouldn't. I'm leaving for Europe tomorrow and must pack. I really don't know what to say." Say goodnight, Jeannie. Three strikes and I was out.

Jeanne Crain, the demure, beautiful sweetheart of *State Fair*, *Margie*, *Pinky* and the dreaded *The Fan*, had outplayed me.

But as I've said, there were many other brave souls who did consent to interviews or provide comments. Some I saw in person, others I queried via phone or mail. I enlisted friends, too, in my often needle-in-the-haystack search for extant quotations on flops—my entreaty: "When you think of failure, think of me."

My deepest thanks to:

Alice Backes
Anne Baxter
John Beal
Eddie Bracken
Lucille Bremer
Macdonald Carey
Janis Carter
Marge Champion
Marguerite Chapman
Nancy Coleman
Jane Connell
Gloria De Haven
Olivia de Havilland
Myrna Dell
Philip Dunne
Charlie Earle
Hector Elizondo
Fritz Feld
Geraldine Fitzgerald
Joan Fontaine
Sally Forrest
Robert Getchell
Coleen Gray
Kathryn Grayson
Jane Greer
Margaret Hamilton

Julie Harris
Rose Hobart
Marsha Hunt
DeForest Kelley
Larry Kert
Barbara Lawrence
Francis Lederer
Joan Leslie
John Lithgow
Joshua Logan
Stephen Longstreet
William Ludwig
Steve Martin
Marilyn Maxwell
Virginia Mayo
Regis Philbin
Cesar Romero
Natalie Schafer
Martha Scott
George Sidney
Frances Sternhagen
Elaine Stritch
Eli Wallach
Ruth Warrick
Cornel Wilde
Marie Windsor

I am especially grateful to Richard Lacey.

Thanks, also, to Patrick Agan, Robert Beck, Ralph Benner, Colin Briggs,

John Cocchi, Jim Connor, Tom Cooper, Kirk Crivello, Maeve Druesne, Eddie Brandt's Saturday Matinée, George Eells, Audrey Fecht, Davind Finkle, Lee Graham, Boze Hadleigh, Ron Harvey, Richard Hegedorn, Jim Jeneji, Jerry Ohlinger's Movie Material Store, Richard Lamparski, Larry Edmunds Book Shop, Leonard Maltin, Dick McInness, Jim Meyer, Eduardo Moreno, Movie Star News, New York Public Library Performing Arts Research Center, Eleanor O'Sullivan, Laura Kay Palmer, James Robert Parish, Lawrence J. Quirk, Tom Stempel, Jorge Tablada and Lou Valentino.

Doug McClelland
Fall, 1989

Flop "Firsts"

"I should have been given the award for
'Worst Performance Ever Given in Movies by an Actress.'"

TALLULAH BANKHEAD:

Thunder Below was my first Hollywood film. It was directed by Richard Wallace, whom we called "Pops." He had once operated a merry-go-round in a carnival; in his youth had been a medical student, later an undertaker's assistant. He was fascinated by cadavers. Once, after a trying day at the studio, he took me to a morgue. Pointing out the departed on the cool slabs, he said: "Tallulah, this should cheer you up. See how peaceful they are?" He was a divine man. For all Wallace's divinity, for all my vitality, *Thunder Below* was a double-jointed dud, maudlin and messy.

❑

EDDIE BRACKEN:

The main reason why audiences rejected *About Face*, I think, is that most of us were too damn old for the roles.

It was a musical version of *Brother Rat*, in which I had appeared years before on Broadway and on the road, and I was now playing a part even younger than the one I had done originally. These were all 19-year-old military school cadets and I was almost 40 years old, for God's sake. Gordon MacRae was too old for it, so were Dick Wesson and some of the others. Even the girls, Phyllis Kirk, Virginia Gibson and Aileen Stanley, Jr., looked a bit womanly for their girlish roles.

One of the few actors in it who was the right age was a new kid whose father was a burlesque comedian I'd known in Chicago. Watching him work, we all thought the boy was absolutely terrible. "What did they hire *him* for? Whose boyfriend is *he*?", we all wondered. We just thought he was overdoing everything.

When we saw the finished film, we were shocked to discover that he had stolen the thing away from all of us! His name was Joel Grey, and *About Face* was his first film. He never knew how we had felt about him, of course, but after he'd run away with the show we felt we could tell him. He laughed—easy for him when he had the picture, such as it was, in his pocket. Of course, he didn't work in movies again for years.

Another thing: when you're performing in a musical, you need good musical numbers. Getting such material is always difficult. There was one number Gordon MacRae didn't want, so they gave it to me. It was a good song, and when he heard us rehearsing it he decided he wanted it after all, so he took it. Gordon was top-billed and under contract to Warner Brothers; I was just visiting there, so what could I say? He was very nice about it, though, and came to apologize for usurping the number.

I had one duet with Phyllis Kirk that was OK, but it was a kind of ballad. As a comedian, I felt that I needed a comedy number to really shine.

I remember another incident that occurred while we were shooting *About Face*. (Or maybe it was *The Girl from Jones Beach*, which I did just before it at Warners.) Anyway, this little girl came up to me on the lot and asked if I would come and perform for her Burbank high school assembly, which I did. Her name was Debbie Reynolds, and she went on to do pretty well herself in show business.

❏

CAROL BURNETT:

After my first film, *Who's Been Sleeping in My Bed?*, I should have been given the award for "Worst Performance Ever Given in Movies by an Actress." I was confused, bored and I missed the [live] audience. Nothing was spontaneous. If CBS ever shows that turkey on their late show, I'll break my contract.

❏

JAMES CAAN:

My satisfaction was there [with his directorial debut in *Hide in Plain Sight*]—all the wonderful reviews. Nice things happened. When you make a picture, you really make it for the people you respect. But I'm not a fool. I want all my pictures to become commercial successes.

But they were such schmucks at United Artists. I had to send my dailies to three undertakers who couldn't understand what they were looking at. The picture was released and nobody knew it was there. I'll never direct again.

❏

OLEG CASSINI:

Despite the boycott [allegedly begun by 20th Century-Fox Studios chief Darryl F. Zanuck, angry that Cassini had married the lot's budding star Gene

Tierney], I did get some free-lance design jobs during this time. The first was for one of Gene's films, *The Shanghai Gesture*, directed by Josef von Sternberg, the man who had made Marlene Dietrich a star in *The Blue Angel*. Both Gene and I were hopeful. A prestigious director, a good cast (including my friend Victor Mature as "Omar the Arab")—perhaps this would lead to other opportunities. But the film was an overwrought turkey destroyed by the critics, who gave Gene her first bad reviews. My costumes were not even mentioned in passing.

As a souvenir of the experience, Gene had brought home carved figurines of each character in the film—they had been used in a particularly absurd dinner scene near the end. When the picture opened and bombed, I took the figurines out to the backyard, lined them up along the top of our fence and executed them with a hunting rifle. "How could you do it?" Gene screamed when she learned about the firing squad. "You know I wanted to keep them!"

"Those characters deserved to die," I told her. "Now at least we won't be constantly reminded of that dreadful movie."

❏

FRANK CAPRA:

The Bitter Tea of General Yen lost money—mainly because it was banned in Great Britain and in the British Commonwealth countries, due to the shocking implications of a love affair between a yellow man (Nils Asther) and a white woman (Barbara Stanwyck). It was 30 years ahead of its proper time. Nor did it receive any Academy Award mentions. Damn those Academy voters! Couldn't they recognize a work of art when they saw one? Nevertheless, *Bitter Tea* will remain forever as one of *my* pet pictures. And it *was* chosen as the film to open Radio City Music Hall.

❏

WILLIAM CASTLE:

The Chance of a Lifetime was a lousy, dull, contrived, miserable script. Chester Morris, a fine actor, played the lead, Jeanne Bates the femme fatale. Every day I viewed the rushes, and my assistants told me what a great job I was doing. I saw the final cut with Irving Briskin, Columbia's "B" unit chief. When the lights came up he uttered the not unexpected, "It's a piece of shit!"

Briskin then took the end of the picture and put it at the beginning, then spliced a section of Reel Four into Reel Two, a section of Two into Four and some of Five into Six. Eight, he trimmed, and Nine, he left alone. After his glowing contribution, *The Chance of a Lifetime* became even more muddled and screwed up than it had been originally, if that was possible.

When the reviews finally came out, I hid in the men's room at Columbia. *The Hollywood Reporter*: "William Castle, in his directorial debut, proves he is totally unfit to handle a motion picture—*any* picture."

INTOLERANCE (Wark Producing, 1916). Director: D. W. Griffith.

◻

SAM COSLOW:

The first musical Arthur Johnston and I were assigned was a vehicle for Kate Smith, the foremost radio songstress of the day. The film was *Hello, Everybody!*, Kate's familiar greeting to open her radio shows. Paramount, at great expense, had hired Fannie Hurst to write the original story.

We turned out a score of eight numbers in short order, but getting Kate's approval turned out to be a bit trying. The demonstration took hours. After each number Kate just looked at Ted Collins, her manager, who would say, "Let's hear it again." We soon gathered that Ted made the decisions for Kate: the selection of songs, her scenes in the script and just about everything else. Each number was played about a dozen times and thoroughly discussed from every angle before Ted nodded approval. The hit of the picture was "Moon Song."

Apparently the only bad decision Collins made was his approval of a shooting script and title, for the film itself bombed. A more appropriate title would have been *Hello, Nobody*!

❏

JOSEPH COTTEN:

The Radio City Music Hall haunted me. Somehow, I felt I had been cheated out of a childhood ambition [to have a film open there]. Imagine my delight when, some 40-odd years later, my dream came true.

I appeared in *Heaven's Gate*, which cost over $40,000,000 and was the most expensive picture ever to open in the Radio City Music Hall. It was such a disaster that it *closed* the Music Hall.

❏

BETTE DAVIS:

Do you know what I used to do with my first picture? Whenever some young actor would ask how I got where I was, I'd show him *Bad Sister*, and we'd end up rolling on the floor with laughter. Seeing how I started out gave them such hope for themselves.

❏

PHILIP DUNNE:

Never was there such a projection room success as *Prince of Players*, with Richard Burton.

Darryl Zanuck was telling everyone that I was a born director. The hard-boiled department heads who had to sit through the dailies of the four pictures then in production on the lot told me the same flattering story. My dailies were always run last, and as one of the department heads put it, "We sit through the other batches making wisecracks, and then, when your stuff comes on, everybody shuts up and the magic begins." The trade reviews were excellent. No longer merely "one of our writers," I was now "one of our ace directors."

By the time I went to New York for the usual pre-release publicity binge, I had noticed that the picture hadn't received much publicity. When I mentioned this to Charlie Einfeld of the publicity department, he said ebulliently, "This picture doesn't need it. It's in the air."

And that's precisely where it stayed: in the air. To put it succinctly, we gave a movie and nobody came. Zanuck remarked, "More people are paying to see the goddam ballet!"

❑

CHARLIE EARLE:

Although Rosalind Russell had been on the screen for 21 years then, *The Girl Rush* was ballyhooed as her "first movie musical, her first VistaVision film and her first in Technicolor." It was produced for Paramount in 1955 by her husband, Frederick Brisson.

Prior to its release, Brisson addressed Paramount's New York publicity staff, of which I was a member. At the end of his great hype about the wonders of *The Girl Rush*, we could hardly wait to see and work on this "exciting" production that brought Russell back to the screen after her successful starring run in the Broadway musical, *Wonderful Town*.

Instead, what unreeled in the private screening room was, to our dismay, an embarrassment, a celluloid lemon. It was poorly scripted and directed, with a batch of surprisingly mediocre songs by Hugh Martin and Ralph Blane of *Meet Me in St. Louis* fame. Even Russell's performance was a disappointment, and Fernando Lamas, her leading man, added little. Gloria De Haven was the only redeeming feature with her tantalizing rendition of "An Occasional Man" and a bubbly champagne production number.

Russell arrived in town to promote the film and meet the press in the Carnival Room of the Sherry Netherland Hotel on Fifth Ave. I was assigned to escort her through the hotel's maze of basement corridors and up to the front of the room for her big entrance. Garbed in the outlandish hillbilly costume she wore for a comic number in *Girl Rush*, she then performed the song, "My Hillbilly Heart," as a live preview. Ironically, just before hitting the stage, Russell told me she was looking forward to her next role as the spinster schoolteacher in Columbia's *Picnic*, calling it "a-change-of-pace," adding in the rapid-fire manner we had all loved in *His Girl Friday*, "That's-what-I-like-a-change-of-pace!"

The Girl Rush proved to be a $2,000,000 turkey that had its premiere in the New York area on the bottom of a double bill in Brooklyn.

Rosalind Russell's change of pace came just in the nick of time.

❑

VINCE EDWARDS:

Frankly, I was discouraged by the poor reviews for *Mr. Universe*. I never liked the plot in the first place. But I took it because it spelled opportunity. After I saw the picture, I was convinced I had done the wrong thing. It was a lousy way to make a debut in the movies—as a big, dumb, blond kid. That kind of character gets you labeled.

❑

DOUGLAS FAIRBANKS, JR.:

The film was called *Stephen Steps Out*. In it were the now dead veterans cigar-smoking Theodore Roberts and husky Noah Beery.

I was publicized as being 18 years old, and the ballyhoo machine got to work at full blast to put over the debut of the younger Fairbanks.

The veterans gave me all the assistance they could, and I applied myself seriously—perhaps far too seriously—to the job of turning in a good performance. There was a big premiere, before which the fanfare of publicity reached its crescendo. Everything the exploiters could do was done. In fact, far too much was done; for, quite simply, the picture was a flop—a dismal and dreary flop.

Sadly, I felt that perhaps my father had been right. I just hadn't the equipment to cope.

EDDIE FISHER:

I tried my best to do a good job in *Bundle of Joy*. In fact, both Debbie [Reynolds] and I worked so hard that we didn't even go home during the last few weeks of shooting. We stayed in a bungalow on the lot.

Then I saw the final cut. As bad as I was, the picture was even worse, a bomb. I had to sit through the whole thing at the Hollywood premiere, but at the premiere in New York, at the Capitol Theater, I couldn't take it again and decided to wait in the lobby. There I met a steady stream of my friends, walking out. At the party after the show, everybody said, "Marvelous! Your voice never sounded better, Eddie. You never danced better, Debbie. Great acting, a great script, great direction, great title, great everything." Great bullshit.

Bundle of Joy laid a financial egg, the songs disappeared without a trace and Debbie's was the only movie career that managed to survive.

HENRY FONDA:

Writer Reginald Rose, director Sidney Lumet and I realized we had something special when we saw the first rough cut of *12 Angry Men* [Henry Fonda's first and last film as producer]. We dreamed of putting it into a small East Side movie house, the kind that held a few hundred people at the most, and we hoped that word of mouth would spread just as it had built with Paddy Chayefsky's *Marty*.

Well, that never happened. I got a phone call from Arthur Krim, the head of United Artists [which had financed the film]: "Get down here as fast as you can."

When I got to Krim's office, there sat Bob Benjamin and the other heads

ROSITA (United Artists, 1923), with Mary Pickford. Director: Ernst Lubitsch.

of the Loew's Circuit. They'd seen our picture and flipped out. They wanted it for Easter Week for all of their flagship theaters across the country. I told 'em I'd like to think on it a while.

"Are you out of your ever-loving mind?" Krim thundered. "All you'll have to do is sit back and hire people to take the wheelbarrows of money to the bank."

The Capitol Theater was Loew's flagship in New York. It's been gone for some time now, but in case anyone's forgotten, it had over 4600 seats. The opening day *12 Angry Men* barely filled the first four or five rows. They pulled it after a week.

❏

JANE FONDA:

Everyone has to start somewhere. But after *Tall Story*, there was nowhere for me to go but up.

❏

PETER FONDA:

The Hired Hand was my first film to direct. We made a darn good film for nine bucks. *Hired Hand* was a classic when it hit the stands. The picture was very well received in Europe and in film festivals. But Universal dumped on it.

I remember they were going to put up a billboard on Sunset Boulevard with a photo of me without a shirt, wearing a cowboy hat and a pistol stuffed in my pants. The billboard was gonna say: "That *Easy Rider* Rides Again!" I went to Universal and said to take it down or I'll take it down with explosives. I really was pissed off! They paid themselves a hefty fee up front to distribute the film. I didn't see a damn dime.

They weren't going to sell my film like that. Needless to say, they took the billboard down.

❏

JOAN FONTAINE:

David Selznick was hounding me to play in Daphne du Maurier's *French-man's Creek* on loan-out.

The film would have been less flamboyant in black and white, a mood movie about a hopeless, daring romance, but Paramount planned to do it in glorious Technicolor and co-star a Mexican actor, Arturo de Cordova. My name would have to carry the film. Director Mitchell Leisen, known for his musicals, would lavish attention on the sets but little on the acting.

I rebelled, Selznick promised contractual changes, more money: "Oh, I can't even tell you all the things I'll do for you when you report to Paramount." I did report. He didn't remember his promises.

De Cordova was not a tall man. Lifts were put in his boots. He teetered as he walked. His wigs were as elaborate as mine. His accent was hardly that of a Frenchman. The costumes, sets and props all swamped the actors. Our acting was stilted, often melodramatic. The spectacle drew laughter at the Radio City Music Hall premiere—halfway through I sneaked out during a particularly raucous audience reaction.

During the filming, Arturo and I were standing in our marks, waiting for a two-shot. Knowing that the film would be a disaster, I asked him why he'd accepted the role. As a popular star in Mexico, he'd certainly taken quite a risk to make his American debut in *Frenchman's Creek*. Overhearing, Nigel Bruce and Basil Rathbone, gossip lovers, twisted my remark. The trade papers made the most of it—I'd supposedly told my leading man to go back to Mexico.

The film was an unhappy one in every way.

❏

WILLIAM FRIEDKIN:

As soon as *Good Times* was released, acid rock came in and wiped out the whole message of Sonny and Cher. They were singing about emotions that were now passé. The film opened to an audience that was rapidly losing interest in Sonny and Cher. But it was made with two people who had absolutely no acting experience and a director who'd never made a feature and whose future was highly questionable. I'm not at all disappointed in it. I can still watch it today and not be embarrassed.

❑

CLARK GABLE:

The studio was just as eager as I to make my comeback after the war a successful picture. I admit I didn't like the story of *Adventure*. But, I blame myself as much as anyone that it wasn't as good as my earlier movies. The trouble was, I had war jitters. Like every other guy back from the service, I was nervous and restless. I was pressing too hard. We were all pressing too hard. Result—it was all very de-pressing!

❑

KATHRYN GRAYSON:

I had been under contract to MGM for many years, then did some things over at Warner Brothers. *The Vagabond King* was my first picture at Paramount, and if God is good to me it will remain my last there. It would take a miracle to get me back to that place

The story, of course, had been done many times before on both stage and screen. We were doing the Rudolf Friml operetta about the poet-rogue François Villon who lived in 15th-century Paris. I played Catherine De Vaucelles, his sweetheart at the French court. To portray the colorful role of Villon, Mrs. Barney Balaban—her husband was President of Paramount—discovered Oreste Kirkop while she was in Europe. He was a tenor from Malta, and the comparisons between him and Mario Lanza, then a big MGM star, were obvious and played up by Paramount.

I got involved because Rudolf Friml was a great friend of mine; I loved his music for *The Vagabond King*. And the money was excellent. So was the supporting cast, which included people like Rita Moreno, Sir Cedric Hardwicke, Walter Hampden, Leslie Nielsen and Jack Lord. However, the script for the picture left a great deal to be desired. The dialogue was terribly stilted—flowery, archaic. Villon had to say things like, "If I were king, the stars should be your pearls upon a string." Lines were forming everywhere then to see *The Blackboard Jungle*, and we were saying things like that. I knew we'd lose them in Kansas City. I didn't realize we'd lose them everywhere else, too.

Victor Young was the musical director, and that caused problems immediately. He insisted on inserting his own music in with Friml's. Furthermore, during my long stay at MGM, we had always gone in first with a symphony orchestra and recorded the soundtrack for our musicals that way.

At Paramount, they were so chintzy that they had Victor Young record our orchestral accompaniment ahead of time, so we all had to sing to his recordings. Consequently, it was Victor Young's interpretation of the music, not ours. I understand that Bing Crosby, who was Paramount's reigning musical star, liked to do it that way; he was so laid back that it may have seemed right for him.

What's more, Michael Curtiz, our director, was having a nervous breakdown throughout the filming. He was a great director who had been much honored for *Yankee Doodle Dandy* and *Casablanca*, but he was in a fog on *Vagabond King* because of his condition. We'd have 500 extras on the set, and Mike would show up without having planned the day's work.

But I got along well with him. He was very sweet to me. I recall that on December 23rd during the shooting, my mother died. I was devastated and Mike called to give me two weeks off. The studio countermanded him, though, and I was brought back to work in three days.

Then there was "Oreste," as he was singly, somewhat infamously billed in the film. He had a beautiful singing voice but didn't understand a word of English and was no actor. Mike Curtiz not only spoke with a heavy Hungarian accent himself but was so disturbed at this time that he could be no help to him at all. And the studio was too cheap to give me any time to work with Oreste beforehand. At Metro years earlier, I had had nine months to help prepare ex-truckdriver Mario Lanza for his first starring films with me, and *he* spoke English. Oreste would stumble over some dialogue and Mike would say to me, "Here, you speak these lines." I'd reply, "I'm not François Villon! It would be completely inappropriate for these words to come from me!" The upshot was that for the picture's release, all of Oreste's speaking was dubbed by some Australian or English actor. He was a delightful, warm human being, though, and we kept in touch through the years. We have mutual friends in London. He never made another American film, but he sang in operas and concertized throughout Europe successfully for years. A while back he had a mild heart attack, so he is now retired and enjoying life with his wife and children on Malta.

Things finally got so horrid on *Vagabond King* that I simply decided to turn my back to the camera as much as possible, hoping not to be seen in the thing!

Paramount did not have a Louis B. Mayer [production chief at MGM], who saw to it that his pictures were done with polish and class. Paramount had money people, but no one who seemed to know or love the picture business as passionately as Mr. Mayer and his associates at Metro. Maybe Y. Frank Freeman, Paramount's Vice President who had charge of the lot, was a knowledgeable and caring man, but it didn't seem to filter down through the studio.

I was signed for 10 weeks on *Vagabond King*, but it ran way over schedule. I was never paid for the overtime. Since this was well over 30 years ago, I am not expecting the check to be in the mail.

HELLO, EVERYBODY! (Paramount, 1933), with Charley Grapewin, Randolph Scott, Kate Smith, Sally Blane. Director: William A. Seiter.

The picture wasn't edited; it was chopped up. Lots of stuff wound up on the cutting room floor, including a bit of Victor Young's incongruous new music. When it came out in 1956, the few people who saw it liked the original Friml music, of course, but wondered where the Young music came from. It just didn't seem to fit the period.

The Vagabond King was such a disaster from every standpoint that it soured me on the movies for many years. Right afterward, I was offered *The Ambassador's Daughter*, but turned it down. Olivia de Havilland took it. Then I was asked to do *Port Afrique*, and refused that, too. Pier Angeli did it. I refused *everything. The Vagabond King* was a traumatic, embittering experience.

Thank God for the wonderful MGM years and films like *Show Boat, Kiss Me, Kate!* and *Anchors Aweigh*—I remember when people everywhere were saying to each other, "How many times have you seen *Anchors Aweigh?*" Fans—many of them very young—write me all the time to say how much these pictures have meant to them. At an appearance in Sacramento recently, a darling little four-year-old girl came up to me and said she'd just seen *Kiss Me, Kate!* (released in 1953!) and now she wanted to be an opera singer! A number of today's opera singers have said they were inspired by my films.

All this makes the low points like *Vagabond King* seem trivial indeed.

❑

BYRON HASKIN:

I directed George Jessel's first film, *The Broadway Kid*, released as *Ginsberg the Great* in 1928. George, as a film comedian, was talented like a clothing store dummy. Later, of course, he became a great raconteur; but that's another matter. He couldn't ever react. Slapstick comedy depends on the ability to "take it." You see the villain, you "take it big." Jessel would see a train coming toward him and show no reaction. It was a real bomb. I couldn't do anything with it.

❏

HOWARD HAWKS:

A very astute and wise man gave me a chance to direct, and I made a picture [*The Road to Glory*, 1926] that I don't think anybody enjoyed except a few critics. And he said, "Look, you've shown you can make a picture, but for God's sake go out and make entertainment." So I went home and wrote a story about Adam and Eve waking up in the Garden of Eden and called it *Fig Leaves*. It got its cost back in one theater. And that taught me a very good lesson; from that time on, I've been following his advice about trying to make entertainment.

❏

SALLY KELLERMAN:

I've had my share of turkeys, but my first film was also my worst. It was called *Reform School Girl* and was released back in the late '50s. My ex-boyfriend, Edd "Kookie" Byrnes, was one of the stars. I played the school dyke and carried a tool case. When I came on the screen, everybody in the theater laughed. I didn't work for three years after that.

❏

STANLEY KRAMER:

I formed a small independent film company out of thin air and used my uncle's office. I took an option on two Ring Lardner stories. I chose, unfortunately, to make "The Big Town." I changed the title to *So This is New York*. The picture was a satire, and George S. Kaufman said satire is what closes Saturday night. We didn't even make it to Saturday night. *So This is New York* closed on Thursday night. It closed all over the country before it opened. Nobody thought the picture was satirical or amusing. It was, and I hesitate to say this because it sounds like a lame excuse, a little bit ahead of its time. It did have funny things in it.

❏

JESSICA LANGE:

When I think back to the *King Kong* experience, I don't see anything really positive. I was put in the position of appearing in a film like that before getting the chance to establish myself as a legitimate actress. I had been doing small theater pieces in New York, and revues—*King Kong* was my first movie audition.

Think about it: this girl is flown to California, is taken to the studio in a limo, walks right into MGM—which had always been my favorite studio—and there's all this hustle and bustle, and the producer and director are there, and they're talking to her and there's all this noise, and it turns out that she's going to star in a $25,000,000 picture. It was like a fairy tale.

But then the picture came out, and it got the kind of negative attention that it did, and all of a sudden I was known—but I was not known as an actress, I was just known as the girl who was in *King Kong*. And after that there was a slide.

☐

CYNDI LAUPER:

In retrospect, I'm not sorry I did it [*Vibes*]. I think they treat everyone badly in that business, but you know, I loved the character but the script wasn't right. I'd like to try it again, but next time I want to make sure the story is there.

☐

ERNEST LEHMAN:

Portnoy's Complaint is a perfect example of biting off more than I could chew. I had no idea how I intended to do it; all I knew was that I wanted to do it. I felt that it would be an enormous hit if it were done well. But I didn't know how to do it, as it turned out.

I think the mistake was in thinking that I had the ability to find a screen drama in that novel, because a film does have to be essentially dramatic. Without being all that formal, it should have a first, second and third act. I think the beauty of that novel is not in its dramatic potentialities. The whole thing was first person singular, somebody lying on a couch talking to his analyst throughout the entire novel. Some of the very best of it was interior. Some of it could be dramatized, some of it couldn't. I would say a novel which is very, very interior probably is not going to make it as a film. There may be exceptions.

Everyone thought my screenplay was excellent. There are those who think perhaps the film might have been better if someone else had directed it instead of me. I would say that *Portnoy's Complaint* was the wrong kind of picture for me to have chosen to direct for the first time.

THE BITTER TEA OF GENERAL YEN (Columbia, 1933), with Barbara Stanwyck, Nils Asther. Director: Frank Capra.

❏

VIVECA LINDFORS:

When Warner Brothers brought me over from Sweden, the first thing they put me into was a mistake called *Night unto Night*. I fell so in love with the director, Don Siegel, that I barely noticed my co-star, Ronald Reagan, or that the picture was so bad the studio almost didn't release it. It was on the shelf for two or three years.

❏

JOSHUA LOGAN:

I gave young, wildly talented Jane Fonda a very poor start to her movie career in *Tall Story*, and right on top of that a shaky debut on Broadway in *There Was a Little Girl. Tall Story* was certainly not a hit, and *There Was a Little Girl* closed after three weeks.

❏

JOSHUA LOGAN:

My first job in Hollywood, as dialogue director on David O. Selznick's production of *The Garden of Allah*, was one of the most peculiar I've had in any medium. Selznick was very concerned about the script's words, which he called "desert poetry."

One day, Charles Boyer, recently arrived from France and sweating over the English dialogue, exclaimed, "I can say 'wiz the,' or I can say 'with ze,' but 'with the' is impossible!" The Austrian Joseph Schildkraut was playing an effete Arab and employing a thick Russian accent.

Our German leading lady, Marlene Dietrich, sidled up to me during pre-production and asked, "You're fwom New York, aren't you? I love people fwom New York. They're so bwight. Tell me, have you wead the scwipt? It's twash, isn't it? Garbo turned it down, and she has that inborn wisdom dose peasants have, you know. I know it's twash."

And she was wight. *The Garden of Allah*, despite Selznick's lavish care, was a dud. One critic wrote: "The dialogue obviously was written by Alf Landon."

❏

ROUBEN MAMOULIAN:

Critics?

Critics made me when my first film, *Applause*, was a commercial flop. It was too far ahead of its time to be a hit with audiences. But critics have never in history influenced any artist. What they are is a creative link—if they're independent and frank and love the medium—between the artist and a large audience.

❏

JAMES MASON:

Arch of Triumph was a major disaster and Enterprise Studios was losing a lot of money and thought, "We'll be able to recoup all our losses with this film, *Caught*." When they gave a sneak preview somewhere it got the most wonderful reception and everyone connected with the film thought, "Well, isn't this nice. Now Enterprise will once again be in the black." And for three months they sat in this glorious situation of knowing that they had this immensely successful film, and then of course when they finally released it nobody went to see it at all, but *nobody*. My first American film was a terrible disaster.

❏

THE SCARLET EMPRESS (Paramount, 1934), with Marlene Dietrich, John Lodge. Director: Josef von Sternberg.

RODDY McDOWALL:

I only directed one film, *The Devil's Widow*, with Ava Gardner. We made it in England 20 years ago [1969]. It had the bad manners to go bankrupt.

❏

ROBERT MERRILL:

I discovered, from a paragraph in *The New York Times*, that I would make my film debut in April, 1951, in *Aaron Slick from Punkin Crick*.

The problem here was not *Aaron Slick*, a title which made me go out and buy a spittoon, but April. That was when the Met's spring tour started, and Rudolf Bing had already advertised me for eight appearances. There was a great back-and-forthing of letters and ultimatums, and I was fired.

I felt I was in the best possible hands in Hollywood, though ... William Perlberg, George Seaton and Claude Binyon, who assured me, "It's going to be a great movie with a great cast." The movie was based on a play which was also "great"; it had been played by every summer camp, backyard, high school and church social group in the country since it was written, in 1919.

After a few days on the set, I realized that Dinah Shore had eleven songs and I had one.

When *Aaron Slick* was released in April, 1952, it had the peculiar distinction of filling boxoffices from coast to coast with patrons demanding refunds. The brains at Paramount discovered that *Variety*'s classic sociological commentary still applied: "STICKS NIX HICKS PIX." The big cities gave it the same KIX.

☐

PAUL NEWMAN:

I began my career most auspiciously. I had the privilege of doing the worst motion picture filmed during the fifties—*The Silver Chalice*.

Everybody thinks it was a disaster just because it was terrible, but I say it wasn't. It's like juvenile delinquency; if you can be the worst kid on your block, you make a name for yourself. How many other actors have you spoken to who can say with complete objectivity that they were in the worst motion picture made in the fifties—a film that cost $4,500,000. That makes me very special.

When they ran *The Silver Chalice* on Los Angeles television three or four years ago, I took out ads in the newspapers apologizing for what was going to happen on channel nine that night. But it backfired. Everybody wanted to know what I was apologizing for, and the picture ended up with the second or third highest rating of any picture that station had ever shown.

☐

SHEREE NORTH:

I hated every moment of that first film I did, *How to Be Very, Very Popular*. Doing something you don't know how to do in front of a lot of people can be quite devastating, you know. It was for me. I knew I was bad. They asked me to try again, so I did—*The Lieutenant Wore Skirts*. That was terrible, too. Then I began taking acting lessons and that changed everything.

☐

LAURENCE OLIVIER:

The cast included no less than Adolphe Menjou, Lili Damita and Erich von Stroheim, with me taking fourth place in equal billing. This first engagement embodied for me all the most horrific aspects of Hollywood. An extravagantly dramatic romance by Maurice Dekobra had, inevitably, been completely rewritten but it was considered that the deal had been worth the money for the sake of the title—*The Sphinx Has Spoken*. Needless to say, by the end of the picture it was decided to change the title to *Friends and Lovers*. It may have been realized that Lili Damita was not exactly sphinx-like. The cast, apart from its eminence, was wretchedly ill-assorted. So my first Hollywood picture died the death of a dog.

FOUR FRIGHTENED PEOPLE (Paramount, 1934), with Herbert Marshall, Claudette Colbert. Director: Cecil B. DeMille.

❏

GEORGE OPPENHEIMER:

Samuel Goldwyn had made an acquisition, Russian actress Anna Sten whom he had imported to make into a new Garbo. The picture chosen for Sten's American debut was *Nana*, Zola's story of a courtesan.

First, however, she had to be taught to speak English. There were a good many jokes about Goldwyn with his accent instructing Sten with hers, but they were unfounded. Goldwyn backed up his confidence in his protégée with the best of everything—an English coach, dancing and singing teachers, speech instructors, a trainer and masseuse, since the lady had a tendency to put on weight. I was given the task of directing a trailer to advertise the epic. In it Sten appeared first as herself and then dissolved into the character, with the lines, "Now I am Anna; now I am Nana." Unhappily her accent was so thick that "Anna" and "Nana" sounded identical.

The country was Sten-conscious and eagerly awaited news of the opening. The reviews were bad, word-of-mouth worse. Sten was a bomb. Goldwyn chose for her second film *We Live Again*, a second bomb, followed by *The Wedding Night*, a two-ton dud despite the presence of Gary Cooper.

❏

LILLI PALMER:

Cloak and Dagger should have been a success: Gary Cooper, directed by Fritz Lang, a decent script. It wasn't. The critics were lukewarm about the picture and Cooper. They praised me, the newcomer, all right, but without the exuberance I'd been hoping for.

❑

ABRAHAM POLONSKY:

Force of Evil, starring John Garfield, was my first film, and I think there's a difference between what I really intended to do and what came off. I didn't know *how*. And then, despite good reviews, it wasn't a successful picture at the boxoffice. Of course it was a difficult picture, and, of course, it was experimental in a way, deliberately experimental. But, nevertheless, I thought that the general weight of it would be obvious, that people would feel it, but it wasn't felt except by very sophisticated audiences.

❑

OTTO PREMINGER:

A small, elderly woman got up from behind a desk to berate me:

"I am Barbra Streisand's mother. I just want to tell you that my daughter auditioned for *Saint Joan* and you did not give her the part. You, a famous director! And you didn't recognize talent when you saw it."

I said, "My dear Mrs. Streisand, please, compare your daughter's career with Jean Seberg's. You should be grateful I didn't cast her as Saint Joan. It might have ruined her future."

Saint Joan was a failure. Many people blamed newcomer Jean Seberg and her inexperience. That is unfair. I alone am to blame, because I misunderstood something fundamental about Shaw's play. It is not a dramatization of the legend of Joan of Arc which is filled with emotion and religious passion. It is a deep but cool intellectual examination of the role religion plays in the history of man. Am I sorry I made the film? No. I loved working on it.

❑

GEORGE RAFT:

I guess I was the first actor in motion pictures to start his own independent company. It wasn't a great success for the simple reason that the first picture I made was badly timed. It was called *Intrigue*, all about China. At the time we made it it was topical, but headlines create a lot of things and by the time the picture was released, well, the headlines were about Russia and they forgot about China.

SYLVIA SCARLETT (RKO, 1936), with Edmund Gwenn, Katharine Hepburn, Cary Grant, Dennie Moore, Brian Aherne. Director: George Cukor.

❏

ROSALIND RUSSELL:

The first lead I played at Metro—it was forced on me, I went down hollering—was in a B movie called *Casino Murder Case*, with Paul Lukas. It was so bad, and I was so bad in it, that it gave my maid Hazel ammunition for seasons to come. "If you don't behave," she'd say, "I'm going to tell people about that *Casino Murder Case*."

❏

DORE SCHARY:

Bright Road—a lovely, warm story of a black boy, J.T. Starring in the picture were two newcomers, Harry Belafonte and Dorothy Dandridge. Emmet Lavery wrote the script and Gerald Mayer, one of our new young directors, did an inspired job; but we couldn't get anyone in to see the picture. It will always be a favorite of mine and a puzzle as to why it could not even return its original low cost of $490,000.

❏

PARNELL (MGM, 1937), with Clark Gable, Myrna Loy. Director: John M. Stahl.

JEAN SEBERG:

Otto Preminger got rid of me like a used Kleenex. I realize that his bullying methods work with some people, but he destroyed my confidence in *Saint Joan*. And he was so cruel to me in *Bonjour Tristesse* that Deborah Kerr and David Niven finally told him off. Oh, I could write a book about Preminger. I'm glad he discovered me and I'm glad he starred me in *Saint Joan*. But after that picture, there was only one way to go—to the bottom.

❑

ROBERT TOWNE:

Bob Evans, when he wants to really hurt me, brings that up [*Villa Rides*]. Actually, it was the first film I did for Paramount. I really hated it. It was weird, though it was one of the most interesting experiences I have ever had working on a film. And it was also one of the least successful. It was a textbook on How Not to Make a Movie.

❑

CATHERINE TURNEY:

Winter Meeting was a project of producer Henry Blanke's for Bette Davis. It was not a successful movie. It looks a little better now on the small screen. It's better suited for television. But it was much too talky.

It was the director Bretaigne Windust's first movie. He had made quite a name for himself on Broadway and came out with a big fanfare. But he directed it like a stage play. And we had an actor, Jim Davis, who was not right for the part at all. So that was kind of a disaster. And Bette was starting to lose her boxoffice appeal. Television was coming in.

❑

RUDY VALLEE:

If I live to be a hundred I can never erase the premiere of *The Vagabond Lover* at the Globe Theater in New York. The place was naturally packed with friends, well wishers and curiosity seekers who had heard us on radio. I made a short speech onstage before it began and then stood in the wings to watch the opus unfold.

About halfway through I became conscious of much movement among the audience and I discovered to my dismay that the theater was half-empty! I had been a party to a resounding flop. It was static and unimaginative. The sound was bad. The performances of the band and myself were amateurish. I was almost laughable with the dead-pan sincerity that I thought was acting.

Outside of these minor reservations it was a real gem! The true, dyed-in-the-wool Vallee fans liked it; but even by the standards of that day [1929] it was the prize turkey of the year and it damn' near ruined us with the public.

Megabuck Misfires

"Though it cost only $5,000,000, it succeeded in losing six."

MORT ABRAHAMS:

The addition of music and the required length of the picture forced us to make certain changes in the story [*Goodbye, Mr. Chips*]. The most logical place to add material was in the relationship between Chips and his wife. Otherwise, the musical sections of the film would have had too many male voices.

Almost none of us liked the idea of utilizing flashbacks; we felt it was a clumsy device. We also updated the story to involve the Second, instead of the First, World War.

In retrospect, I don't feel the story lent itself to a roadshow production. We were forced to create new material that, simply, didn't work. And, of course, we were unfavorably compared to the original film. I think we'd have been much better off if the picture had been only two hours long.

❑

DANA ANDREWS:

I put my own money in a film and lost a lot of money. I learned a lesson: don't ever put your own money in a motion picture, because with all the practice that writers have and all the experience that producers have, they never know whether a film's going to be a hit.

Enterprise was the company with which I made my own film called *No Minor Vices*, with Lilli Palmer, Louis Jourdan and Jane Wyatt. Enterprise went under, you know, and this was one of the pictures that helped that, but the big one was *Arch of Triumph* which cost about four and a half million dollars and I don't think it *grossed* that much.

❑

THE RETURN OF DR. X (Warner Brothers, 1939), with Humphrey Bogart. Director: Vincent Sherman.

JULIE ANDREWS:

The public couldn't accept me as a spy in *Darling Lili*, and that disappointed me awfully. The opening scene was the most difficult thing I have had to do; it was shot in a darkened theater, and it was done in one enormous take. They kept moving cables around and pulling curtains away, and it was a nightmare. There were 360-turns of the camera all around me. And we had to do it twice! Once in Dublin in a theater, and then, because the stage was too bumpy, in a studio! And then the film was not successful. Very sad.

❑

NORBERT T. AUERBACH:

There were offers to buy United Artists. *Heaven's Gate* was not the only reason for the sale [to MGM]. However, had the picture done well, as we had hoped, the sale might not have taken place.

❑

CHARLES BOYER:

Cutting *Arch of Triumph* has improved it considerably. It was terrible for four hours, but now it is only terrible for two hours.

❑

SAUL CHAPLIN:

Star! came out at a time when suddenly the generation gap opened up and the movie audiences no longer wanted to see this kind of musical. They wanted *Easy Rider*. Remember, after *Sound of Music, all* the musical films bombed, including the big ones—*Paint Your Wagon, Hello, Dolly!, Goodbye, Mr. Chips*. By the way, *Star!* didn't lose anywhere near the money that those others lost. As far as I'm concerned, if we gave Fox one picture that's made as much for them as *Sound of Music* and they lose maybe $12,000,000 on another, they shouldn't really complain. I think that audiences did not want to see Julie Andrews in this sort of role. They simply did not want her playing a real person.

❑

MICHAEL CIMINO:

During the last five months, I have not read anything that has been written about *Heaven's Gate*. Since it closed in New York and we went to work editing a shorter version, I had to ignore the violence of the reaction by the press if I were to keep my own enthusiasm for the project. We all believed in what we were doing. We still do. The reaction was so extreme in the press, so out of proportion to what seemed justified, that we had to ignore it. If the attacks on the film had been well reasoned . . .

❑

JAMES COCO:

I have never done anything where I was miserable that was ever a success. The worst experience was making *The Blue Bird* in Russia. *Everyone* was miserable. My room was the game room and everybody gathered there and played cards all night. The last time I saw Ava Gardner she was drinking vodka out of a milk bottle and yelling, "Get me out of here!" I knew that movie would be a bomb.

❑

FRANCIS FORD COPPOLA:

One exhibitor said *One from the Heart* was the worst film he'd seen in 10 years. That's what all the San Francisco exhibitors said about *Apocalypse Now* three years ago. So it can only be the worst film he's seen in *three* years.

❑

LINDA DARNELL:

I didn't know what it meant to struggle—but I found out. After three years, people wearied of seeing the sweet, innocent young things I was playing and I landed at the bottom of the roller coaster. I didn't work for a year—and then I went bad on them in *Summer Storm*. So bad that I was chosen to play Amber in *Forever Amber*.

I thought I was the luckiest girl in Hollywood. They talked around the studio about it being another *Gone with the Wind*. But Amber didn't do right by me. Somehow or other we fumbled the ball.

Amber has continued to haunt me. I lost out to Jeanne Crain for the part of the young Negro girl in Darryl F. Zanuck's production of *Pinky* because Mr. Zanuck feared audiences might think Pinky had something of [the racy] Amber in her.

I have had, too, to lead the most circumspect life of any actress. If I did anything that even looked bad, people would say, "Oh, well, you know, she was Amber. Type casting."

❑

CLINT EASTWOOD:

Paint Your Wagon was a mistake. At $8,000,000, the original budget, it would have been a bargain, but at $20,000,000 it was a disaster. The company

ICE FOLLIES OF 1939 (MGM, 1939), with Joan Crawford. Director: Reinhold Schunzel.

was terribly jaded, demoralized, and not even a tight director like Don Siegel could have saved it from suicide.

❏

ROBERT EVANS:

I always believed in the film [*Darling Lili*]. I was wrong. Producer-director-writer Blake Edwards was going so far over budget in the picture and spending money so capriciously that I had to look into it. The picture was the biggest financial fiasco Paramount has ever had.

❏

GERALDINE FITZGERALD:

Why did *Wilson* fail? A good question. This biography of our 28th President was the dearest thing to producer Darryl Zanuck's heart, and he did not stint. At a cost of $5,000,000, it was said to be the most expensive picture yet made.

Zanuck supervised everything, even the clothes. My wardrobe as Edith Gault, the second Mrs. Woodrow Wilson, alone cost about $30,000, an enormous sum in 1944. I remember that when the real Mrs. Gault-Wilson, who had been criticized for extravagance in the White House, saw the film and my costumes, she exclaimed, "I never had anything like *that!*"

The New York premiere was spectacular, too. Zanuck and Wendell Willkie, whom he looked on as a sort of latter day Wilson, were there, as was I, and the crowd was so large and wild that all the cars were being rocked to and fro; people inside were in real danger of having them knocked over. Then —everybody disappeared. There was no business.

Originally, the screenplay was to have been more candid about Mrs. Gault as well as the people who blocked the League of Nations. But when it was learned that most of them were still alive, they decided to take it easy. Consequently, my role, the second Mrs. Wilson, didn't have the bite it otherwise might have had.

The reviews for *Wilson* were respectful, some even excellent. *Life* magazine made me its cover girl and called our film "one of the best pictures Hollywood has ever made." But many of the notices indicated that the film could have used a little more humanity. The political aspects, including that long convention sequence, were beautifully done, but I think that with history it's often the human things that we remember most. In school I recall learning that the 100 Years War was started when some ambassador was thrown out of a window. My teacher, a nun, said, "Now I don't want you girls to remember just that," but of course today that's all I remember about the 100 Years War—a man was thrown from a window.

During the filming of *Wilson*, my four-year-old son Michael came on the set to watch some of the shooting. When I asked him how he liked it, he replied, "All right, but it would have been better if you'd put on your clown suit." That was his way of saying that the picture could have used some humor.

Not surprisingly, he grew up to be a director.

❑

AVA GARDNER:

I was up until four A.M. at that goddam premiere of *The Bible*. Premieres! I will personally kill that John Huston if he ever drags me into another mess like that. There was must have been 10,000 people clawing at me. I get claustrophobia in crowds and I couldn't breathe.

Christ, they started off by shoving a TV camera at me and yelling, "Talk, Ava!" At intermission I got lost and couldn't find my goddam seat after the lights went out and I kept telling those little girls with the bubble hairdos and the flashlights, "I'm with John Huston," and they kept saying, "Is he from Fox?" There I was fumbling around the aisles in the dark and when I finally found my seat somebody was sitting in it and there was a big scene. On top of it all, I lost my goddam mantilla in the limousine.

Then Johnny Huston takes me to this party where we had to stand around and smile at Artie Shaw, who I was married to, baby, for Chrissake, and his wife, Evelyn Keyes, who Johnny Huston was once married to, for Chrissake. And after it's all over, what have you got? The biggest headache in town. Nobody cares who the hell was there. Do you think for one minute the fact that Ava Gardner showed up at that circus will sell the picture? Christ, did you *see* it?

I went through all that hell just so this morning Bosley Crowther could write I looked like I was posing for a monument. All the way through it I kept punching Johnny on the arm and saying, "Christ, how could you let me do it?"

❑

TERI GARR:

Francis Ford Coppola's Zoetrope Studios collapsed and he still owes me money from *One from the Heart*. He's a great artist, but he was so hurt by the film's failure he's divorced himself from everyone involved with it. As Martin Sheen said, "I wouldn't work for Francis again even if he paid me."

❑

LILIAN GISH:

Intolerance, reputed to have cost $1.9 million, was the costliest production up to that time and for years after.

THE BLUE BIRD (20th Century-Fox, 1940), with Al Shean, Shirley Temple, Johnny Russell, Cecilia Loftus. Director: Walter Lang.

When D. W. Griffith finished editing, it ran approximately eight hours. He planned to exhibit it in two parts, but exhibitors refused to handle it. Cut down to two and a half hours, the film was much too tight. How could he tell four stories of such magnitude in so brief a time?

In the first four months at the Liberty Theater, New York, *Intolerance* outdid *Birth of a Nation*. Then attendance began to fall off. In other cities it was the same story—a first surge of attendance, then a drop to almost nothing. "I don't know where to go or where to turn since my great failure," Mr. Griffith wrote me. He told me sadly of wandering through darkened theaters, barking his shins on empty seats. Eventually withdrawn, it is one of the few pictures that has never had a second run in neighborhood houses. It had not nearly begun to pay for itself. Mr. Griffith started to pay off his million-dollar debt. It took him years.

Many reasons have been advanced for the failure of the film. *Variety* said it was "hard to follow." I believe that had he shown the film in two four-hour screenings as he had planned, it would have been successful. But there were other reasons for the failure. He should have left the details of other productions to his assistants. He should have finished *Intolerance* as quickly as possible to keep down the costs. And he should have given his players the kind of publicity and exploitation that was by then starting in the industry.

Another factor was timing. In 1916 and early 1917 the country was pre-paring for war. Yet here was a picture that preached peace and tolerance.

In the years since the failure of *Intolerance*, I have lived to see its elemental power affirmed. All teachers of film that I have ever talked to, and numerous critics, have said that *Intolerance* is the greatest film ever made.

❑

WILLIAM GOLDMAN:

Nobody knows what will work. It's all blind guessing. You are guessing public taste two and three years down the line. You don't know who's going to be a star and who isn't. If we *knew* what was going to work, we wouldn't spend eight million dollars making *Nickelodeon* and one million making *Rocky*. We'd be making nothing but *Rocky*s. Nobody knows.

❑

HOWARD HAWKS:

We made a lousy picture that had a lot of great stuff in it called *Land of the Pharaohs*. Everybody in that was a jerk—you didn't have anybody to root for. I didn't know what a pharaoh talked like, either, and I did a lousy job.

❑

KATHARINE HEPBURN:

Sylvia Scarlett was supposed to be magical and hilarious comedy. Well, we took the picture to the preview and it started and not a sound from the audience. And Natalie Paley, who was in it, said to me, "Kate, why don't they laugh?" And I said, "Well, Natalie, they don't think it's funny!"

They didn't know what it was about; they were leaving in droves. I got up and went to the ladies room and a woman was just lying there in a dead faint. I thought, "Well, that picture killed her, obviously." It was a disaster and it had been quite expensive for those days [1936]—over a million dollars.

❑

CHARLTON HESTON:

55 Days at Peking was one of the most disagreeable experiences of my entire life. First of all, we had no script at all. The lines were made up from day to day. The only reason I did the thing at all was as a favor to screenwriter Phil Yordan, who told me he had several kids to feed and no money. I shouldn't have listened to a word he said.

As for Ava Gardner—well, I must be careful. But let's say she wasn't the most disciplined or dedicated actress I ever worked with. A lot of the time she wasn't available for scenes. I think she was scared to death of her part. I can't really blame her. None of us should have made that piece of crap in the first place.

❑

ALFRED HITCHCOCK:

I had no special admiration for the novel *Under Capricorn*, and I don't think I would have made the picture if it hadn't been for Ingrid Bergman.

She was the biggest star in America and all the American producers were competing for her services, and I made the mistake of thinking that to get Bergman would be a tremendous feat; it was a victory over the rest of the industry, you see. That was bad thinking, and my behavior was almost infantile. Because even if the presence of Bergman represented a commercial asset, it made the whole thing so costly that there was no point to it. Had I examined the whole thing more carefully from the commercial angle, I would not have spent two and a half million dollars on the picture—at the time a lot of money.

Did the film lose a lot of money? Yes, it did, and the bank that financed it reclaimed the picture.

❑

DUSTIN HOFFMAN:

Ishtar: How can you open any movie when the audience has heard so much negative stuff about it first? "How dare they spend that kind of money?" And who's saying it? Gene Siskel and Roger Ebert, God bless 'em, who are probably the highest paid film critics in history. But it's all right for them to make millions while kicking the shit out of us.

I don't mind saying that I like the movie. I don't think it's great, but I'm not sorry I made it. In many ways I can't even evaluate it, because it's the only movie I've ever been on that was attacked like that. Before *Ishtar*, I never realized there was this desire to kill a film. That was sobering. And it's all OK, because . . . it's not cancer and it can only hurt you so much.

❑

JOHN HURT:

Michael Cimino made this gigantic film—*Heaven's Gate*—without an emotional or intellectual center. He gave himself a brilliant narrative on a plate and then stubbornly refused to use it. It starts with two characters, one of whom is brilliant at college but can't cope with the outside world, the other of whom scrapes by at college and then gets out to find life is an oyster. It's a wonderful structure, which gets lost under the mound of detail. I remember arriving on the set when they were shooting a scene that in the script was described in a sentence as, "Averell passes the cockfight on the way to the bar." When I got there, they were on the third week of shooting the cockfight, which really says it all.

ANGELS OVER BROADWAY (Columbia, 1940), with Douglas Fairbanks, Jr., Rita Hayworth. Directors: Ben Hecht, Lee Garmes.

❏

JOHN HUSTON:

I thought it would have a big audience. And one hopes for a film to be universally admired. Not to be considered just an art film. It got the New York Critics Award, but the fact that there wasn't a multitude clambering to see *Moby Dick* was a great disappointment.

❏

JENNIFER JONES:

As far as I'm concerned, *Tender is the Night* was never made. The original script was good, but by the time the gremlins got it, it wasn't. Every film is a gamble and it's a miracle when one good moment comes out.

❏

LARRY KERT:

I was doing an all-star stage presentation called *A Musical Jubilee* up in Toronto when I got a call from lyricist Fred Ebb who said there was the part of Liza Minnelli's boyfriend plus a musical number in a big film then being prepared and I should get to New York to discuss it. I met Martin Scorsese, the director, at the Sherry Netherland Hotel, talked about *New York New York* a bit and went back to Toronto. Two days later I got a call to report to Los Angeles for two weeks to shoot my role in the film.

It was my first real movie part in 32 years! In 1935, I had played the five-year-old son for whom Fredric March stole the bread in *Les Misérables*. During the 1940s, I was Roddy McDowall's stand-in and stunt double on all his *Lassie* and *Flicka* films. But I am known for my work on the musical stage.

Imagine my horror, then, when *New York New York* opened and I found that my whole sequence had been cut! I was no longer in the picture. According to the powers-that-were, the film ran too long and the last 30 minutes, my portion of the picture, was deemed too late to introduce a new, important character. I was on the soundtrack album for the film, but not in the film!

At best, the reviews were mixed. Four years later Martin Scorsese restored my part in the picture and reissued it. He invited me to a seminar he was giving at the time, and when someone in the audience asked, "We love that number with Larry Kert in the film—why was it cut?", he replied, "Larry is in the audience. Why don't you ask him?" When I stood up, everyone cheered. I felt somewhat vindicated.

To be frank, when I first saw the completed *New York New York*, it certainly wasn't what I had expected. I realized I was just a tool. I never get to look at the camera. I only look at Liza, then she looks at the camera. I never have a moment—I give it all to her. When I was recording the music, I thought the picture would be more. My nose was bent out of shape for a while.

Why did it fail? I don't know. Of course, the only real thing in it was the actors. The snow, the trees, the sets—they just seemed too fake for that kind of realistic story. I would have taken a more realistic approach to the movie.

But I had a good time making it. Scorsese has great style, Robert De Niro's lip-synching to Georgie Auld's saxophone playing is superb, Liza sings some wonderful songs. And I enjoyed working with choreographer Ron Field—this was his last major movie before he died.

You know, a lot of people don't consider *New York New York* a failure. Just because it failed at the boxoffice doesn't mean it was *really* a flop. I watch the complete videotape of it occasionally and there is a lot of entertainment in the picture.

❏

HARRY KURNITZ:

The Spirit of St. Louis, a movie about Charles Augustus Lindbergh, is still mentioned with reverence in the West Coast counting houses because, though it cost only $5,000,000, it succeeded in losing six.

❑

ERNEST LEHMAN:

When did I realize *Hello, Dolly!* wasn't working? After the first review, a rave in *Daily Variety.* I still have it. It came out on a Friday, and I had exactly one weekend in which to dream that maybe this picture was going to be OK after all. And then the roof fell in, with the exception of a few good reviews here and there. It got to the point where I decided it would be better for me personally not to read the awful reviews.

There is no way to make a really good picture out of anything based on *The Matchmaker.* Because half of it is about two silly young clerks and their romantic adventures. There was never enough about Dolly Levi. I realized that when the picture flashed on the screen at the Broadway premiere at the Rivoli Theater—you know, this big gala premiere, and it suddenly occurred to me, "Oh, my God, all these people are here to see a Barbra Streisand picture." And I know how much of this picture doesn't have her on the screen. The show's title was sort of a misnomer, because there was not very much about Dolly Levi. When I saw the play and Carol Channing came out at the end and was taking all these tremendous bows, I kept thinking, "Hey, wait a minute, you're acting as if you're the whole show." Gower Champion was as much the show as she was. It was the staging that made it magical onstage—so, as a movie, I tried to overcome this flaw in the story with production values—gargantuan sets, beautiful costumes.

It was such a huge success on the stage that it didn't seem possible that it couldn't succeed as a movie. Well, it cost a lot of money, and we didn't succeed.

❑

MITCHELL LEISEN:

Frenchman's Creek: she falls in love with a pirate, leaves her husband and comes back in time not to get caught. It's dull as dishwater and a lousy picture. I did it or got suspended.

Joan Fontaine was furious that David Selznick had sold her to Paramount for $2500 a week and he was only paying her $1200. She dug her heels in and said, "I'm going to give you $1200 worth of work and that's all." I was stuck with Fontaine and Arturo de Cordova, a Mexican from the Bronx. He could never pronounce the "g" in "ing"—he'd say "huntin'" and "fishin'." You could retake for days to get one good take out of him. Somehow we finally got him to say "going" and editor Alma Macrorie had countless copies made and cut the "g" in everywhere.

Fontaine and de Cordova were fighting all the time. She pranced in one day and said she was sorry for being so difficult, but after all, the whole picture rested on her shoulders. The whole company of distinguished British

TWO-FACED WOMAN (MGM, 1941), with Greta Garbo. Director: George Cukor.

actors was so insulted they refused to work with her and we lost a lot of time patching that one up.

It took us 104 days to get it in the can, but most of the overage was due to the fact that we got marooned in the fog on location and most of the time we could only shoot half the day.

❏

JACK LEMMON:

The Great Race made $25,000,000 and still hasn't broken even after they got through paying Natalie Wood and Tony Curtis and me.

❏

VIRGINIA MADSEN:

Dune was being touted as bigger than *Star Wars*. That was my big break, although it wasn't my big break at the boxoffice. I still haven't had that. But it was a big break within the business because it got me in the door and got me some other work.

❏

JOSEPH L. MANKIEWICZ:

Alice in Wonderland was a disaster, but a well intentioned disaster. The costumes and headpieces were so heavy that the actors couldn't carry them, so they had doubles walking through all the master or long shots. But it had a fantastic cast—just everybody: Cary Grant, Cary Cooper as the White Knight, Richard Atlen as the Cheshire Cat, W. C. Fields as Humpty Dumpty, Jack Oakie as Tweedledum, Alison Skipworth as the Duchess, Edna May Oliver as the Red Queen and many others. A girl named Charlotte Henry played Alice.

❏

STEVE MARTIN:

I knew *Pennies from Heaven* was a gigantic career mistake, but I loved the thing so much. I loved the language, the writing, the script. I thought it was an original movie done in an original style. I thought it had something to say. I still feel that way. Besides, if I have a career 15 years from now maybe it won't look like such a blunder.

A lot of people come up to me now and tell me they saw *Pennies* in film class. That makes an impact. It might have been esoteric when it was released but more and more people are beginning to understand it better. First, they had to get over seeing *me* in it, then they had to figure out what was going on. There were a lot of humps to get over.

❏

AL PACINO:

Revolution—I wish it hadn't turned out that way [a $19,000,000 fiasco, out of theaters in three weeks]. How could I not care? But I never felt my career was over. I always go back to work. What else can I do?

❏

GREGORY PECK:

After the many years Jane Fonda put in to get *Old Gringo* made, it's a pity to see it destroyed in 48 hours. *Old Gringo* made less than $2,000,000 at the boxoffice, a disastrous return for the $25,000,000 romantic extravaganza. People didn't go right away. And by the time they wanted to go, the picture wasn't playing anymore.

❏

ROBERT REDFORD:

How do I feel after putting so much work into a picture [*The Great Gatsby*] that fails? It's like robbing a bank and then discovering you carried the wrong bag out, and all you've got for your trouble is a sackful of old rags. But most things fall short of the mark, and that's the chance you take. The mistake, it seems to me, is to linger over it. I think the hype on *Gatsby* was damaging. It was offensive to a lot of people.

❏

DIANA ROSS:

I think *The Wiz* was maybe just too big, and maybe we lost some of the magic on that grand scale. It was an important story line of finding yourself and searching for direction. Maybe it was so overblown nobody got it. I don't know why it was so important for me to play Dorothy, but I'm going to stick to my instinct that it was the right move for me.

❏

DORE SCHARY:

My biggest and most embarrassing failure was *The Prodigal*. In all candor, I hustled Lana Turner into playing it opposite Edmund Purdom.

The sorry fact is, I liked the script. I thought it would draw an audience. What I forgot was that Cecil B. DeMille had an exclusive on the Bible. Poor Lana swayed her way through the film, but it was a hopeless task. The script was lifeless.

I MARRIED AN ANGEL (MGM, 1942), with Nelson Eddy, Jeanette MacDonald. Director: W. S. Van Dyke II.

That year [1955] Wade Nichols, editor of *Redbook*, awarded us [MGM] a large silver cup as the studio of the year for *Bad Day at Black Rock, Blackboard Jungle, Trial, Love Me or Leave Me* and *Interrupted Melody*. In his presentation, he admitted he was tempted to fill the prize with manure in tribute to *The Prodigal*.

❏

JOHN SCHLESINGER:

They say in the film business that you are only as good as your last picture. On the plane to Los Angeles for the premiere of *Far from the Madding Crowd* I was sitting next to a publicity man for the company [MGM]. We knew after the New York opening that the film was not going to be a great success, so he said to me, "Be careful what you do next. What is this *Midnight Cowboy* thing? It doesn't sound very promising to me."

❏

MARTIN SCORSESE:

Right after *New York New York*, during those two and a half years from 1976 to 1978, I went through a lot of problems. The film was not successful, and I was very depressed. I finally came out of it when I was in the hospital on Labor Day weekend in 1978, and [Robert] De Niro came to visit me and he said, "You know, we can make this picture [*Raging Bull*]."

❏

GRADWELL SEARS:

It was anticipated throughout the entire motion picture industry that *Arch of Triumph* would be a boxoffice sensation. Instead, it has proved to be the most disappointing picture and probably the greatest commercial failure in the history of motion pictures. No satisfactory explanation has yet been offered by anybody in the motion picture trade for the unprecedented failure of this picture.

❏

GEORGE SIDNEY:

I don't know why *Jupiter's Darling* missed. Certainly it was a great challenge to make and we all had fun meeting that challenge, or trying to.

It was the last picture I did at MGM for years; our leading lady, Esther Williams, left for good. Fifteen years before, I had directed the test that got Esther her contract there and also directed the picture that made her a star, *Bathing Beauty*. Her movies made a fortune for the studio. You could say

WILSON (20th Century-Fox, 1944), with Alexander Knox, Geraldine Fitzgerald. Director: Henry King.

that Fox froze the screen for Sonja Henie and we wet it for Esther Williams. I built an underwater camera for her, and after we'd shot this water ballet between her legs I remember telling her, "I'm going to show the American public more than your husband ever saw." She was always a pleasure to work with. There were some problems shooting *Jupiter's Darling* (which turned out to be an expensive picture), but never with Esther.

The property was based on an old Robert E. Sherwood play called *The Road to Rome* which had been on the shelf at Metro for years. For some reason, they just decided to take it down, dust it off and turn it into a musical aquacade for Esther. The story had to do with the conqueror Hannibal [Howard Keel] and his elephants. Now elephants and horses are natural enemies. We had this chariot race where the horses and elephants—which we borrowed from a circus—suddenly, unexpectedly went mad. It was chaos! You have to run elephants in a circle to stop them when something like this happens.

For purposes of plot, all the elephants had to be painted different colors. For obvious reasons, watercolor paint was to be used. So of course the day we were to shoot an assistant came up to me and said, "Some idiot painted these elephants with watercolors, and it comes right off, so I had them painted in oils"! I said, "Call the lawyers." I don't recall how we got the oil paint off the elephants, but it wasn't easy.

Later, when the pack was broken up I bought one of the elephants, a lovely lady named Babe, and kept her in Culver City—there's an ordinance that you can't have an elephant in Beverly Hills. I lived with a circus when I was a kid and had always wanted one.

Another time, a guy was sitting in a loo on the back lot when Esther's pet leopard in the film broke loose, climbed to the top of the open outhouse and looked down at the guy, whose constipation problems were solved immediately.

Jupiter's Darling was distinguished by one thing, at least: it had the longest swim in history. For one sequence, Esther dove into the water at Catalina, California, where we began the bit, and came up in Silver Springs, Florida, where we went to finish.

❑

STEVEN SPIELBERG:
I'll spend the rest of my life disowning this movie [*1941*].

❑

ELAINE STRITCH:
Despite the outcome, I had a divine time on *A Farewell to Arms*!

I was doing *Bus Stop* on Broadway with Kim Stanley when the Hollywood producer David O. Selznick saw me in it and engaged me to go to Italy where they were going to shoot most of *A Farewell to Arms*. I was to play Jennifer Jones' girlfriend at the hospital. It was a great thrill for me. Although I seemed to specialize then in playing older women, I was very young, had never been to Europe and had only done two films. And David Selznick, the producer of *Gone with the Wind*, wanted me!

I didn't want to go alone, though, so I asked David if I could bring my girlfriend Liz Smith, who today is the well-known columnist. He said yes, so off we went to Rome where we spent our spare time working on my autobiography—me talking, Liz typing. (The book hasn't been published yet, but it will be someday.)

Even though my role was not that large, I spent eight weeks on the film. It was an enormous, lavish undertaking; David hoped it would be another *Gone with the Wind* and do for Jennifer Jones, his wife, what that production did for Vivien Leigh. But of course it turned out to be his swan song.

It got off to a bad start when John Huston, who was already on location to direct the picture, had a disagreement with Selznick and walked off. His statement was, "It was a case of one Alp and two Hannibals." Selznick said, "I asked for a first violinist and instead got a conductor." Charles Vidor then came on as director. Not to be outdone, afterward he remarked, "What Selznick really wanted was a piccolo player." Scenes took forever because of the

SUNDAY DINNER FOR A SOLDIER (20th Century-Fox, 1944), with Anne Baxter, John Hodiak. Director: Lloyd Bacon.

thousands of extras sometimes just milling around in the background; costs mounted. I remember we shot in the Vatican Railroad Station for a week.

Rock Hudson and Jennifer were our stars. Rock was wonderful fun; we had a great time together. And I think his performance in the film is one of his best. Jennifer is also very good. She was a lovely girl whom I adored. Selznick was terrific, too—all that was great.

I really can't say why the picture failed. I was too young and green to know. I could tell you exactly why if it were a play; I have much more experience on stage than I have on screen. I just don't know enough about camerawork, lighting or the other components that comprise a motion picture. Film is a *total* mystery to me.

I just know that I loved doing *A Farewell to Arms*. I was a young girl on her first trip to Europe, making a big movie and having a ball!

❑

ELIZABETH TAYLOR:

The final humiliation was to have to see *Cleopatra*. The British Embassy trapped me into it. They requested me to take the Bolshoi Ballet as my guests to a screening of *Cleopatra*. I couldn't very well say no. When it was over, I raced back to the Dorchester Hotel and just made it into the downstairs lavatory before I vomited. I'm being sued by 20th Century-Fox and one of their complaints is that when somebody asks me what I think of the film, I tell them.

❑

LEA THOMPSON:

The "H" word—that's how I refer to *Howard the Duck*. I'd never seen the press go after something like that. I was in such shock. I wasn't prepared.

You can say anything about the movie—I'm not defending it—but you have to realize how much work it was, six months, every single day. I was so committed to that duck—I had to fall in love with a mechanical ILM [Industrial Light and Magic] effect, and in order to do that you have to *believe*. So, yeah, it was really disappointing.

❑

SPENCER TRACY:

The last few pictures I've tried, God knows I've failed. You know what happened to *The Old Man and the Sea*. And a critic or two took care of *Inherit the Wind*. Young people today want the thrill of a *Psycho*, for the love of God. I don't get to the young people. What the hell do they want to see me for? They don't go to see an old man. The older people go because they think they *might* see something good.

The 30 years have gone by awfully fast. My rewards have been doing things like *The Old Man and the Sea*, though it was a flop—my days at Metro—*Captains Courageous*, which was my best role.

❑

LANA TURNER:

MGM studio chief Dore Schary told the press he hoped to make *The Prodigal* one of "the really significant spectacles of all time." But when I read the script I wondered what Schary had been drinking.

I was to play a creature called Samarra, the high priestess of Astarte, goddess of the flesh, the temptress who incited the prodigal son of the Bible to leave home. The prodigal they named Micah and, to play him, chose Edmund Purdom, a young man with a remarkably high opinion of himself. His pomposity was hard enough to bear; worse yet was the garlic breath he brought back from lunch. My lines were so stupid I hated to go to work in the morning. Even the costumes were atrocious.

❑

AN AMERICAN ROMANCE (MGM, 1944), with Ann Richards, Brian Donlevy. Director: King Vidor.

LIV ULLMANN:

I'm ashamed about *Lost Horizon*, but I stayed in a big rented house in Hollywood and the film was full of famous actors and how could we know what it was going to be like? I had fun and now I'm paying for it.

☐

KING VIDOR:

I was determined to tell the story of steel from the viewpoint of an eager immigrant in *An American Romance*. Brian Donlevy and Ann Richards were made up and tested in all the various ages from youth to full maturity called for in the script, and they gave performances of striking conviction.

When the picture was previewed at Inglewood, Louis B. Mayer came to me on the sidewalk in front of the theater, put his arm around my shoulders and said, "I've just seen the greatest picture our company has ever made."

However, an order came from the New York office to cut half an hour. They cut the human elements of the story instead of the documentary sections, explaining that this was the only way a half hour could be taken out without complications in the musical soundtrack. In other words, the film was edited according to the soundtrack and not according to the inherent story values.

At the lowest emotional level I have reached since I have been in Hollywood, I went to my office, packed up and moved out of the studio. The

THE CONSPIRATORS (Warner Brothers, 1944), with Hedy Lamarr, Paul Henreid. Director: Jean Negulesco.

picture was not a big boxoffice success. Many of the inhabitants of Beverly Hills and Hollywood have never seen the film and many do not even know it was made. I spent three years of my life on the project and MGM spent close to $3,000,000.

❑

WALTER WANGER:

I lost a great deal of money on *Joan of Arc* and [Ingrid] Bergman's escapades, which didn't exactly help project her image as a saint.

When Howard Hughes put out that damn picture *Stromboli* right ahead of it, I lost over a million dollars. You see, I had a deal with Metro, and some of the conditions failed to work out. There was a break in the film market abroad. They wanted to change things, and I refused to, which I regret. I should have stayed with Metro. Overnight I made a deal with Hughes and RKO. He got entranced with Bergman and when she fell in love with Rossellini, this thing broke. Rossellini made *Stromboli* with her—nobody would finance it but Hughes; and he had my picture which hadn't been released yet. He brought out *Stromboli* first and it was a disaster. But with the exploitation of it, he killed the respectability of my picture.

In Europe they didn't give a damn. *Joan of Arc* did very well there. But I lost too much in the American and English market.

❏

RUTH WARRICK:

Initially, there was great interest in *Arch of Triumph*. It was from an internationally popular Erich Maria Remarque novel and a new studio, Enterprise, had been formed mainly to film it—which turned out to be at tremendous expense.

Ingrid Bergman and Charles Boyer were set for the romantic leads, and there was a huge talent search for someone to play the rich but tragic American girl involved with Boyer. *Everyone* wanted this part. At various times, actresses mentioned for the role of Kate included Joan Crawford, Barbara Stanwyck, Claire Trevor, Sylvia Sidney, Norma Shearer, Frances Dee, Ann Dvorak and Bette Davis. Afterward, I heard that 32 women were tested for the part, and that it was my test that won it for me. There were enormous headlines trumpeting my signing, predicting this would make me a big star at last.

Now at the time a writer friend of mine had a secretary who was into what today they would call "channeling"—as she'd be typing letters, some unexplained message would just pop out of her typewriter onto the paper. I was terribly excited about getting *Arch of Triumph*, so one day I asked her what would be the result, career-wise.

She replied, "It will mean absolutely nothing to you."

Crushed, I said something like, "What do *you* know."

Well, the picture was a complete disaster, a victim of terrible miscasting. Ingrid Bergman was the first one cast—that should have warned people right off the bat. Like everyone else then, I admired her as an actress but here she was supposed to be playing this frail, poor little Parisian drifter. This big, blonde, healthy Swedish girl! And in the most glamorous Edith Head gowns!

In the opening scene, when she's on the bridge contemplating suicide, and Charles Boyer comes up to her—well, he comes up to about her *nose*! Then there was a scene in the script where they go to her apartment and he was supposed to carry her up the stairs. At least they realized this would have been totally ridiculous, so it was not filmed.

In her autobiography, Bergman called Boyer one of the nicest people she'd ever met, but the truth is they did not get along. For one thing, she couldn't wear high heels with him, which annoyed her. Nevertheless, he was still dwarfed, and resented it. They were like boxers, a heavyweight and a lightweight—they'd go into their scenes, then go to their corners and glare at each other. She had her "handlers," he had his "handlers." They almost had to negotiate before they did a scene.

Most of my scenes were with Boyer, who had really pushed to get this assignment and was somewhat more aptly cast than Bergman. They seemed to turn out well, his reputation for scene-stealing notwithstanding. Now in Hollywood during those years not that many actors were adept at using props to call attention to themselves. But Boyer was a theater man, too. I remember

FRENCHMAN'S CREEK (Paramount, 1944), with Cecil Kellaway, Joan Fontaine. Director: Mitchell Leisen.

one scene we had together in the café. We rehearsed it; our director, Lewis Milestone, said, "Fine, let's shoot it." When the cameras began to roll, Boyer suddenly pulled out this huge silver cigarette case that had been nowhere in sight during rehearsal. He lit his cigarette, puffed and puffed and blew the smoke all around my face!

I laughed! I just laughed! Then I said, "*Now* I know what they were talking about." That calmed him down.

Otherwise, he was a lovely, charming actor to work with. At one point during the filming, Boyer, Charles Laughton and I were on location in the hills behind Malibu and didn't want to eat the unappetizing food provided by the studio. So we decided to take turns bringing the food from home. Just sitting there in the fresh air, munching and listening to these two extraordinary men, was worth everything that happened with *Arch of Triumph*.

The film was previewed in Santa Barbara. They had overshot wildly. It was then four hours long, unheard of in those days, and people walked out. The [opinion] cards were terrible. So the studio decided to cut it in half. There was about a 45-minute episode involving me in the hospital where I was dying of cancer. *Arch* was shot in 1946 (though not released until 1948) when cancer was like AIDS—no one discussed it. So they felt my whole hospital segment would be a good one to discard. I was left with very good billing, which they couldn't change, but only a brief, nothing café scene with Boyer. It taught me one thing: don't count ahead of time on what's going to be great.

Lewis Milestone had every confidence in my work but could do nothing against the studio. (A couple of years before I had worked with "Milly" on *Guest in the House*. One day he was carried off the set with a ruptured appendix, and as he left he told everyone, "Ruth is shooting the rest of the day." He let me direct!)

Looking back, *Arch of Triumph* seemed almost foredoomed. There was too much pre-publicity, an over-determination to make the "great" picture, too much expectation. I saw how hostility between the stars can destroy a film. If there is not a true affinity, a chemistry, between them, the picture will suffer. Soon after the débâcle was released, Enterprise Studios, having produced just nine films, folded after being in business only a couple of years.

❏

FRANK WESTMORE:

To this day, on the Warner Brothers Burbank lot there's an unusual monument both to [makeup artist] Perc Westmore's influence with William Randolph Hearst and to Hearst's unbelievable profligacy in all matters concerning his protégée, Marion Davies.

Elaborate musical numbers were very popular in movies in the 1930s. One day in his Warner office, thoughts of such a spectacle stirred Perc's creative juices as he read the script of Marion's next picture, *Cain and Mabel*. Perc conceived the idea of a gargantuan pipe organ, the stops of which would open to spew forth dozens of tap-dancing young ladies playing violins and other instruments. In the midst of this holocaust, Marion and co-star Clark Gable would get married.

Miss Davies adored it; Hearst's eyes misted over, too. [Jack] Warner said it was great and [dance director] Busby Berkeley applauded, albeit sadly: "We don't have a sound stage high enough to fit it all in."

Hearst said, "How much would it cost to raise the roof of Sound Stage Seven?" Warner said about $100,000. "Done!" shouted W. R. And that's why, if you visit Warner Brothers today, you will see an exceptionally tall, thin stage.

Even with Clark Gable's charisma and Perc's ingenuity, *Cain and Mabel* bombed. Marion made only one more picture.

❏

CORNEL WILDE:

Forever Amber was in trouble even before shooting began.

In a search he hoped would rival the hunt for Scarlett O'Hara in *Gone with the Wind*, Darryl Zanuck, the head of 20th Century-Fox, brought a little blonde named Peggy Cummins over from England to play the lusty Amber

THE HORN BLOWS AT MIDNIGHT (Warner Brothers, 1945), with Alexis Smith, Jack Benny.
Director: Raoul Walsh.

St. Claire. I was cast as her lover, Bruce Carlton, and after filming for over a
month it became clear that Peggy was wrong for the role. She was a pretty
girl, but she was too young and just wasn't getting it. (Later on, she would
prove herself a very good actress.) John M. Stahl's direction lacked inspiration,
too. Zanuck, who had paid plenty for the best-selling novel by Kathleen
Winsor, was dropping a bundle to film it. When everyone began telling him
that Peggy wasn't working out, he stopped production and removed her from
the picture. This created more headlines than the search for her had done,
but they were hardly positive.

All the footage shot by Stahl was scrapped when we began again with
Linda Darnell as our new Amber and George Sanders as England's King
Charles II, replacing Vincent Price.

Why did Zanuck hire Otto Preminger to direct the second version? I
think to torture the actors.

I had just done *Centennial Summer* with Otto, and he was impossible.
He made a habit of making the most insulting, sarcastic remarks on the set.
I argued with him constantly on *Amber*, not because of his behavior to me,
the leading man, but because of his cruelty to extras or the little bit player
with maybe three lines. I became the public defender. Otto was a constant
pain in the ass; I did *not* enjoy working with him.

On the other hand, Linda was a very sweet, likeable person, very kind
and generous. But I didn't think she was quite right for Amber, who was a

feisty, explosive dame with an obvious sexuality. Lana Turner might have been better, or Susan Hayward. Linda was beautiful, of course, but too gentle and docile.

It's been written that I never wanted to do *Forever Amber*, that I fought against it. True, I wasn't crazy about the long black wig I had to wear: it made me look like Joan Bennett. But it was only the *second* version I tried to resist. I knew from experience what Preminger would be like, but of all the actors under contract there they insisted I was the only one for Bruce Carlton. Also, I'd read the book and that was another reason I didn't want to do it: as I say, I felt that Linda, with whom I'd also just done *Centennial Summer*, was miscast.

When *Forever Amber* didn't do well, I wasn't too surprised. Zanuck had spent a fortune on it, claiming it was the most expensive picture ever made which it may well have been. But when he cast dear Linda as the tempestuous Amber he sealed its fate. Otto's direction has to take some of the blame, too. It was often ponderous. He'd devise these shots that went on for three minutes, without a break; there was no reason for that. Some of these got boring.

In addition, the film was condemned by the Legion of Decency, yet it was nowhere near as racy as the book. It was nowhere near as *anything* as the book.

The picture should have been called *Forever Trouble*.

❏

DARRYL F. ZANUCK:
Unless these two pictures, *Wilson* and *One World* [never made], are successful from every standpoint, I'll never make another film without Betty Grable.

❏

DARRYL F. ZANUCK:
Wilson? We lost our ass.

❏

RICHARD D. ZANUCK:
Star! is my Edsel.

Career Crushers

*"If it hadn't flopped, I might have become
a star instead of a waiter."*

DESI ARNAZ:

I started filming *Four Jacks and a Jill*, which I hope nobody remembers. I wish I could forget it myself. Good title and it didn't have a bad cast: Ray Bolger, Eddie Foy, Jr., and Anne Shirley. But we had a director—no use mentioning his name. I don't think he's around anymore, and if he is nobody knows where. Maybe he's been hiding ever since. He was originally an editor. I played a dual role: prince and taxi driver. After that we did *Father Takes a Wife*, with Adolphe Menjou and Gloria Swanson. I played an operatic tenor. RKO did not have another picture for me, so I went off salary. I had made $20,000 in a short time, but my career as a motion picture actor had not benefited. Both pictures were lemons.

❏

LAUREN BACALL:

Confidential Agent was a horror. The critics had said that I was the sun and the moon and the stars when *To Have and Have Not* came out. When *Confidential Agent* was released they all said they had been wrong, and I should be sent back to where I came from. They put me up on the top rung of the ladder, and then they pulled me down, and I spent the next 20 years trying to get back up.

❏

CHUCK BARRIS:

Toward the end of 1979 I decided to try something new. I wrote, directed and starred in a motion picture, *The Gong Show Movie*. It was to be my last hurrah.

If the movie was a success, I would have something to do for the rest of my life: make motion pictures. If the movie failed, it would be one blunder too many. I would remove myself, one way or another, from the public eye.

It took me 40 days and nights to shoot the movie, and five months to edit it. Then I had to tour the country to promote the goddamn thing. The most succinct early review was the *Albuquerque Tribune*: "Life is cruel enough without Chuck Barris around."

The Gong Show Movie was a flop. It opened in theaters across the country on a Friday and closed three days later. I became a recluse.

❏

JOAN BENNETT:

In 1958, my husband, Walter Wanger, began negotiations on what film critic Judith Crist called "A Monumental Mouse," *Cleopatra*, and he proceeded to repeat the mistakes of *Joan of Arc*, but on a much more magnificent scale.

By the time *Cleopatra* was released in 1963, it had almost wrecked 20th Century-Fox, forced the retirement of its president, Spyros Skouras, and made its stars, Elizabeth Taylor and Richard Burton, the hottest boxoffice in movie history. Walter sued Fox for having dismissed him during the last days of the film's production, and Spyros Skouras sued Walter for having libeled him in his book, *My Life with Cleopatra*. The suits were settled out of court. Until his death in 1968, Walter never produced another film.

❏

JACK BENNY:

The Horn Blows at Midnight—when the horn blew at midnight, it blew taps for my movie career.

❏

INGRID BERGMAN:

In my opinion, *Stromboli* was a very touching picture and a very true, believable story. But people were so taken by the private scandal [the Bergman-Rossellini love affair] that they were against it from the beginning. I remember reading in *Variety* when the picture came out in several movie houses at the same time that American exhibitors would see if the movie were a success, and if it weren't, they'd ban it "upon grounds of morality"!

❏

TURHAN BEY:

Nineteen fifty-three's *Prisoners of the Casbah* was my last picture. It was one of the most amusing scripts I'd read, but when I saw the film I was horrified.

ADVENTURE (MGM, 1945), with Greer Garson, Clark Gable. Director: Victor Fleming.

Columbia scored it with "canned" music and it just didn't fit. Unfortunately, the picture was made at a time when I had to wear a toupé, and when I saw the fencing scenes I felt my career should stop right there ... and it did. Three or four days into shooting, I became terribly ill and they had to give me some injections to keep me going. I had trouble remembering my lines—it was *agony* getting through that picture.

Our leading lady was wonderful Gloria Grahame. *Prisoners* had to be a great disappointment as she had just made a great success in *The Bad and the Beautiful*. She tried to do something with the stereotyped Princess role; inject her own personality into the routine part. But this didn't meet with the approval of the director or producer, so she had to play in an ordinary way. And the results of the final film were not what we had expected.

❑

PETER BOGDANOVICH:

At Long Last Love—in my family we began calling it The Débâcle. The one thing it proves is that I didn't know how to make a musical. I've recut it three times at my own expense. I just got the bill from 20th Century-Fox for $30,000 for the last one. The version that's being shown on television now is very different from the one that played theatrically. I finally arrived at what that movie should have looked like three years ago.

❏

MARLON BRANDO:

The Freshman—it's going to be a flop, but after this, I'm retiring. I'm so fed up. This picture, except for the Canadian crew, was an extremely unpleasant experience. I wish I hadn't finished with a stinker.

❏

LOUISE BROOKS:

At the time these pictures [*Pandora's Box, The Diary of a Lost Girl*] were released as silents everybody wanted to see talkies, so that my films went unnoticed, and I decided I was a great failure. Everyone said I stunk.

❏

MARGE CHAMPION:

Jupiter's Darling was a special favorite of mine. I never thought it was much of a movie to hang your heart on, but I LOVED working with those elephants. It was like being with a circus for three or four weeks. Each cow [female elephant] had her own personality. Gower and I got to know them all because we fitted our big dance number around their talents.

At the end of shooting, George Sidney, the director, held a "wrap" party for them and us. He ordered a truckload of watermelons brought to the back lot at MGM. The elephants went crazy—throwing them up in the air with their trunks, squashing them with their big feet, lapping them up, rind and all.

I can only venture guesses as to why *Jupiter's Darling* never made money. It came at the end of the big musical vogue . . . Esther Williams was preparing to retire to marriage and motherhood . . . it was set in ancient Rome which removed it even further from the average person's experience. Also, it was pretty silly except for the marvelous musical numbers. CinemaScope didn't help, either, because at that point [early 1955] there weren't that many theaters yet equipped to project it.

❏

CAROL CHANNING:

I was over at RKO—remember them? But the scripts weren't always the best in town. The worst script in my life was for *The First Traveling Saleslady*, starring Ginger Rogers when I was at RKO. It was so bad Ginger's mother used to come on the set and suggest alternative endings and lines to say. We helped close RKO, which isn't easy for two little girls to do.

YOLANDA AND THE THIEF (MGM, 1945), with Lucille Bremer, Fred Astaire. Director:
Vincente Minnelli.

❏

MARGUERITE CHAPMAN:

The Amazing Transparent Man was filmed in Dallas, Texas, with oil money.
They needed a money loser, and they sure got it. It was never publicized. I
don't know of any theaters that played it, though a few little fleatraps somewhere may have had a death wish. The first I saw it anywhere was on television
about five years later.

When I arrived in Dallas everyone on the picture was by the motel pool.
Les Guthrie, our director, had just done three films in a row for these people
and told me, "I've never had so much trouble. All I need now is for the motel
to burn down."

Later that evening, I was in my room where I'd just bathed. I was wearing
my robe and rolling my hair. Suddenly, the roof of the motel caught fire and
it was spreading toward where I was. Quick as a flash, Les rushed in—to save
me, I thought. Instead, he grabbed my studio clothes lined up by the drapes
and ran out with them. "What about me?" I yelled as Les and the wardrobe
flew through the door to safety.

A minute later, James Griffith, one of the actors in the film, hollered in,
"I've got to save my guns! I'll be back for you!"

Afterwards, we were all safely outside when the press came and took photos. I was still in my bathrobe, my hair half in rollers. The motel was saved. Les came over to me and said, "I don't care if we *are* shooting in the morning, I'm gonna get drunk tonight." I went back to my room and had a few beers myself.

The next morning, we were filming out in the woods in the most incredible quiet for a movie location. Everyone was tiptoeing around—they all had hangovers. I wasn't tiptoeing, though—my scene was in a car!

The odor from the fire was so foul that I asked if I couldn't please be moved to a hotel. So they put me on the 13th floor of a Dallas hotel. I no sooner got settled in than a waiter blithely announced, "Oh, this is the room where a lady jumped to her death from one of the windows"! *Everyone* who came in said this to me. The day after the picture finished, I called a couple I knew in Fort Worth and pleaded with them to come and get me. "I can't stay in this room a minute more," I said. They came. After a while trouble popped up there, too. My friend's husband tried to rape me!

There was a plus side to the whole Texas movie career massacre, though. I got paid for the picture and bought some nice clothes at Neiman-Marcus. And I got to know Larry Marcus. He invited me to a beautiful garden party where the guests included Greer Garson. These things made the whole nightmare worthwhile.

What do I think of *The Amazing Transparent Man*? What would *you* think of something called *The Amazing Transparent Man*?! Pukesville!

It was my last movie.

❑

CYD CHARISSE:

Silk Stockings was one of the best films I did, followed by the absolute worst. MGM loaned me to Universal for a tidbit called *Twilight for the Gods*, based on the Ernest Gann book.

It started out as a pleasant enough assignment—most of it was to be shot in Hawaii, and my co-star was Rock Hudson. Rock was then married to Phyllis Gates and the four of us had a great time for a while. But one day Phyllis told me she was going home and, as it turned out, that was when she and Rock separated. That kind of put a pall on things.

But the worst thing that happened, as far as I was concerned, was the director, Joseph Pevney. He took a good book—a best-seller—and did not seem to know what to do with it.

❑

RENÉ CLAIR:

Flame of New Orleans was a big flop, and a great handicap in my American career. When I started in Hollywood, they were enthusiastic about welcoming people they knew in Europe. We really had great possibilities. But you know how Hollywood is. If they get too much on you and you fail, finish; that happened to me in *Flame of New Orleans*. Maybe it was a little too subtle for that time.

❑

PETULA CLARK:

Finian's Rainbow is still one of the happiest experiences of my life, although I seldom talk about it or my movie career because the critics hated both of the musicals I did [the other: *Goodbye, Mr. Chips*]. Today they are considered flops, which is probably why my movie career flourished and died so quickly.

❑

HANS CONRIED:

That was the film that might have changed my life—*The 5,000 Fingers of Dr. T*, under the direction and overall oppression of Mr. Harry Cohn. The picture was to be a big one, and Ted Geisel (Dr. Seuss) wrote it, designed the costumes, designed the scenery. A good deal of money was spent; it was a great, beautiful picture.

The Americans have never made a really successful fantasy, although of course this was a comedic one. The picture was badly cut in fear of the reappraisal after it was made, even if it was evident to those knowledgeable but inartistic heads of studio that it might have been an artistic triumph rather than a financial one. But in an attempt to make it one, they cut over 11 musical numbers and re-shot for one whole week. I had never had any such part before, never have since and probably never will again. We rehearsed for eight weeks before I was engaged to shoot for eight weeks, an extravagance that I as a bit player had never known.

The picture never made its print money back. It was comparable only to *Wilson* as one of the great money-losers of all time; it would stop conversations for some years thereafter at any Hollywood gathering. If you mentioned it people would laugh, and if you were connected with it you might cough embarrassedly.

If it had been a success, with my prominent part in the title role, it would have changed my life.

❑

JACKIE COOPER:

I realized that there was nowhere for me to go after films like *Stork Bites Man, Kilroy Was Here* and *French Leave*. I didn't want to spend the rest of

DEVOTION (Warner Brothers, 1946), with Olivia de Havilland, Paul Henreid, Ida Lupino. Director: Curtis Bernhardt.

THE DIARY OF A CHAMBERMAID (United Artists, 1946), with Reginald Owen, Hurd Hatfield, Francis Lederer, Paulette Goddard. Director: Jean Renoir.

my life in D pictures, and that was what they were. In the past I had known what it was like to be in really first-rate films, and it was degrading to be seen in such schlock.

❑

BETTE DAVIS:

My first film with Bogart was a deadly thing called *Bad Sister*. We were both under contract to Universal and (no wonder, after seeing *Bad Sister*) we were both fired from the studio. There was a legend at that time that if you were fired from Universal, you would eventually make it to the top.

❑

JIM DAVIS:

When *Winter Meeting* flopped, I couldn't get another acting job for a year. Things got so bad, I ended up wheeling concrete on construction sites for a while.

❑

GEORGE DOLENZ:

Vendetta was a very expensive mess, but Howard Hughes, who owned the studio [RKO], was determined to showcase his latest protégée, Faith Domergue, in it.

We worked on the picture for years. It was filmed and refilmed. Hughes kept bringing in different directors to look at the film and often shoot part of it—Max Ophuls, Preston Sturges, Stuart Heisler, Josef von Sternberg, Don Siegel and, finally, Mel Ferrer, who got director's credit on the screen. Each time they made it, I played a different character (although I was always the leading man).

Well, *Vendetta* wasn't released; it escaped. If it hadn't flopped, I might have become a star instead of a waiter.

❑

STANLEY DONEN:

I never felt that *The Little Prince*'s financial fiasco—or that of any other film of mine—was the result of the way it was handled by the studio. I don't think the picture has in it the elements that the audience likes in a movie. They like razzle-dazzle; they like flash. They are not very pleased about the whole musical form any longer. I always used to say I don't know for whom we are making it. I only know *I* like it.

IT'S A WONDERFUL LIFE (RKO, 1946), with Thomas Mitchell, Carol Coomes, Donna Reed, James Stewart, Karolyn Grimes, Sarah Edwards, Jimmy Hawkins, Larry Simms, Beulah Bondi. Director: Frank Capra.

DIANA DORS:

They brought me over here as a sex bomb, a supposed threat to Marilyn Monroe. And who did they give me for leading men? George Gobel in *I Married a Woman* and Rod Steiger in *The Unholy Wife*! I should have had Bill Holden or Cary Grant. I had to carry the whole burden myself, and the pictures fizzled. I was a sex bomb, all right—with the accent on "bomb."

IRENE DUNNE:

It Grows on Trees was kind of a cute story—money suddenly growing on trees in my backyard. Maybe if we'd had a bigger director and a "name" leading man, it might have been successful. But we didn't and it wasn't. My movie career was over.

NIGHTMARE ALLEY (20th Century-Fox, 1947), with Coleen Gray, Tyrone Power. Director: Edmund Goulding.

CHARLES DURNING:

I think that the time for actors of my age and my range is over in movies. Right now, films are made for kids.

One of the things that I think put a clamp on me was that I did this great film, *Mass Appeal*, and critically it's terrific, but nobody's going to see it.

❏

ROBERT EVANS:

I didn't make one dollar on the film [*The Cotton Club*], and look what I got for it.

❏

DOUGLAS FAIRBANKS, JR.:

My next job offer came from Ben Hecht, a brilliant playwright. I didn't even try to disguise my delight. I had long admired Hecht's colorful command of "big city" language and his priceless inventory of offbeat characters. The screenplay was called *Angels over Broadway* and I thought it a gem. Hecht (who had little knowledge of movie making) insisted that he and I should be co-producers, Lee Garmes co-director.

Preview audiences were warmly approving. Ben and I were satisfied that it was a very good picture, and most of the critics seemed to agree. Unfortunately, these press laurels were written on wet paper. The public stayed away in disappointing droves. Looking at the film again after many years, I can see why. It had some fine but perhaps overstylized Hechtian dialogue; both Tommy Mitchell and I greatly overacted; dear Rita Hayworth, though very pretty, was very inexperienced; the photography by Lee Garmes was fine; but the whole thing was just too fanciful and, aside from a few melodramatic instances, too fey.

I had no good job offers at all after *Angels over Broadway*.

❑

ALICE FAYE:

Going back [to 20th Century-Fox for the 1962 remake of the musical *State Fair*] crushed me. The studio was in such chaos you couldn't even tell who was running it anymore. I think they hated me because I was too young to play Pat Boone's mother. I had absolutely no direction from José Ferrer. I was lit wrong, photographed badly ... and they made me play opposite Tom Ewell! Do you *know* Tom Ewell? The whole thing was a nightmare. I never even saw it on TV. It was awful. I don't know what happened to the picture business, but I'm sorry I went back to find out.

❑

JODIE FOSTER:

I've never done a film people liked. And I've stopped second-guessing whether my films would do well or not. Ever since *The Hotel New Hampshire*, I don't even try. I thought it was going to be a huge success, and it bombed. I still don't understand what happened, and I'm the only one. Everybody else said to me, "What do you mean you don't understand?! It was horrible!" People either liked it, or despised it so intensely that it became the bane of my existence. That film blew it for me for a while.

❑

GRETA GARBO:

Two-Faced Woman—they're trying to kill me—they've dug my grave!

❑

TAY GARNETT:

Walter Wanger and I bought the rights to a book, *Send Another Coffin*, and Ken England sweated out a funny script with a fresh, flippant approach to the standard murder mystery. We finished ahead of schedule—which

THE SEA OF GRASS (MGM, 1947), with Spencer Tracy, Katharine Hepburn. Director: Elia Kazan.

should have warned me. With a feeling of "Well done," I humored myself and went to bed with a ten-Kleenex case of flu. Walter agreed to finish the final odds and ends.

The film had been booked into a San Francisco theater whose owner I respected as a perceptive showman. As we strolled across the lobby, he met me, eyes blazing: "You dirty double-crossing s.o.b.! I bought this picture as *Send Another Coffin*. What in the hell was the idea of changing the title to *Slightly Honorable*? That won't sell matinée ticket number one."

"I don't know what you're talking about," was all I could say.

The theater owner showed us to the cheap seats, growling, "You'll know what I'm talking about after you've taken a look at your own private disaster." What we saw was a badly mutilated, unfunny comedy cut with a jigsaw and reassembled with a Mixmaster.

One hundred and fifty prints were en route to theaters, catastrophes bearing *my* name as director. I realized exactly how bad *Slightly Honorable* must be when the officer at the United Artists gate (who had been parking my car) asked me for identification one morning.

❑

GREER GARSON:

A couple of years ago, along with the whole Metro-Goldwyn-Mayer studio, I wanted something too much. Clark Gable, our friend and home-lot hero, was back from the wars and everybody wanted to make his return picture a bang-up hit. I played opposite Clark. Maybe we all tried too hard. *Adventure* wasn't good at all. That was strike one, to mix a metaphor.

Then a friend of mine sent me an Enoch Arden story I thought particularly good and timely for those post-war days. But it wasn't made until two years later, very much out of date, and censorship robbed it of what punch was left. I loved doing it (although that's when I almost drowned at Big Sur), but *Desire Me* was a sad mistake. No alibis, though. Just strike two.

I steeled my red head for the blows and they came, the cracks by the columnists and critics. It was good for a titillating gossip hint in one column that "Deborah Kerr is being groomed at Metro to take over Greer Garson's place as First Lady." We had a lot of fun out of it, Deborah and I. I think I invited her over once for arsenic sandwiches.

❏

ALEX GOTTLIEB:

Some agent had pawned off a property on Jack Warner and he wanted me to have a screenplay prepared. The book was about an adopted, illegitimate child taunted by the people in her small town who ended up, at 17 or so, in the arms of a man old enough to be her father—in fact, believed by the town to be exactly that. It was a lot of soap for an audience to swallow.

I got Charles Hoffman to do the screenplay for *That Hagen Girl*, which everyone thought was pretty good. I went back to Warner and asked who he thought we should cast in the picture. He said, "Well, the guy is easy, we'll get Ronnie Reagan or one of those guys. The girl is tough. Who do you have in mind?" I said, "What about Shirley Temple?"

Shirley had not done much real acting lately. I was surprised to find she was frightened and very nervous when I met her. Her acting capabilities were quite limited. Director Peter Godfrey did what he could, but we needed a trained actress like Anne Baxter or Teresa Wright. I, somehow, had thought that all those years in films meant Shirley could act. She never really understood the character she was playing. I had made a terrible error in judgment, and all through production I knew it would turn out terrible and, boy, was I right.

To add to the awfulness of the film, Reagan and Temple had no chemistry together.

❏

LIVING IN A BIG WAY (MGM, 1947), with Gene Kelly, Marie McDonald. Director: Gregory LaCava.

FARLEY GRANGER:

Edge of Doom—that's where it brought all our careers.

❑

KATHRYN GRAYSON:

I don't know why, but people out here are always tricking me. They promise a good script and I say I'll do it if the script is good, but it never comes through. Like on *The Vagabond King*. I had script approval, but I never got to see it until too late. It was hideous. In the four years since I did it, I've had a bad case of nerves where movies are concerned.

❑

JOHN GREEN:

In 1947 I was brought to Universal-International by William Goetz and Leo Spitz to rescue Deanna Durbin's career. I'd say I finished her off!

She got a reputation for being difficult. However, when I was working with her she was fascinating, a good enough actress and still sang like an angel. We got her weight down and made two very bad pictures. The first was *Something in the Wind* for which I served the multiple tasks of being her psychiatrist, vocal coach and music director of the film. I also wrote the score. Leo Robin wrote the lyrics. The second film was *Up in Central Park*. It was death to do that kind of [costume] picture in black and white, but the budget wouldn't permit doing it in color.

Both pictures were disasters. The public just did not want Deanna Durbin at that time, although she was very good in them. The soundtracks of her voice were wonderful.

❑

MARGARET HAMILTON:

We had a great time making *The Sin of Harold Diddlebock*; we felt we were getting a very funny film. Harold Lloyd was the star and Preston Sturges the writer-director.

Preston was wonderful: he would give the actors their head, allow them to improvise and develop their scenes and characters. If a scene was working well, he would let us keep going as long as the scene was playing. Later, he would cut and edit it all himself. Unfortunately, the powers at United Artists and, later, RKO took the picture away from him, cutting here, trimming there, until most of the humor was obliterated.

It was re-titled *Mad Wednesday* and by Thursday was out of theaters. Harold Lloyd never made another picture, and I don't think Preston ever had a successful film again.

❑

KATHARINE HEPBURN:

No, it didn't worry me that I was labeled boxoffice poison in the thirties. They were right. The films I made at the time—*Sylvia Scarlett, Break of Hearts* and *A Woman Rebels*—bored *me*, so no wonder they bored the audience. Another, *Quality Street*, was actually quite repulsive. But I was young at the time and I could survive.

❑

JAMES HILL:

I heard a lovely voice. "Mr. Hill . . . ?" When I turned, I found an attractive young girl of 19 or 20 looking intently up at me from her deep violet eyes. Well, she went on to tell me that of all the films she had ever seen in her life, her very favorite was one I had produced, *The Sweet Smell of Success*. Now I wasn't about to disillusion her by telling her the picture had lost so much money it had just about landed our company in chapter 11. So I had to settle for the truth by telling her it also happened to be *my* favorite. This so delighted her that she admitted she had never bought a man a drink in her life, but would like to buy me one now. Given her great good taste in films, it seemed sheer ingratitude to wreck her entire day by refusing her.

❑

DENNIS HOPPER:

Before I'd made *The Last Movie*, I'd gone around to all the universities selling *Easy Rider*, and everyone was saying, "We want new kinds of movies." So I made a new, different kind of movie. But if I'd really listened to what they were saying, really taken a moment to interpret it, I'd have realized they meant, "We don't want to see anything too extreme to jar our sensibilities, which are already rattled by drugs and protests and so forth." But I didn't see that. I just took what they said at face value, and I made a movie which stopped my directing career. It won the Venice Film Festival, but the film was never seen.

❑

MILT JOSEFSBERG:

A memorable radio moment had Jack Benny and Rochester driving up to the studio gate. The guard shot at them and Jack said, "Don't you recognize me? I'm Jack Benny. I made a movie here at Warner Brothers—*The Horn Blows at Midnight*. Didn't you see it?" And the guard answered, "See it? I *directed* it!"

❑

ELIA KAZAN:

We had another showing of *The Last Tycoon*, and this confirmed we had a dud. Many people, including some of producer Sam Spiegel's friends, got up and left without a word. A close friend of mine came to me, kissed me and walked off without a comment. Bobby De Niro was there; he didn't respond to the film. David Lean seemed to rather like it—how could anyone tell—but he did not like De Niro. He said Bobby wasn't a leading man, that he played the individual scenes acceptably but was not interesting overall, the way a star should be.

Only Jeanne Moreau sincerely and passionately extolled the film. Which was a sign of what was coming: the French would again like a film of mine that audiences in the United States did not. Should I go live in France?

As I began to pack my books, my records and my diaries to send back East, it hit me that this was indeed my last film and that it was a kind of death for me, the end of a life in the art where I'd worked for so long. It was all over.

MOURNING BECOMES ELECTRA (RKO, 1947), with Rosalind Russell, Kirk Douglas, Nancy Coleman, Michael Redgrave. Director: Dudley Nichols.

❏

HOWARD KEEL:

Kismet was a bomb. I never worked so hard in my life, but I was up against great odds. The whole thing was done with too heavy a hand.

❏

BERT LAHR:

Unfortunately, the Hays office cut the picture [*Zaza*] to shreds, but I got the notices. If it had been a hit, I would have been made as a dramatic actor.

❏

VERONICA LAKE:

I turned to a role in *The Hour Before the Dawn*, a film version of W. Somerset Maugham's novel about pacifism and its ramifications. I now recognize this film as the beginning of a great slide down for Veronica Lake.

There I was at the peak of my popularity and with only a glowing future in store. Yet *The Hour Before the Dawn* started me on a long series of bad films that never did a thing for my career. I never even knew I'd begun the slide until it was too late to grab a rung and try to halt the fall.

❑

LIBERACE:

Sincerely Yours was my big try for stardom in the movies, but no one noticed it or me. Maybe I should have worn my candelabra on my head, Carmen Miranda style.

❑

SOPHIA LOREN:

A Countess from Hong Kong had been in Charlie Chaplin's desk drawer for 20 years. I heard tell that he had originally written it for Paulette Goddard and got it out and updated it after he saw me in *Yesterday, Today and Tomorrow*.

Marlon Brando was cast in the male lead. I liked Marlon, and I admired him enormously as one of the greatest actors in films, but he was obviously better suited to dramatic roles than to comedy. To make matters worse, he and Charlie did not get along. As for myself, I adored Charlie.

The critics called it old-fashioned. The movie's failure was heartbreaking for Charlie—it was his last film. Perhaps if it had succeeded, he would have made more. As far as I was concerned, what I learned from him as a director, and as a man, made the experience, for me, a triumph.

❑

GROUCHO MARX:

I signed to make a film for United Artists, *Love Happy*. It was terrible and I tried to blot it out of my mind.

One memory, however, lingers. The producer called me one day. "We have three girls here," he said. "Why don't you come and pick one out?" I would be picking the girl who would be doing a sexy vignette in the film.

Three girls lined up when I arrived. "Which one do you like?", the producer asked. They walked for us. "You must be crazy," I replied. "There's only one. The blonde." The girl was signed. For her one scene, she wore a dress cut so low I couldn't remember the dialogue. Very soon other men throughout the world would be suffering similar fevers, for the girl was Marilyn Monroe.

Love Happy marked the last time the Marx Brothers acted together for a film.

MONSIEUR VERDOUX (United Artists, 1947), with Martha Raye, Charles Chaplin. Director: Charles Chaplin.

❏

SAMUEL MARX:

The market began to turn downward—*Variety* headlined its October 30, 1929, issue: "Wall Street Lays an Egg." MGM chose that week to introduce John Gilbert to talkies in *His Glorious Night*, made by Irving Thalberg. On the same page as its stock market story, the paper reported: "Audiences Laughing at Gilbert." His voice elicited such hilarity that in some parts of the country, according to the trade journal, people were throwing fruit and veg-ctablcs at the screen.

The star's second talking picture, *Redemption*, was as disastrous as the first. Audiences drew a cruel inference that if his voice sounded sissified, feminine tendencies must go with it.

John Gilbert died on January 9, 1936, alone and in an alcoholic stupor. He was 38.

❏

JACKIE MASON:

I will never make another movie. Making movies is murder; it's not for me. It means working four months straight, talking to the walls from early morning until 12 at night. It's a disgusting way to live.

There was not only last year's *Caddyshack II* that was a critical and

73

commercial disaster, there were four other films made with a huge percentage of my own money.

One was called *The Stoolie*, and was directed by John Avildsen before he became famous making *Rocky*. I made the vehicle to make myself a star and it flopped. You would have never heard of the other three I did—they flopped even worse.

❑

JAMES MASON:

I played an angel in *Forever Darling*, with Lucille Ball and Desi Arnaz, but there was nothing heavenly about the boxoffice returns. I love Lucy, but I hated our picture, the worst I ever appeared in. And Lucy and Desi did no more movies together.

❑

BETTE MIDLER:

After *Jinxed*, I slept all day and cried all night. I was drinking to excess. I was miserable.

❑

RAY MILLAND:

In 1948, I rebelled and refused to do a picture, the first and only time I was to take a suspension in 21 years at Paramount. And with good reason. The movie was a turkey called *Bride of Vengeance*.

The story was about the Borgias, a very lush and expensive picture to make. It had the top director on the lot, Mitchell Leisen, Paulette Goddard and half the contract list. But the story? Whew! I can still smell it. The critics lacerated it unmercifully, and after five days in release it was yanked, and as far as I know it has never been shown since. Leisen was let out, so was Goddard, so was the producer [Richard Maibaum], and so was the unfortunate leading man [John Lund] who replaced me. Even the assistant director was demoted.

The producer eventually migrated to England and is still there, because I passed him on the street. I stuck out my hand to say hello and he cut me dead.

❑

ANN MILLER:

I finished off my early RKO years in a dud—a B called *Tarnished Angel*, with Sally Eilers. She played a part like that great lady preacher, Aimee Semple

THE LOST MOMENT (Universal, 1947), with Susan Hayward. Director: Martin Gabel.

FOREVER AMBER (20th Century-Fox, 1947), with Cornel Wilde, Linda Darnell. Director: Otto Preminger.

McPherson. I think it was one of the last movies Sally made, and I couldn't blame her.

We had a scene together in a meeting hall where Sally was preaching to a flock of people. And right behind her was a real live camel. Sally was wearing a long white gown, holding a Bible and preaching, "It is easier for a camel to go through the eye of a needle than for a rich man to enter the Kingdom of Heaven." I was sitting on a dais in the center of the stage.

Suddenly, the real-life camel started doing what comes naturally. The sound man screamed, "What's that noise? Is it raining?" It sounded like Niagara Falls. And then suddenly the camel relieved himself of a big flop, flop, splashing everyone within reach. We were all drenched. Sally's gown and shoes were sopped in buckets of camel dung. That ended the day's shooting. And that picture was my last under my RKO contract; I asked for my release.

❑

VINCENTE MINNELLI:

Those who look at my career categorize *Yolanda and the Thief* as my first interesting failure. It was based on a sophisticated fable by Ludwig Bemelmans and Jacques Thery. The story was naive, however, and much of the public couldn't accept a simple story in an avant garde setting. Film buffs say the picture was ahead of its time—it had great style.

If there was one casualty it conceivably could have been Lucille Bremer (as Yolanda). Nothing was spared to show off her extraordinary dancing ability. However, she lacked star quality. But then, Lucille never wanted to be a star, and it probably showed. She got married as quickly as she could, leaving pictures. Her "defection" is sad in a way, for I consider her one of the finest dancers I've ever worked with.

❏

MARIA MONTEZ:

Siren of Atlantis gave off such a smell, I had to leave town. In fact, I had to leave the country! One important New York newspaper said it should be given prizes for worst picture and worst acting of the year [1949].

❏

ROGER MOORE:

It's a period in my life I just laugh about now. I remember my biggest part was opposite Lana Turner in a bomb called *Diane*. *Time* said, "Lana Turner as Diane de Poitiers walked on the screen in a clattering of heels and a fluttering of false eyelashes, followed by a lump of English roast beef." I was the English roast beef. Then they [MGM] asked me to leave. "Just check in your wardrobe and clear out" is the way they put it. I arrived in America on April Fool's Day, 1954. I should have known that meant something.

❏

GEORGE MURPHY:

The last film I made was for Metro in 1952. But I'm afraid the only reason *Talk About a Stranger* may be of interest is that in it I appeared opposite a very lovely young actress named Nancy Davis. Today Nancy is better known as Mrs. Ronald Reagan.

After we read the script of *Talk About a Stranger*, Nancy and I talked it over and agreed it wasn't very good. We tried to persuade the studio to shelve the project, but to no avail. The finished product was so horrible that I don't think it was ever released. Every year since then, around Christmastime, I have promised Nancy that I would get a print and run it—but thus far she has been spared that pleasure.

❏

PATRICIA NEAL:

Kirk Douglas was my escort to the premiere of *The Fountainhead*. Jack Warner had already screened the film, and he sent me a wire stating that I was the greatest thing to hit Hollywood since Garbo.

I had the grim feeling all through the screening that I would not emerge a champion, a feeling that was not dispelled by the crowd. When Kirk and I moved out into the bright lobby it seemed that everyone just turned their heads and looked in the other direction. One familiar face did not avoid me. Virginia Mayo gave my hand a squeeze and said, "My, weren't you *bad*!" I hoped she meant the character I played, but I knew my career as a second Garbo was over before it began.

The Fountainhead was a bomb.

◻

JACK NICHOLSON:

After *Goin' South* bombed, I couldn't get arrested as a director.

◻

GEORGE OPPENHEIMER:

I claimed the dubious distinction of having written the picture that drove Greta Garbo off the screen.

Two-Faced Woman was the last film Garbo made. However, even had it been a good picture, which it most definitely was not, I believe that Garbo was ready and eager to quit. Why this particular story was chosen for her remains one of those mysteries that pockmark the industry. It was taken from a German plot that had already served, to no great effect, as a film some years before. In addition Garbo, who had never been famous for her taste or interest in clothes, allowed co-player Constance Bennett to help pick out her wardrobe. The results were not nearly so felicitous as Bennett's own gowns. In fact they were disastrous.

Then someone sold director George Cukor on the idea that Garbo did not, as legend went, have big feet. He conceived the notion that Melvyn Douglas, who played her husband, should praise her extremities and, in a bedroom scene, lift one of them up to reveal its beauty. At the first preview Garbo's bare foot looked larger than legend and elicited one of the loudest and rudest laughs I have heard in a theater. The scene was promptly cut.

◻

DOLLY PARTON:

I had no control over the movie [*Rhinestone*], but it was the first project I did after I was ill and had been out of work for 18 months, and it was a hit with me. Being around [Sylvester] Stallone was fun—I really enjoyed doing it. It was a disaster—but fun, cute.

◻

ARCH OF TRIUMPH (United Artists, 1948), with Charles Boyer, Ruth Warrick. Director: Lewis Milestone.

VALERIE PERRINE:

Did the failure of *Can't Stop the Music* hurt my career? I never think that. But something must have. I thought it was badly rapped, and I thought it was undeserved. I've certainly done movies much worse than that.

❏

VICTORIA PRINCIPAL:

I think I have an irrational fear of features. I did something called *The Naked Ape*, which is arguably one of the 10 worst movies ever made. That began such a painful period in my life, and I always connect it to features.

❏

GILDA RADNER:

I bounced back after the miscarriage [while filming *Haunted Honeymoon*], but not too long afterward I caught a cold that was going around. The studio in England could get very damp and chilly, and the cold settled in my respiratory system and wouldn't go away. I never felt 100% well after that.

On July 26, 1986, *Haunted Honeymoon* opened nationwide. It was a bomb. One month of publicity and the movie was only in theaters for a week—a boxoffice disaster.

THAT LADY IN ERMINE (20th Century-Fox, 1948), with Cesar Romero, Betty Grable. Directors: Ernst Lubitsch, Otto Preminger.

❑

ALYSON REED:

Frankly, the bad notices for *A Chorus Line* didn't bother me that much. I could live with them. It was the aftermath. Before the papers hit the stands I had offers for three movies, a lead in a TV mini-series and a chance to appear on *The Tonight Show*. Within a day, the offers were withdrawn and I didn't work for close to a year.

THAT LADY FROM SHANGHAI (Columbia, 1948), with Orson Welles, Rita Hayworth. Director: Orson Welles.

❑

DONNA REED:

It's a Wonderful Life, with Jimmy Stewart, is my favorite film, but it was a boxoffice failure.

A year or so later, I was cast in *The Stratton Story* (about one-legged baseball star Monty Stratton). My co-star was Van Johnson. But something happened with Van, and they cast Jimmy Stewart. I was thrilled, because I thought we were pretty good together. But, as it turned out, I was taken off the film and replaced by June Allyson. I was told that Stewart was fighting for his professional life, and I said, "What do you think *I'm* fighting for?"

I had four more years in my contract at MGM but, after that, I never worked there again.

❑

JEAN RENOIR:

The Woman on the Beach was made at the request of Joan Bennett, who said, "They've asked me to make a film at RKO. I've two or three scenarios, come and make it with me." At first the producer was to be Val Lewton. Then other projects interested him more and I practically became my own producer. I've never shot a film with so little written scenario and so much improvisation.

I was intrigued by a love story in which the attractions were purely physical, in which feelings wouldn't intervene at all. I made it and was very happy; it was rather slow, maybe, so we arranged some previews. It was very badly received and we returned to the studio pretty depressed. I was the first to advise cuts and changes. Joan Bennett's husband, Walter Wanger, came to showings and gave me his point of view. I reshot numerous scenes—about one third of the film, essentially the scenes between Joan and Robert Ryan, and I put out a picture that was neither flesh nor fish, that had lost its *raison d'être*. I'd let myself be too influenced by the Santa Barbara preview. I'm afraid I was too far ahead of the public's mentality.

❑

EDWARD G. ROBINSON:

Late in 1949 I went to London to make a picture called *My Daughter Joy*. In this country it was called *Operation X*. In either country it should have been called unspeakable. Then the drought set in. I became an absolute pariah. The only thing I could do if I wanted work was to return to the stage.

❑

RICHARD RODGERS:

The Phantom President, with George M. Cohan and Claudette Colbert, was made early in 1932 and released just in time for the Roosevelt-Hoover election campaign. I think even Hoover was more popular than the film.

❑

JOHN SCHLESINGER:

I'm always scared because one's success and failure these days is so rapidly judged on what the film will gross. There were people going around after *Day of the Locust* saying, "He must never be allowed near a camera again."

❑

DANIEL SELZNICK:

The single most painful experience of my father's [David O. Selznick] life has to have been *A Farewell to Arms*. The worst moment actually was at the Roxy Theater when the film was opening. He wanted to sit there with me. I hoped to Christ that it would be wonderful. And I sat there in shock.

Beginning with the excessive degree of hysteria in Jennifer's [Jones] performance, everything was wrong. There was my father sitting with me waiting for me to tell him what I thought of it. I don't even know what I said. But the reviews were so harsh that whatever I said would have been mild in comparison. He had been hoping for Academy Awards across the board, and I don't even know if there were any nominations. Here was a man who was a genius and a giant in the industry, and he lost it somehow.

Watching him in those last years and admiring him as I did was terrible, just terrible.

❑

DAVID O. SELZNICK:

A Farewell to Arms hasn't come off. The thing that bothers me is that I don't know why. God knows I gave it everything I could. And yet it didn't come off. Maybe my kind of picture is out of style. Maybe I'm an anachronism. I just can't figure it out.

❑

NORMA SHEARER:

On these last two [*We Were Dancing, Her Cardboard Lover*], nobody but myself was trying to do me in.

❑

SID SHEINBERG:

I don't fault Frank Price [ex-president of Universal Pictures] for the decision to make *Howard the Duck*. That is a bullet that could have hit anyone at the studio. Those people who claim that *Howard the Duck* was a catalyst in Frank Price's departure, that's ridiculous.

Of course, some smart ass could say, "Well, are you saying that if *Howard the Duck* had been a $200 million picture, he wouldn't be here?" Of course, I'm not saying that. We would have convinced ourselves that the problem didn't exist for a little while longer. But Frank Price and MCA weren't working.

❑

CYBILL SHEPHERD:

Eleven years later, I'm still getting slammed because of that movie [*At Long Last Love*]. And it's really hurtful. I used to have moments of real despair, where I felt like I'd never do anything ever again. But just when I absolutely felt like giving up, someone would give me the littlest bit of encouragement. I knew I could sing and act. Deep down, I knew my career wasn't over. But I needed to prove it to myself.

UP IN CENTRAL PARK (Universal, 1948), with Deanna Durbin, Dick Haymes. Director: William A. Seiter.

❏

DINAH SHORE:

Making movies was so boring. You sat around interminably. And I never thought I was photogenic, I thought I looked horrible on the Technicolor screen. To this day, if I hear some of those recordings and see those movies my knees start knocking. Now those monumental successes are played on TV at three o'clock in the morning. I've become an insomniac's nightmare! Anyone who stays up to those ungodly hours to see *Aaron Slick from Punkin Crick* deserves what he gets.

❏

JEAN SIMMONS:

The movies I did at RKO—*Androcles and the Lion, Angel Face, Affair with a Stranger, She Couldn't Say No*—practically put my career in the toilet. They were not good. Not for me, anyway.

❏

ROBERT STACK:

Back in the 1950s, I got the best reviews of my life in that good movie with the terrible title, *The Bullfighter and the Lady*. Even *Time* magazine singled me out as a young actor with great potential. Much of the potential went out the window on my next film, *My Outlaw Brother*, a piece of Limburger that put a temporary damper on the careers of Robert Preston, Mickey Rooney and me—and finished off Elliott Nugent, the well known Broadway director.

❏

SYLVESTER STALLONE:

It's all cyclic—you can't stay on top forever. With *Rhinestone*, you'd have thought we all got together and decided how we could fastest ruin our careers. There was a change in director early on, to Bob Clark, who directed *Porky's*. We should have called it *Dorky's*. "You saw him in *Rambo*, now he's back as the Dork."

❏

MAX STEINER:

Two on a Guillotine—they criticized the picture and I didn't like it and that was the end [of his years at Warner Brothers]. It wasn't a picture, it was an abortion. There was a big mistake in the thing, the guillotine was placed in the wrong place, you know. They should have cut off William Conrad's head for producing the thing. They said I killed the picture. That, I wouldn't take after 29 years.

❏

ANNA STEN:

I feel toward *Nana* as a mother toward a sick baby, a crippled child. Full of sadness, full of affection, borne with love. The first version, the one that was discarded [directed by George Fitzmaurice, who was replaced by Dorothy Arzner], was not a bad picture. But it wasn't good enough to satisfy Mr. [Samuel] Goldwyn, or myself, either.

It is hard to say just what went wrong, because everything was wrong. When I saw the rushes and the rough cut I was amazed to see that not only I but all the players reflected their unhappiness upon the screen. Even the gay scenes seemed clouded with woe. Believe you me, there was plenty of it.

❏

SUMMER HOLIDAY (MGM, 1948), with Mickey Rooney, Gloria De Haven, Agnes Moorehead, Walter Huston, Selena Royle, Jackie "Butch" Jenkins. Director: Rouben Mamoulian.

JAMES STEWART:

Well, Frank [Capra] got *It's a Wonderful Life* together. We went to the preview. And the picture went out. Did no business. And it not only did no business—the fact that it did no business hindered the continuation of Frank's company, Liberty Films, that he had formed with George Stevens, Willie Wyler and Sam Briskin. Frank made a few more pictures, but I think it discouraged him a little.

❑

LILY TOMLIN:

I think the failure of *Moment by Moment* was much more devastating to Jane [Wagner, the writer-director]. She didn't really even want to work again for a long, long time.

It came out of our old show, *Appearing Nitely*, which I was playing on Broadway in 1977. John Travolta came to see it. We had always been kind of drawn to each other because we sort of resemble one another. We'd see each other at the Emmys or places like that and we always said hi. He came to the show one night and loved it so much he went to Robert Stigwood, with whom he had a contract to do another movie, and he said, "I want to

86

do it with them [Tomlin and Wagner]." So Stigwood called and said, "I want to show you some scenes from this movie John has done called *Saturday Night Fever* because he wants to do his next movie with you two."

John wasn't a big star yet. Jane and I looked at *Saturday Night Fever* and thought he was really wonderful, so we said, "Okay, great." Jane was asked to write a script and it all kind of snowballed. Then John and his manager wanted Jane to direct it. I don't think we had any idea what that meant, never having had something to do with a lot of other people and certainly never having made a movie, in that sense. We went into it like we'd go into anything else—expecting it to work out and make something of it. And even when we finished nobody had any idea we were going to get murdered for it. I should never have played it the way I played it. And I also think the initial intention of the movie was quite different—we just couldn't make it come out—but we were quite innocent about it.

Until John and I started out on a cross-country press junket [for *Moment by Moment*], we had no idea how the press was going to beat up on us. Here we were, going from city to city, to face this onslaught. I think if it had been a less consequential pairing—but *Saturday Night Fever* and *Grease* had come out and John was a big star. I was popular and riding off the end of *Appearing Nitely*, which had been a big success. I think people live with the fear that it is going to happen and it usually happens to some degree to most people, if they're around long enough. And, plus, they beat it to death! You couldn't pick up a magazine for three or four years! Just when I'd think it'd finally been put to rest, I'd pick up a magazine with some terrible piece about it and of course I couldn't do an interview because you have to take that whole trip back.

Jane got a tremendous amount of fallout and John did, too. But everybody suffered, believe me.

❏

JOHN TRAVOLTA:

I was in a pretty bad state of mind. I was really feeling the loss of my mom. Plus, *Moment by Moment* had just been released and had created a negative storm.

❏

JOHN TRAVOLTA:

Moment by Moment—that was the first time I heard the words, "Your career is over."

❏

DREAM GIRL (Paramount, 1948), with Macdonald Carey, Betty Hutton, Patric Knowles. Director: Mitchell Leisen.

LANA TURNER:

It was the only time in my career I ever felt ashamed of a movie I made. It seemed fine when I made it, but by the time it was edited—and butchered—it ended up playing as the second half of a 1973 Halloween double bill under the title *The Terror of Sheba*!

☐

JIMMY VAN HEUSEN:

After the first preview of *Honeymoon Hotel*, which was originally called *His and His*, the head of the studio said, "Take out four songs!" It was a terrible flop. How can you have a picture with Robert Goulet with no songs?

☐

GORE VIDAL:

Myra Breckinridge was not just a bad movie, it was an awful joke. And I have you, Mr. Alpert, to thank for that. You once reviewed a film called *Joanna*, made by an English pop singer named Michael Sarne. This film was like 52 Salem commercials run back to back—people running in slow motion through Green Park, girls with long hair and lots of plummy dialogue.

Richard Zanuck and David Brown, then running 20th Century-Fox, suddenly asked me to see *Joanna*—one of the 10 worst films. The next thing I knew they said, "Well, he's directing *Myra Breckinridge*, and he will also write the script." I said, "What has he done to justify giving him a major film to direct, a movie about Hollywood, a town he has yet to visit?" They said, "*Joanna* is a great flick." I said, "It's a terrible picture." They said, "Just look what the critics say." And there was the Hollis Alpert review. Seared on my memory is that review. I said, "What about the other reviewers?" They said, "What difference do they make? He's the best."

Anyway, Michael Sarne never worked in films after *Myra Breckinridge*. I believe he is working as a waiter in a London pub where they put on shows in the afternoon. This is proof that there is a God and, in nature, perfect symmetry.

❏

HAL WALLIS:

Despite the fact that every Hearst paper gave Marion Davies' pictures rave reviews (the critics valued their jobs), the public remained indifferent. When we made *Ever Since Eve*, we were in real trouble. The best thing about this picture was that my wife, Louise Fazenda, had one of her finest comic roles, a publisher with women's lib ideas. But Marion was showing the effects of drinking, overeating and late hours. She was 41, and it showed. *Ever Since Eve* was her last picture with us, and the end of her career. As much as we all loved her, we were relieved—because her pictures were losing money and Harry Warner was screaming.

❏

JACK L. WARNER:

An outsider would gather that we have made nothing but money, that all our films returned a profit, and that all our ambitious ideas fall neatly into place. But I have had some wooden nickels that were beauts.

We put together a story line, named it *Sincerely Yours* and engaged Liberace to play a singing, piano-playing lead. Joanne Dru, Dorothy Malone and William Demarest were in the picture that made Liberace so happy he sent me an autographed picture: "To Jack Warner for making possible the opportunity to realize one of my lifelong ambitions."

I don't really know why his lifetime ambition went haywire. The first two or three days in most cities was remarkably high—it did $20,000 in San Francisco in two days—but after that the theaters ran out of vicarious elderly mothers. Liberace made no more pictures for us.

❏

A SONG IS BORN (RKO, 1948), with Danny Kaye, Virginia Mayo. Director: Howard Hawks.

WILLIAM A. WELLMAN:

That dumb [Jack] Warner, my great hate: he raped my *Lafayette Escadrille* (originally called *C'est la guerre*), the story of a very dear friend.

I had made it as a tragedy. It was previewed as a tragedy; it was the only preview I ever had where people stood up as the picture ended and said nothing. Then there was a beat and a beat and a beat and they suddenly started cheering. And that dirty, rotten bastard decided that killing Tab Hunter—don't laugh—was impossible. At the time, he'd made a record that had sold two million copies. So they changed it to a happy ending and called it *Lafayette Escadrille*; it didn't have a damn thing to do with the Lafayette Escadrille. All the guys that were still alive from the Escadrille thought I was nuts.

I told Warner that if I ever caught him alone, which is damn near impossible what with all those disgusting yes-men, I'd put him in a hospital.

I shot the happy ending, came home and said, "Dotty, I'm tired. I've worked too hard and I made a deal with a man I hate, knowing he's wrong. I'm never going to make another picture." And I never have.

MAE WEST:

One day, Gregory Ratoff, the actor-producer-director, came to my apartment, and after kissing my hand, clicking his heels, sighing like someone too full of food, talked about doing a "peecture" with me, *Tropicana*, based on a successful Broadway musical. It sounded good and Ratoff has an accent that has an accent.

Weeks went by and no word. Finally, he came to my apartment again, and following a deep, shark-like kiss on my hand, he said, "Dollink, we can't make the story I told you, but the name *Tropicana* we'll make." When he finally got it to me on paper, it had a trite flatness. I tried to get a release from my commitment. Ratoff pleaded in three languages: "I will be ruined if I have to give back the money and call off the picture. Besides, Dollink, I have no money. A man got to live in style. I was raised in the Czar's own house." I made the picture.

I did manage to write the only good scenes for myself in it, but there wasn't enough time to change the story and make it into a good picture. It was released as *The Heat's On*. Along with mine, the fine talents of Victor Moore and Billy Gaxton were wasted on an inferior story. I sometimes wonder if Gregory didn't *talk* the Czar out of Russia.

❑

BILLY WILDER:

I was absolutely baffled by the reaction [to *Kiss Me, Stupid*]. I've seen many a picture, believe me, that was far more suggestive and dirty. I don't mind reading a slew of reviews that say it was bad. It probably was bad. But what hurt me was that old pals said I set out deliberately to make a dirty picture.

After the picture came out, I went to Europe and walked through the snow and got it out of my system and came back and sat down with my esteemed colleague, I. A. L. Diamond. For 12 weeks we sat and stared at each other. He said we were like parents who have produced a two-headed child and don't dare to have sexual intercourse again.

❑

ESTHER WILLIAMS:

If *Jupiter's Darling* had been my first picture, there wouldn't have been a second.

❑

SHELLEY WINTERS:

The last film I did at Universal was something called *Playgirl*. It was so bad that the actress who played the lead [Colleen Miller] moved back to

Chicago, married a millionaire and is very happy. Maybe she made the wisest choice.

❑

WILLIAM WYLER:

I don't think Larry [Olivier] had much faith in the story. He kept asking me, "Why are you doing this picture?" I saw *Carrie* as portraying a period of America that was very interesting. As it turned out, Larry was right.

Biographical Bombs

"If that's my life, I didn't live."

BRIAN AHERNE:

I was with my mother and father in Rome when a cable from [agent] Bill Hawks brought me an offer from producer Mervyn LeRoy to star in *The Great Garrick*, by Ernest Vajda.

A short time before I left Hollywood, Vajda had come to my house to tell me this story, and, encouraged by our enthusiasm, had acted the various parts with gusto. He had rushed home in great excitement to put it down on paper. On the way he stopped in at a cocktail party where, after a couple of drinks, he had a fine time retelling the story, with embellishments, no doubt, to Mervyn LeRoy. Mervyn offered to buy it for a movie, and Vajda accepted. Time went by and he failed to deliver a script to either of us. It seemed he had forgotten it! We all had to remind him of pieces of his own dialogue. Mervyn did manage to make a picture for Warner Brothers, but the story was never as good as it had been at the first telling.

Co-starred with me in *The Great Garrick* was the young and entrancing Olivia de Havilland. I little thought that I would one day marry her younger sister, Joan Fontaine. The picture was to flop at the boxoffice—so badly, in fact, that Jack Warner told Hawks he never wanted to see me on the lot again.

❑

ED ASNER:

Fred Astaire and Ginger Rogers were full of affection for each other in their last RKO picture together, *The Story of Vernon and Irene Castle*, when they played a married couple for the first time.

The Castles were a real-life dancing partnership from the time of the first World War. Astaire sought to recreate scrupulously the dancing style of that period. But his effort to alter the formula wasn't welcomed, or maybe it just came too late. The team seemed to have run out of ideas for Astaire-

THE PIRATE (MGM, 1948), with Gene Kelly, Judy Garland. Director: Vincente Minnelli.

Rogers vehicles; or perhaps the chemistry that had been so potent in 1933 had lost its attraction in the more knowing climate of the late thirties.

For whatever reason, audience responses to the Astaire-Rogers pairing began to cool. The film lost $50,000.

❑

ALICE BACKES:

When we heard that Universal was looking for an actress to play Hedda Hopper, the Hollywood gossip columnist, in *Gable and Lombard*, my agent immediately submitted me. Hedda was a colorful lady who was famous for, among other things, her wild hats. When I went for my interview with the casting people and Sidney Furie, the director, I just happened to wear a cute hat. I got the part.

Gable and Lombard was fun to do, although judging by its subsequent small audience it was not much fun to watch.

It was a massive production, with huge sets and a large cast. Where did it go wrong? So many "docudramas" have been made in recent years that you simply don't know anymore where truth ends and fiction begins. It's like our four-day holiday weekends today—we no longer know what's real, what any of our holidays or presidents' birthdays are anymore because of them. I

UNFAITHFULLY YOURS (20th Century-Fox, 1948), with Lionel Stander, Barbara Lawrence, Kurt Kreuger, Rudy Vallee. Director: Preston Sturges.

think *Gable and Lombard* would have been much better if they had stuck to the truth more. Real life is so much more interesting than anything people can dream up. For instance, Clark Gable did not join the service until *after* Carole Lombard was killed in the plane crash. In our film, they had him joining while she was still alive.

They just kept "creating." They'd say, "How about we do this?" ... "Let's see if this works." There were so many days when the production people came in with new ideas for that day's shooting that simply strayed too far from the truth. For my first scene in the picture, I was to work with Red Buttons and, as Gable and Lombard, our stars James Brolin and Jill Clayburgh. At the last minute, on the set, they came to us and said, "Why don't you make up what you want to do in this scene?" We kept the original intent of the script but created our own scene. It seemed to work all right. But the film as a whole would have been better served by sticking to the truth.

Jill had a particularly large burden to carry. Her every appearance seemed to say, "Now we'll have some dirty words." As Lombard, she was required to swear a lot. To all reports, Carole *did* swear like a trooper, but the words came trippingly off her tongue—people would do double takes and ask, "Did she say what I think she said?" She did it with *style*. But the profanity in our film was just too blatant. *Gable and Lombard* got an "R" rating, not because of any explicit sex but because of the profanity. When it was to be shown on TV, the editor, a friend of mine, said it took him three months to get all the swear words out. And you know something? It was a much better movie then. It played much better on TV. It went easier on the mind.

But in theaters, people who might have loved to go, who remembered Gable and Lombard, just didn't want to have to deal with the profanity, to expose their children to it. I was practically the only one who came out of it unscathed with some nice personal reviews. In *Daily Variety*, Army Archerd said, "Alice Backes has Hedda down to a hat pin." Other people who had known Hedda Hopper also told me I had managed to be very like her. This has encouraged me to think seriously about putting together a one-woman stage play as Hedda.

❑

CARROLL BAKER:

With John Michael Hayes at times handing in pages of script only three or four days in advance of filming, we somehow managed not only to get *Harlow* onto celluloid but also to bring the movie in well within that skimpy, squeezed, impossible shooting schedule producer Joseph E. Levine had dictated in his race with the Electronovision version [of the same story].

The actors and director had not been given rehearsal time. There was no time for rushes. A team of editors stood by to cut the film the second it was hot out of the developing room. Electronovision beat us into the movie houses, but only just. We had been very close behind, just close enough to add to the public's confusion and to damage our own potential.

Levine had been the first to call our movie a bomb, and he had blamed the rival version. However, it soon became and has since remained Carroll Baker's *Harlow*.

❑

ALEC BALDWIN:

When this movie [*Great Balls of Fire*] was done, people said to me, "Hey! *Batman*" and "Hey! *Lethal Weapon 2*" and "*Indiana Jones*," and all those other movies. And I said, "*Great Balls of Fire* is going to be the best movie of the summer." When it came out and flopped, I was totally shocked. Then I saw it and I could see that there was something wrong with it, but just on the strength of Dennis Quaid's performance alone, I thought the movie was going to be great. People say Dennis was over the top, but that's what Jerry Lee Lewis *was*. He was a total madman. He was insane.

❑

INGRID BERGMAN:

When I saw *Joan of Arc* recently on television—it's hard to realize it was made more than 30 years ago—I saw it had that smooth, glossy quality

JOAN OF ARC (RKO, 1948), with Richard Derr, Ingrid Bergman, Ray Teal. Director: Victor Fleming.

THE KISSING BANDIT (MGM, 1948), with Frank Sinatra, Kathryn Grayson. Director: Laslo Benedek.

of Hollywood. All the battle scenes were done in the studio; the towers of Chinon and the French villages were painted backdrops. I didn't think I looked like a peasant girl at all. I just looked like a movie star playing the part of Joan. Clean face, nice hairdo.

❏

KEEFE BRASSELLE:

Some people think that *The Eddie Cantor Story* almost ruined my career. But they are so wrong. *The Eddie Cantor Story* made me famous and a fortune. I was able to play Las Vegas for 15 weeks at $25,000 per week. The role also gave me an absolute, immediate international reputation.

❏

KEEFE BRASSELLE:

When I saw the rushes of *The Eddie Cantor Story*, I realized there was something wrong with it. When I read the reviews, I knew what it was: everything.

❏

JAMES BROLIN:

Gable and Lombard. Did you see that? No. Well, I took Clark Gable and complicated the hell out of that guy. A very sad person. Nobody wanted to see that about Gable. He married women for their position in society, and then finally his marriage to Carole Lombard [Jill Clayburgh] was a true love affair, which ended in disaster and really destroyed the guy. A guy cannot survive when he is putting away a quart of booze a day.

But in a way that movie was successful: it gave us an impossible exercise to do, and everyone should have one of those in their lives.

❏

RICHARD BURTON:

Prince of Players has become a collector's item. You have to look hard to find it.

❏

EDDIE CANTOR:

The Eddie Cantor Story—if that's my life, I didn't live.

❏

LETTER FROM AN UNKNOWN WOMAN (Universal, 1948), with Louis Jourdan, Joan Fontaine.
Director: Max Opuls.

JILL CLAYBURGH:

Gable and Lombard? There isn't enough money to make me do something like that today. But let's face it, I had to do whatever I got then and be grateful for it, and some were dumb things and some were better—only *semi*-dumb things.

❏

GARY COOPER:

If you saw me in *The Adventures of Marco Polo*, you belong to a very exclusive club.

❏

ADAM FIELDS:

Why did *Great Balls of Fire* fail? It wasn't a great movie. The beginning was *Bye Bye Birdie* and the ending a Dennis Hopper drama. It was a film trying to be everything. Besides that, Orion Pictures rushed its release and production to make their money back as soon as possible, and were more involved placating star egos than getting the Jerry Lee Lewis story right.

❏

NIGHT UNTO NIGHT (Warner Brothers, 1949), with Viveca Lindfors, Osa Massen, Ronald Reagan. Director: Don Siegel.

ROBERT GETCHELL:

Bound for Glory was my second screenplay, written close on the heels of *Alice Doesn't Live Here Anymore*. Both of those screenplays were quickly produced, and I had, at the time, the terribly mistaken, short-lived feeling that I would spend the rest of my life choosing what subjects I wanted to write about, writing, then watching with a smile as the scripts became movies.

Within a matter of three weeks, United Artists had committed to my first draft of *Bound for Glory* and were looking for a director. Hal Ashby was chosen (to my delight, since I admired his *Harold and Maude* and *The Landlord*), and casting began. Very quickly, they settled on Richard Dreyfuss.

"I'm saved," I thought, since Dreyfuss fit exactly the Woody Guthrie I'd written. Guthrie was short, irascible and charming. He was a drinker, a fighter and a skirt-chaser, as well as a man who had a highly developed social and political awareness. Dreyfuss was perfect; also *hot*, having just made *Jaws*.

Then came the trouble. Dreyfuss asked for half a million, which Ashby thought too high. "He's not the fucking *shark*!", said Hal.

Then somehow, maddeningly to me, Hal decided that tall, laconic David Carradine was the perfect choice to play short, feisty Woody. And that, basically, is the answer, as far as I can give it, as to why *Bound for Glory* didn't do better. It was *miscast*. Though it was nominated for six Academy Awards, including Best Picture, the star was ignored. Cast Joan Fontaine in *All About Eve* and you have a miscarriage. Cast James Mason in *Meet John Doe* and it will not work. Cast Tom Hanks in *Rambo* and people will not come to see it. Cast David Carradine as a funny, woman-chasing, short gadfly with a social conscience, and people will not be interested. *Were* not interested. That's my answer. Others might have a different one.

Though beautiful to look at, the movie has a slight stink of sanctimoniousness which I'd hoped to avoid (much of the humor was removed from the shooting script). *And the star was wrong.*

☐

SAMUEL GOLDWYN:

The Adventures of Marco Polo was the biggest flop I produced—yes, more than *Nana*.

☐

SHEILAH GRAHAM:

I thought I was lucky when Jerry Wald at 20th Century-Fox bought *Beloved Infidel*, a book mostly about my time with Scott Fitzgerald.

He invited me to the preview in Long Beach. I sat alone, not wanting his other guests—the director Henry King, the cameraman, his secretary— to watch me while I watched my life unfold on the screen.

I sat there in the darkness absolutely frozen. Why didn't I feel anything? It was supposed to be my life up there. Why didn't I cry when Scott died as I had almost 20 years before? Why didn't I giggle at the end when Deborah Kerr was kneeling on the sands of Malibu to the accompaniment of the theme song, "Oh My Beloved Infidel"?

"Well, what do you think of it?" said Jerry. "I didn't feel anything," I said flatly. "Ah, that's because you're too close to it." They were both so pathetically eager for me to like it. The film was terrible. "It's too long," I said, for want of anything else. This annoyed Mr. King. "I love every foot of it," he said.

The critics agreed with me. I received just one statement from the studio, and was delighted to read (a year after release) that so far it had made $3 million. While I was figuring out how much my five percent would come to, my eye wandered to the other side of the page. *Beloved Infidel* had cost $5 million and was $2 million in the red.

☐

MERV GRIFFIN:

I'll never forget the press screening of *So This is Love*. It was held at the Hollywood Pantages Theater. When I came on the screen, I literally slid on the floor and Rita [Farrell], who was with me, got the giggles. Afterwards, out in the lobby, Hedda Hopper came up to me, gave me a hug and said, "You

THE BEAUTIFUL BLONDE FROM BASHFUL BEND (20th Century-Fox, 1949), with Betty Grable, Rudy Vallee. Director: Preston Sturges.

were magnificent. You're going to be a big star." Unfortunately, the movie didn't do too well. It opened the day after CinemaScope came out and there we were, stuck up on that postage stamp when everyone was talking about "wide screen."

❑

DEBORAH KERR:

I was heartbroken that *Beloved Infidel* did not do what it should have done, but, on the other hand, I understood Gregory Peck's point of view, and I was happy to work with him. [Peck had insisted that this biography of Hollywood columnist Sheilah Graham be altered to begin when his character entered her story.]

The film wasn't all bad, but it became disjointed, between Sheilah's original story, the film script and Peck's own writers, and I was unable really to characterize, because half the poor woman's personality was cut out. It was difficult for me to pick up the threads halfway through her life and, for my own self, be genuine. I wasn't able to show where she came from, and what she was, and why she became the way she was later on.

❑

BEATRICE LILLIE:

Gertie [Lawrence] and I were seldom apart. That made me somewhat intrigued to see how, in a 20th Century-Fox production called *Star!*, I was altogether erased from history. Gertie, as played by Julie Andrews, never had a friend named Beattie.

I'll tell you what happened. The creators of *Star!* for the sake of accuracy were offered the use of my name. But in typical Hollywood style, they wanted *all* or nothing. That is to say, the right to impersonate me throughout and also do one of my numbers, "March with Me." When the answer was, "No, thank you very much," they omitted all mention of Beatrice Lillie. I was deleted from the script as though I'd never existed. Pity. I'll bet Gertie has had a good laugh at the deplorable boxoffice fate of an inaccurate movie.

❑

STEPHEN LONGSTREET:

I worked on *The Helen Morgan Story*, but it was a dud. The actress playing Helen, Ann Blyth, was too refined and not able to catch the full seamy character, and the director, Michael Curtiz, was Hungarian and had no idea of Americana. It was, by the way, one of Paul Newman's first pictures. He was only fair.

❑

IDA LUPINO:

Olivia de Havilland and I worked very hard on research when we were cast in *Devotion*. Strangely enough, she was cast as Charlotte [Bronte] and I was cast as Emily. Olivia said, "It's strange we've been cast in these roles. Let's really go for the way they were."

Charlotte was blonde and near-sighted, wore glasses, and Emily was very dark and she had a falcon she used to have chained to her arm, and a mastiff dog. So we did our tests, and I went for the dark wig parted in the center and Olivia wanted to go blonde. The next thing we knew, Mr. Warner said, "I will have no such thing! Olivia will play with the dark hair and curls, and Ida will play with the long red hair. And she's going to have a sheepdog." The two of us were just destroyed. Mr. Warner said, "I'm not going to have the two of you wandering around looking like that!"

And we said, "Well, we can just see the notices now, and all the Bronte Societies, you know."

Sure enough, they tore *Devotion* to pieces. You see, it altered the performances so much.

❑

SIREN OF ATLANTIS (United Artists, 1949), with Maria Montez. Director: Gregg Tallas.

DANIEL MASSEY:

Noel [Coward] loved the job I did of imitating him in *Star!* He auditioned me beforehand, for he had casting approval on his character. Afterward, I asked him what it was like watching himself. He said it was like staring into a youthful mirror. Then he said he had one tip for me: "You put in too many 'dear boys,' dear boy."

Of course, *Star!* was a big financial failure because Julie Andrews was not playing a governess; she was a real-life woman who drank and swore and had a sex drive. Yet the leading man was her gay friend, and her husbands were minor characters, and she spent all her time quarreling with them. Mostly, it was about her lavish lifestyle, with marvelous songs thrown in, and lots of close-ups of Julie Andrews in costume.

It was a wonderfully tuneful flop.

SAL MINEO:

I don't really know what happened with *The Gene Krupa Story*. Susan Kohner said it was the lousy script (she had to say lines like, "You made love a dirty word!"). But I've seen movies with lousy scripts become hits, before and since.

Some people said including marijuana in the plot was a major turn-off - and didn't help us with audiences or publicity-seekers, because Hollywood was very, very uptight then [the fifties].

I think the supporting cast could have been better. Or at least better known. They were expecting me to carry the whole picture, so they put someone like Gavin McLeod in as my father. I mean, he was okay, but no great talent or personality, frankly speaking.

What really happened was, Sal Mineo got to the top, got to star in a movie they built around me and when it didn't live up to their expectations, when I couldn't make silk out of dross or whatever, I was the fall guy. Everyone who had been gunning for me, who had it in for me, loudly proclaimed *I* was why *The Gene Krupa Story* failed. It was tough. Not a good time for me. And I'm not sure my movie career ever recovered fully after that.

DONALD O'CONNOR:

[One of the main reasons *The Buster Keaton Story* failed was because] it was so damned dishonest. It wasn't Buster's life. They called him a technical advisor but they never listened to him. I remember talking to him right after we'd shot a scene of him as a boy in the circus going on for his father who had just died. I asked Buster, "What kind of circus was it?" He kind of looked

LOVE HAPPY (United Artists, 1949), with Otto Waldis, Marilyn Monroe, Groucho Marx.
Director: David Miller.

at me and said, "I was never in a circus." So I asked him, "Well, how old
were you when your father died?" "Forty-five," he said.

❏

MANDY PATINKIN:

I was devastated by the way *Daniel* was received. It was like being lined
up against the wall and assassinated. Whether one thought it was flawed or
not, it had so much that was worthwhile. It just didn't deserve that kind of
annihilation.

❏

GREGORY PECK:

Both Deborah Kerr and I did *Beloved Infidel* to finish off commitments
we had with Fox. There was some disagreement about whether this was the
saga of Sheilah Graham or the last episode in the life of Scott Fitzgerald. I
pushed in Fitzgerald's direction, naturally. There are outrageous, funny drunk
scenes, very true to life, judging from all I've read about Fitzgerald. Not a
huge success.

❏

VINCENT PRICE:

We knew during the filming that *The Story of Mankind* was heading downwards; the script was bad to begin with and it worsened with daily changes. I remember one puzzled visitor asking Ronnie Colman, "Is this picture based on a book?", and he replied in that beautiful, soft diction of his, "Yes. But they are using only the notes on the dust jacket."

❏

DORE SCHARY:

Nineteen fifty-two was a good year with the exception of one acute disappointment—my misadventure with *Plymouth Adventure*, the story of the voyage of the Mayflower to America. [Loew's, Inc.-MGM executives] Nick Schenck, Eddie Mannix, Joe Cohn had pleaded with me to cancel the expensive picture. But my instinct told me the naysayers were wrong and I bullied myself into a production with a script by Helen Deutsch and direction by Clarence Brown. Some people liked *Plymouth Adventure*, but there weren't enough direct descendants of the original Mayflower passengers to help it cross over to success. The picture proved to be a bummer, and I could feel the hot breath of the board of directors.

❏

PAUL SCHRADER:

I would say, without reservation, one should never make a film like *Patty Hearst*. It violates the commercial precepts of moviemaking.

I think the prevailing reason we go to movies is to have some sense that we can control our lives. You know, we can't control our lives. But in a movie, people do. Things get settled; a person takes action. In real life, there aren't many problems. There are only these fucking murky dilemmas that never get solved. Life is one long moral Vietnam [War], and you can't get out of it.

And so, to make a movie about a passive character—a person who is not in charge—is to in some way go dead against why you want to see a movie. As I came to understand that in the preparation of *Patty Hearst*, I knew that this could never be a commercial film. It was not something that I told the people who were making the film, but I knew it just couldn't become a commercial film, because it didn't have that voyeuristic identification element.

❏

THE FOUNTAINHEAD (Warner Brothers, 1949), with Patricia Neal, Gary Cooper. Director:
King Vidor.

JEAN SEBERG:

I have two memories of *Saint Joan*. The first was being burned at the
stake in the picture. The second was being burned at the stake by the critics.
The latter hurt more.

LEON SHAMROY:

Cleopatra was an awful tough business; it nearly killed me. There was
no script, you never knew what they were doing from day to day, and I had
to take over from Jack Hildyard, who did the [early] Rouben Mamoulian
footage. I saw some of the Mamoulian stuff; I thought it was terrible. There
were one or two good photographic moments in my version—when Rex
Harrison has a fit, for instance. But as for the rest!

SIDNEY SHELDON:

A man named Bob Smith came to me with the idea [for *The Buster Keaton
Story*], I liked it, had Paramount buy it and I produced it, made Bob a co-
producer. I directed it, and Bob and I wrote the script.

Buster did not *help* on the stunts on that picture. He alone created and did everything himself. He *was* the stunts in that picture. He was brilliant! All the tricks that our star, Donald O'Connor, did, all the stunts that he did was Buster Keaton, his brain child, his creation. And that was about the only good thing in it.

I take responsibility for the failure of that picture. I allowed myself to be rushed into it with a script that wasn't ready because the studio gave me a star and shooting date.

❏

MARY STEENBURGEN:

I was heartbroken that *Cross Creek* didn't do well. I don't know why it didn't; I thought it would. I thought it was a lovely film and was so happy with it.

❏

MARY STEENBURGEN:

Melvin and Howard—it's like the Little Movie That Could. It keeps trying to make itself a hit, with no help from Universal. Everything good that could happen to it has happened and it's not even playing anywhere. It got rave reviews, it's on every 10 Best list in the country, and now Universal is being shamed into re-releasing it. But they took out an ad campaign that literally kept people out of the theaters and they've done nothing to help it. That's the tragedy of this business. You work your ass off and nobody cares.

❏

GLORIA SWANSON:

Nero's Mistress had a stellar international cast including Brigitte Bardot, Vittorio De Sica and Alberto Sordi, but it was so bad that six years elapsed between the shooting in Italy in 1956 and the picture's release in a dubbed version in the United States in 1962.

❏

ELIZABETH TAYLOR:

God, when I think of some of the movies, like *Beau Brummell*. I never saw that film until after Richard [Burton] and I were married. It was on television and Richard turned it on. I had to change stations after about five minutes—I mean, *I* was so embarrassing in it.

❏

BRIDE OF VENGEANCE (Paramount, 1949), with Paulette Goddard, Macdonald Carey.
Director: Mitchell Leisen.

BEYOND THE FOREST (Warner Brothers, 1949), with Bette Davis, David Brian. Director: King
Vidor.

ELI WALLACH:

I got into *Act One* at the last minute. They were already shooting.

After looking at the rushes, Dore Schary, who was producing, directing and had written the screenplay, decided that the actor playing the role of "Warren Stone" was not working out and called me in to do it. My character, though given this other name, was based on the famous—or infamous—Broadway producer, Jed Harris. (When Laurence Olivier played Richard III, he was asked where he got the inspiration for his interpretation and replied, "Jed Harris.")

I only worked one day on *Act One*, and it only involved one scene in a bathroom. The bit was based on a well known if possibly apocryphal story about Jed Harris.

I had no qualms about accepting so small a part because everyone expected the film to be a smash. It was based on Moss Hart's wonderful, best-selling autobiography—I can still remember the excitement in the book when Moss gets his first Broadway production and tells his parents to move, leave everything behind. George Hamilton, who starred, has some of the upper class air that Moss had, but unfortunately not his fire.

Why didn't the picture succeed? Sometimes you just can't translate into visual terms what a guy pours out of his heart and imagination onto a page. Recently, in England they asked a youngster which he preferred, radio or TV. He replied, "Radio, because the pictures are better."

Some years ago my wife, Anne Jackson, and I did a well received off-Broadway production comprised of two short plays, *The Typists* and *The Tiger*. When we were going to make a movie of *The Tiger*, we were told we had to open it up, that you couldn't make a whole movie in one room as we had done with the play. Well, we opened it up and all the good things the play had fell out—all the tension and substance. The picture, which was re-titled *The Tiger Makes Out*, did not do well.

Some things are like good wine; they don't travel. And that's what I think happened with *Act One*. A fine book simply resisted being turned into a fine movie.

❏

JACK L. WARNER:

The most disastrous failure we ever had was *The Spirit of St. Louis*, a multi-million-dollar production we made in 1956 with Jimmy Stewart as Colonel Lindbergh. The exhibitors are still moaning. We could afford to take a jolting loss with that picture because we had money in the bank, but during the early twenties every nickel counted when we bombed with such pictures as *Ashamed of Parents*, *Parted Curtains* and *Your Best Friend*.

❏

JAMES R. WEBB:

I worked very hard on the script [for *Alfred the Great*], writing it and rewriting it to achieve an historical drama much more adult than most. Our choice of Clive Donner as director was a mistake, but we had hoped that being a very modern type he would get a novel approach that would appeal to youth.

Unfortunately, directors and actors in London were going through a non-verbal phase [in the sixties]. They thought they could get across all necessary emotions and plot points with virtually nothing said. This was sort of rebellion against their Shakespearean training. I had written some of the speeches almost poetically though I used a minimum of archaisms. But neither the director nor the actors wanted any part of this.

The upshot was that a British TV writer was hired—largely, I think, to put Donner's ideas and words down on paper—serving as little more than an amanuensis. Before they were through, the script had been changed almost beyond recognition and some of the plot made simply laughable. Pictorially the picture was beautiful, but it was murdered by the critics and was a financial disaster.

❏

RICHARD WIDMARK:

Saint Joan! That's one I should have done in a closet! I was always interested in Shaw's play and in that part [the Dauphin]—but I was no more right for it than the man in the moon! And [director Otto] Preminger compounded it by beating on poor Jean Seberg. That was the most unpleasant experience I think I've ever had. I got along very well with him, though it was awful to watch what he was doing to Jean. I used to have dinner with him and Graham Greene, who wrote the screenplay. After I saw the movie, I realized I should've shot both of them!

❏

MARIE WINDSOR:

To me, as too often happened, *The Story of Mankind* was just another job. However, I *was* very impressed with the big names that had been scheduled to be in the film. When my agent told me I would be working only one or two days and that most of the other actors had also been set to work for such limited periods, I began to wonder what kind of a chopped-up production this would be.

At that time, I seem to recall that the producer-director-writer, Irwin Allen, had a reputation for low-budget pictures. I never dreamed the film would ever become the kind of buff classic it apparently has turned into. It certainly is obvious in its lack of production values in almost all areas, and

I still can't figure out why all those big stars [Ronald Colman, Hedy Lamarr, Virginia Mayo, the Marx Brothers, etc.] agreed to do it in the first place. To many of them it surely couldn't have meant "just another job."

Dennis Hopper was just beginning to be noticed and I was very happy to be working with him. Even then he was one of those pleasant and "prepared" actors. Our scene, as Napoleon and Josephine, was shot very fast and our working together seemed to be over almost as quickly as it began. A lot of water has gone under the bridge with Dennis, some of it, as you know, troubled. I'm delighted he got his wonderful act together. Dennis is not only a heavy talent, but a very nice man. I didn't see Dennis for several years after *Story of Mankind*, but each time I did he always had a warm hello. So many actors were being rushed through wardrobe, makeup and shooting, I believe the only other actor in it whose path I crossed during my short time on *Mankind* was Vincent Price, who stopped by to chat.

The idea of doing Hendrik van Loon's book was a good one, but it's the kind of idea that demands top-notch quality, with better writing and production values than our film got. In some ways, it almost seemed like a glorified high school movie with a great cast. I don't rate it very high on my list of films. Sometimes I even forget I was in it. Still, I can't say it's on the bottom of my list, because I've done more than my share of tacky movies.

❑

ROBERT WISE:

What went wrong with *Star!*? We didn't know at the time, but I saw it last week at the British Film Institute. My wife had not seen it before and we sat down and analyzed it. It had too many musical numbers and we didn't get Gertie Lawrence's character enough on screen. The numbers were great but there was not enough development of Gertie herself. It was hard to capture her. Too bad, because there was a lot of good work, and I know that Julie [Andrews] was disappointed.

Political Prey

*"It came at a time when anyone who didn't wrap
the flag around himself was a Commie."*

ED ASNER:

Hearst's newspapers imposed a countrywide ban on advertising and publicity for *Citizen Kane*. Many of the major cinema chains were scared off and refused to take the picture. It was a disaster at the boxoffice. But the critical reception was overwhelmingly favorable.

❑

GEORGE AXELROD:

The Manchurian Candidate? Satire closes on Saturday night. Political satire starts dead. The movie went from failure to classic without passing through success. That the movie has not been seen for years is not mystical. It's economically based, fanciful bookkeeping by United Artists. I've got a lot of other failures available. Perhaps it's time for *Paris When It Sizzles*. I took Bill Holden, Audrey Hepburn, Marlene Dietrich, Noel Coward and the city of Paris and made an absolute stinker!

❑

RICHARD BROOKS:

I wrote and wanted to direct *Crisis*. Cary Grant was the one who said, "If he can write it, why can't he direct it?" He was very kind and I learned a great deal from him. I was very lucky, because with José Ferrer and Grant I was with very professional people.

Originally, the way I wrote the story was that Grant was a surgeon, a widower. He had a little girl, and he never had a chance to be with her, so he took her on a vacation to South America. But MGM at that time felt, well, if you've got Cary Grant why d'you want to have a kid in it? You've got to have a dame. A woman materialized in the picture.

114

THE FAN (20th Century-Fox, 1949), with Jeanne Crain. Director: Otto Preminger.

BORN TO BE BAD (RKO, 1950), with Joan Leslie, Joan Fontaine. Director: Nicholas Ray.

When they saw it, they said, "Gee, Cary in a serious picture, that could be a disaster." So they advertised the picture, "Carefree Cary on a Happy Honeymoon," and of course no one went to see it.

It was banned in all South America, Central America and Mexico. It was banned in Italy because the dictator in it was hanged by his heels; so was Mussolini. Wherever there was a little trouble in any country, it was banned. No one has ever seen the picture except Cary and myself!

But I took John Huston to see it, and he said, "It's a good picture. Next time, don't listen to so many people."

❏

CHARLES CHAPLIN:

Monsieur Verdoux is the cleverest and most brilliant film I have yet made. It had a run of six weeks in New York and did very good business, but it suddenly fell off.

Grad Sears of United Artists said, "Any picture you make will always do business for the first few weeks, because you have the following of your old fans. But after that comes the general public, and frankly the press has been continually hammering at you for more than 10 years and it's bound to have penetration; that's why business fell off."

He showed me the *Daily News* and the Hearst papers. One had a picture of the New Jersey Catholic Legion picketing outside the theater showing *Verdoux* in that state. They were carrying signs that read: "Chaplin's a fellow traveler"; "Kick the alien out of the country"; "Chaplin, the ingrate and Communist sympathizer"; and "Send Chaplin to Russia." The picture was booked by all the big circuits, but after receiving threatening letters from the American Legion and other pressure groups they canceled the showings.

All hopes of a $12,000,000 gross for *Verdoux* vanished. It would hardly pay its own cost; the United Artists company was in a desperate crisis.

❑

KEVIN COSTNER:

Fandango: people who see that movie—it was only out for a week because it ran into political problems [with the studio]—say to me that it's the best coming-of-age movie they ever saw. The thing is, if it's a good movie, whether it does any boxoffice or not, you and I are gonna love it, and anybody who finds the movie five years from now will go "Cool movie." That happens with *Fandango* all the time.

❑

BETTE DAVIS:

Storm Center was highly controversial. The McCarthy era was not over. Someone else had been slated for the part [Mary Pickford], but I was told she chickened out. It was about book-banning, and I was a librarian, you see, and I defended the right to have all kinds of books in a public library. So it had no romance and it was controversial. It did not make money.

❑

EDWARD DMYTRYK:

In Hollywood, we had a number of private showings of *The Reluctant Saint*, and the reactions were gratifying. I failed to pick up an ominous undertone.

Ruth Waterbury, a veteran fan-mag editor and critic, approached me after one showing. "I didn't want to come tonight, Eddie," she said. "I expected to be completely bored. But I enjoyed it thoroughly."

A few—very few—people thought I had to be kidding. They couldn't believe that an ex-Communist and self-professed agnostic would make an honest film about a levitating saint. Like Ruth, most of the people expected to be bored and stayed away.

Columbia didn't know how to sell it—and neither did I. It was just one

CRISIS (MGM, 1950), with Cary Grant, Paula Raymond. Director: Richard Brooks.

of those pictures people love *if* they happen to catch it, but something discourages them from wanting to see it in the first place. It was perhaps the only film I've ever made that honestly never came out of the red.

❑

KIRK DOUGLAS:

Stanley Kubrick had a script called *Paths of Glory* about the greed for fame in the high command in World War I France that led to the needless deaths of so many men. "Stanley, I don't think this picture will ever make a nickel, but we *have* to make it," I told him.

It was a truly great film with a truly great theme: the insanity and brutality of war. As I had predicted, it made no money. A picture can't make money unless people pay to see it, and people can't see it if it's been banned. Oh, they never banned it outright in France. Just the usual "high level talks" between the French government and United Artists. It was also banned from the Berlin Film Festival in 1958 when France threatened to pull out. Even the Swiss were not neutral on *Paths of Glory*. They called it "subversive propaganda directed at France." It was not shown in France and Switzerland until the 1970s.

I never thought of *Paths of Glory* as anti-French. I love France, have done many things for France, for which they gave me the Légion d'Honneur. More important—they gave me my wife.

❏

JOAN FONTAINE:

Letter from an Unknown Woman was made in 1948 under the banner of our Rampart Productions. My husband, William Dozier, was president; I was vice president, as well as star of the picture.

John Houseman, who produced *Letter*, brought the Stefan Zweig novel to my husband, I believe. Howard Koch, a collaborator on *Casablanca*, wrote the screenplay and we imported German-born Max Opuls to direct his first American film. Ultimately, the picture made no money, a victim of inner-studio friction. William Dozier and William Goetz were jockeying for head of the studio, Universal, at the time. Mr. Goetz got the job, I think, and consequently our production didn't get the proper promotion.

It all comes down to this: if someone in charge doesn't like your picture, nothing is done with it. *Letter from an Unknown Woman* was an old-fashioned romance. When it came out, Hollywood was into weighty contemporary social themes (such as my sister Olivia de Havilland's *The Snake Pit*), and the neo-realism period from Europe had begun, so even some of the critics dismissed our picture. Today, however, *Letter* is highly esteemed. I adore it.

❏

ROSE HOBART:

I really don't recall much about *Bride of Vengeance*, as it was while I was having costume fittings for it that I discovered I was pregnant. I had been told all my life that I couldn't have any children. Since I was 43 at the time, it came as quite a shock, and everything else faded into the background.

As a freelance player who got feature billing, my agent would call me and tell me to go to Paramount (in this case) and pick up a script, and if I okayed the part I would sign the contract. As to the shooting of *Bride of Vengeance*, I felt that the stars Paulette Goddard, John Lund and Macdonald Carey were fairly mild interpreters of the Borgias. I never read the whole script, because all I had received were the parts in which I appeared, and I never saw any of the rushes—usually only the stars were allowed to see them. I never saw the picture after it was released, either, having read the reviews which were pretty dreadful. Since I was also busy getting used to being a mother, I had no inclination to go and see it. Besides, it came and went so fast!

I'm sorry, but I really remember very few of the 45 pictures I made before I was blacklisted. This happened, incidentally, around the time *Bride*

THE MUDLARK (20th Century-Fox, 1950), with Alec Guinness, Irene Dunne. Director: Jean Negulesco.

of Vengeance was released [1949]. I was brought up before the House Un-American Activities Committee because I was a member of the Actor's Lab, a theater group whose participants included many liberals, myself among them. I had to sign a paper saying I was not and never had been a Communist. The word still went out from the studios not to hire me.

Bride of Vengeance was my last film.

❑

JAMES WONG HOWE:

The North Star was a Sam Goldwyn film starring Dana Andrews, Ann Harding, Anne Baxter, Farley Granger, Walter Huston and Walter Brennan. Erich von Stroheim played a sadistic Nazi doctor. Lillian Hellman wrote it. It was a good film. We were friends with the Russians at the time they made it. Goldwyn wanted to make the Russians sympathetic and show how the poor peasants were fighting the war and getting massacred. It was a propaganda film, you could say. However, it didn't make any money because when it went into release, the whole relationship between America and Russia had changed.

❑

MARSHA HUNT:

Actors and Sin was one of the most unusual films I ever did, and an interesting one. I only wish more people had agreed with me. A pair of English films, *Quartet* and *Trio*, recently had been very successful with their format of several unrelated Somerset Maugham short stories. This gave Ben Hecht, who was one of our top screenwriters, the idea of filming two of his stories for a single feature.

He decided on "Woman of Sin," a comedy about the picture business with Eddie Albert and Ben's daughter Jenny as a nine-year-old who writes a lurid novel and sells it to the movies; and "Actors Blood," a drama about the theater with Edward G. Robinson (an irreplaceable man and artist with whom I'd worked 10 years before at MGM in *Unholy Partners*), Dan O'Herlihy and myself as a temperamental actress who is first thought murdered but later revealed a suicide. The titles of the two stories were then combined to make the title of our picture: *Actors and Sin*.

Ben Hecht not only wrote the screenplays but served as producer and director—the latter two being areas in which he did not have a wealth of experience. The shooting was not without turmoil. The astonishing thing is that the whole film, which was done in rented space at one of the independent studios in Hollywood, was shot in five days! My segment was filmed in two days, but because Ben's daughter was so young and inexperienced hers took three. The budget for the picture was miniscule. We all worked for absolute minimum, which in the early fifties was *very* minimum. We were promised that when the film made money, we would get some more. I never saw a penny.

I remember that for the scene in which I was to be found dead, there was supposed to be a large portrait of me on the wall—all slashed. Because they were saving nickels, Ben asked if I had a painting of myself, which I did, a very interesting one; so they had it photographed, slashed the copy and hung it up. When my friends saw the film and observed the portrait which they knew from my home, they gasped in horror, thinking it was my painting that had actually been shredded. For a dressing room scene where a portrait of me was also needed, I sent back to Sardi's Restaurant in New York for the caricature of me which hung on the wall there; Vincent Sardi very kindly sent it out and we used it in the scene.

I was very impressed with Dan O'Herlihy, who had recently come over from Ireland's Abbey Theater. Not long after he played my husband in *Actors and Sin*, I received a call from someone about to make a picture called *The Adventures of Robinson Crusoe*. He asked if I thought Dan would be up to doing Crusoe. "Now remember," advised this man, "whoever plays the role will be alone for much of the movie—he'll have to be superb to bring it off." I gave Dan a complete rave. I like to think it helped him get the role which ultimately won him an Academy Award nomination.

I was never really satisfied with my performance in *Actors and Sin*, though.

THE RED BADGE OF COURAGE (MGM, 1951), with Audie Murphy, Bill Mauldin, John Dierkes. Director: John Huston.

Anything that is shot that fast is sort of like a rough dress rehearsal. This was a bravura role and I wish I had had more time to do it. The first showing here in the Los Angeles area was a benefit for the Oakwood School in the San Fernando Valley. A number of children from show business backgrounds attended this progressive school which had been started by the actor Robert Ryan, but it was operating at a deficit. It's still in existence.

Why didn't *Actors and Sin* do better? Several of us on the production were known to be liberals, an extremely unpopular political belief at that time. Also, the picture was produced on such a shoestring that there was no money for promotion. And if you didn't have a chain of theaters lined up to show it, your picture, as we used to say, came out with a hush.

❑

NUNNALLY JOHNSON:

Some exhibitors were against my production of *The Senator Was Indiscreet*, starring William Powell, before a print had left the studio.

It was, I suppose, what we now call (maybe we did then, too) the "rightists." I was utterly unconscious of them, of what possible feelings they might have had about it as we worked. I didn't know that a senator was sacrosanct. God, they say enough about them when they're running against each other! I felt that we might have had some fun with this fellow and I was wrong.

There were at least half a dozen organizations like American Legion posts or conventions or things like those that had condemned the picture before it was released—before they'd seen it—as being subversive or some such thing. It came at a time [1947] when anyone who didn't wrap the flag around himself was a Commie.

❑

EVELYN KEYES:

The Prowler was the best film I ever did, a well thought-out, well constructed script. Dalton Trumbo wrote it, but I didn't find that out for 20 years because he was on the political blacklist; they had to use someone else's name on the screen. I had a small interest in the picture, but never saw a nickel. It opened during the height of the Red scare of the fifties and many exhibitors were frightened off by the alleged left-wing sympathies of director Joseph Losey and producer Sam Spiegel. It flopped. Losey had to move to Europe to work.

❑

ROBERT LEWIS:

In April of 1947, *Monsieur Verdoux* had its New York premiere—a sickening evening. Chaplin's awareness of his atrocious publicity resulting from a paternity case, as well as his much misunderstood political statements, prepared him somewhat for the at times frightening reception of some organized, hostile members of the audience.

Insane booing greeted such lines as, "Millions are starving and unemployed." Agonized groans greeted Verdoux' reply to his child who asks him what sort of man Santa Claus is: "Very kind—to the rich." But the angriest response was to the scene just before his execution. "Have you no remorse for your sins?", the priest asks Verdoux, who comes back with, "What would you be doing without sin?" Charlie once told me of a terrifying, recurrent nightmare from which he suffered all his life. He'd be performing a comedy act in front of a large audience, and no one would be laughing. His nightmare had become a reality.

"They couldn't take it, could they?", he kept repeating. "I kicked them in the balls. I hit them where it hurt."

❑

AARON SLICK FROM PUNKIN CRICK (Paramount, 1952), with Adele Jurgens, Alan Young, Dinah Shore, Robert Merrill. Director: Claude Binyon.

MARY PICKFORD:

I worked on *Secrets*, only to burn the negative and write off a $300,000 loss. Another misadventure followed, *Kiki*, before I returned to *Secrets* and made what I consider a creditable picture. Unfortunately, *Secrets* opened in 25 key cities on the day that President Roosevelt declared the bank holiday. Very few people were spending money on entertainment in the weeks that followed, and while the film was well received it was a financial disaster.

❑

JANE POWELL:

In 1933 America was in the grip of the Great Depression and hundreds of thousands were without jobs. Hungry people lined up at the soup kitchens and the homeless slept wherever they could. United Artists bought Ben Hecht's story about a hobo mayor elected by the homeless people camped in New York's Central Park, and Rodgers and Hart wrote the songs, including "You Are Too Beautiful."

The star of the movie was the man who started talking pictures in 1927—"The Jazz Singer" himself, Al Jolson. *Hallelujah I'm a Bum* was filmed not in Central Park but at the Riviera Country Club of the Pacific Palisades, near Hollywood and Santa Anita Racetrack. When *Hallelujah I'm a Bum* was completed, the studio found it had a musical social satire about a very real and very desperate situation. In the dark days of 1933, before Roosevelt's election and the New Deal, the public stayed away in droves from its stark reality.

Nevertheless, *Hallelujah I'm a Bum* is a marvelous product of its time.

❑

MARTHA RAYE:

Monsieur Verdoux, with Charlie Chaplin, is my favorite of my pictures, and no one saw it. When it came out in the late forties, Charlie was in hot water—they were calling him a Red, among other things—and he got excommunicated from the United States. Our picture was boycotted. I've always felt the blacklist rubbed off on me, too: it was 15 years before I got another movie, *Jumbo*. In the early seventies, Charlie was welcomed back and given an honorary Oscar. I met him at the ceremony. The first thing he said to me was "Ah, Madame Verdoux!"

❑

ALLEN RIVKIN:

I had some censorship problems during the Korean War with *Prisoner of War*. The Defense Department had at first okayed it. And then, when the picture was finished, they changed their minds and wanted us to pull the picture. Dore Schary wouldn't let them. He said, "We made it. I don't care if anyone sees it. We're going to release it." But it got the lowest possible advertising budget, ads the size of a postage stamp. And the picture went down the drain. It starred Ronald Reagan, and that, of course, didn't mean a goddamned thing at the boxoffice. It was a good picture, too.

❑

RICHARD RODGERS:

Hallelujah I'm a Bum was the first and probably the last musical ever made in Hollywood that concerned itself almost entirely with the problems of the Depression.

During those years so many people lost their jobs, money and homes that they were forced to live wherever they could find a few yards of vacant ground. In our picture we focused on bums living in Central Park, with Al Jolson playing the part of Bumper, their leader, Harry Langdon playing Egghead, a radical who calls the police "Hoover's Cossacks," and Frank Morgan as a Jimmy Walkerish mayor. We tried to keep the score relatively light, but we were defeated by the theme.

The subject of homelessness at a time when it was such an urgent national problem didn't strike many people as something to laugh and sing about.

❑

LEON SHAMROY:

Wilson I was very proud of; Ernest Palmer started [photographing] it, but Zanuck took him off after a week: Darryl had been spoiled by my style. I ran the picture recently for Henry King [the director], and it's still great, but it was a pacifist picture when war was on, they couldn't show it to the troops, and making it was a mistake.

❑

JOSEF von STERNBERG:

I returned to the treadmill to make the last two of the seven films with Marlene Dietrich. These two, in which I completely subjugated my bird of paradise to my peculiar tendency to prove that a film might well be an art medium, were not bad, but audiences and critics turned thumbs down.

The Scarlet Empress, the penultimate film, deserved to be a success by any standard then existing or now prevalent, but with few exceptions it was greeted as an attempt to assassinate a superb actress. The film was, of course, a relentless excursion into style, which, taken for granted in any work of art, is considered to be unpardonable in this medium.

My last and most unpopular film of this series was to be called *Capriccio Espagnol*. This was negated by Ernst Lubitsch, in full charge of the studio [Paramount], and though he was unable to interfere with my production, he set his seal on it by altering the title to *The Devil is a Woman*.

Though Mr. Lubitsch's altering the sex of the devil was meant to aid in selling the picture, it did not do so. The Spanish government made protestations that caused the work to be withdrawn from circulation. The ostensible reason given was that the Guárdia Civil had been shown to be ineffectual in curbing a riotous carnival during which the action of the film takes place.

❑

CORNEL WILDE:

No Blade of Grass is a definitive story of the world ecological tragedy. It's not just another science fiction caper or documentary. One environmentalist called it a prophecy. Now the story is coming true. People are starving to death in Asia and Africa. Wars are being fought for good. It's a peculiar thing to watch things happen which were only imagined when I produced and directed the picture [in 1970].

TALK ABOUT A STRANGER (MGM, 1952), with Harry Hines, George Murphy, Nancy Davis, Ed Cassidy, William Tannen. Director: David Bradley.

MGM brass was afraid *No Blade of Grass* would frighten people. The studio wrote it off without giving the picture a chance to prove itself.

The first sneak preview in Westwood, California, was super. MGM dismissed it saying the college audience was kooky. A Hollywood sneak was ignored because it was claimed the theater was packed with my pals. Then I asked Jim Aubrey, head of Metro, to sneak the picture in any city he chose. He settled for Sacramento. The audience went crazy. People hung around the lobby for 45 minutes discussing the impact of what they'd seen. It made no difference. The studio refused to get behind the picture. I raised all kinds of hell. But MGM gave it an abortive release. It died.

❑

SHELLEY WINTERS:

We knew when we saw the first rushes that we were part of something classic and timeless. *Night of the Hunter* is probably the most thoughtful and reserved performance I ever gave. The studio released the film very quietly, and the public seemed to ignore it. I believe [director] Charles Laughton had been "named" by someone and was therefore blacklisted. A decade later, both in Europe and in the U.S., the film was finally recognized as a unique poetic achievement.

❏

JAMES WOODS:

Can you imagine? Here I am, working all my life, doing good work, asking for that chance to play a lead role with a great actor, and promising that I won't let anybody down. Then [director] Sergio Leone calls me and tells me that I have the role of a lifetime [in *Once Upon a Time in America* with Robert De Niro], and I say, wonderful. This will be the role that turns my entire career around. Three weeks before release, they have the assistant editor of *Police Academy* chop it to ribbons. I mean, do you think maybe I was suicidal?

It got slaughtered by the critics, as it should have. What chance in hell did the studio think the picture was going to have of pleasing the critics when they've already created the political scandal of interfering with a great artist's film? It was such a stupid move. They were dead in the water.

Did you know that Warner Brothers forgot to submit composer Ennio Morricone's name for an Oscar that year? Let's point out that the film did not get one Oscar nomination. I made a great film and they killed it. So I live with what I live with, and they live with what they live with.

❏

WILLIAM WYLER:

Carrie was cut in America. We had a scene in a flophouse which, at the time of the Un-American Activities Committee, was said to show our country in an unfavorable light. That went and so did the suicide of Hurstwood, played by Laurence Olivier. The cuts didn't help. The picture died anyway.

❏

MICHAEL YORK:

Justine was *so* sad. I only saw it once in Paris. It should have been so much better. It's very easy to apportion the blame, but that's not being fair. In the first place, Joe Strick started directing the picture and did all the location work in Tunisia. When the film was taken to Hollywood, he was fired and George Cukor took over. It's to his credit that he took on a film without any real preparation. But his main concern was actually to get the thing done. And I think that shows. It just didn't work out. Also, I think when you extract a plot about gun running-to-the-Palestinians from an essentially literary book that delights in verbal conceits and the sheer play of language, you're not getting the whole story.

❏

DARRYL F. ZANUCK:

When I produced *Wilson*, which was based on the life and career of the President, I was told that it would be looked upon as propaganda for the Democratic Party in the upcoming election and that Republicans might boycott it.

The Republicans didn't boycott it, but the American public did. It just happened not to be popular entertainment in spite of the fact that it received probably the best reviews of any film I have ever made; and in spite of the fact that Fox spent more on advertising and publicizing it than they did on *Cleopatra* or *The Longest Day*.

❏

FRED ZINNEMANN:

Behold a Pale Horse was a big flop everywhere in the world except Lebanon. It was a smash there because Omar Sharif was born there. My mistake on that picture was in assuming that people remembered and still cared about the Spanish Civil War. Apparently they don't because nobody cared about the movie.

Ego Eulogies

"Let him have one good, resounding flop and he'll be adorable."

DANA ANDREWS:

My worst picture? Probably *Enchanted Island* with Jane Powell. Director John Huston originally had the rights to it, but when he sold the story, the new producer's wife completely re-wrote it, took out everything of quality in it and we were given the worst dialogue you could ever imagine to try to say. I don't think anyone ever made any sense of it. Disgraceful!

❏

JOAN BENNETT:

All proceeds from the successful *Scarlet Street* went into the next Walter Wanger-Joan Bennett-Fritz Lang film, *Secret Beyond the Door*. But Fritz was a real Jekyll-Hyde character, calm and purposeful one moment, off on a tirade the next. At script conferences he was rebellious, on the set he was outrageous and demanding. I remember he wouldn't use doubles for Michael Redgrave and me for a sequence in a burning house. We fled terrified through scorching flames time and again. Fritz and I had some thrilling arguments during the filming. When he was in a successful period, he was impossible and Darryl Zanuck told me, "Let him have one good resounding flop and he'll be adorable." He got it in *Secret Beyond the Door*. It flopped and Fritz was adorable at once.

❏

MARLON BRANDO:

I *tried* on *A Countess from Hong Kong*, but I was a puppet, a marionette in that. I wasn't there to be anything else, because [Charles] Chaplin was a man of sizeable talent and I was not going to argue with him about what's funny.

I must say we didn't start off very well. I went to London for the reading

ACTORS AND SIN (United Artists, 1952), with Marsha Hunt, Edward G. Robinson. Director: Ben Hecht.

CARRIE (Paramount, 1952), with Laurence Olivier, Jennifer Jones. Director: William Wyler.

of the script and Chaplin read for us. I had jet lag and I went right to sleep during his reading. I was miscast in that. He was a mean man, Chaplin. Sadistic. I saw him torture his son—Sydney Chaplin played a small part in the movie. I said, "Why do you take that?" His hands were sweating. He said, "Well, the old man is old and nervous, it's all right." Chaplin reminded me of what Churchill said about the Germans, either at your feet or at your throat.

He tried to do some shit with me. I said, "Don't you *ever* speak to me in that tone of voice." I told him he could take his film and stick it up his ass, frame by frame. That was after I realized it was a complete fiasco. He wasn't a man who could direct anymore. I don't even like to think about it.

❑

CLAUDETTE COLBERT:

I had just had an appendectomy before starting *Four Frightened People*, and the first day on location—with nurse—producer-director Cecil B. DeMille put me in a swamp up to my shoulders. A real swamp.

The nurse yelled, and he said, "I've waited 10 days already!", so in I went. Two days later I was bedridden with a 104-degree temperature; I simply thought I was going to die. Mr. DeMille was very apologetic about his behavior. "It's just an act," he told me. "People expect that of me. I'm not really like that underneath." By that point, I didn't care what he was really like underneath.

But I liked the old boy. I think I was the only woman who ever talked to him as an equal. As it turned out, *Four Frightened People* was the only DeMille picture that ever lost money, and I was in it—up to my shoulders.

❑

JANE CONNELL:

I knew at the first screening of *Mame* that we had a turkey on our hands. It started off excitingly, but very soon my two teenage daughters, who were kids of the sixties and didn't give a damn whom they offended, began to moan, "Ughhh!" I had to keep squeezing their hands to keep them quiet.

When the stage *Mame* opened on Broadway in 1966 starring Angela Lansbury and with me as the misfit secretary, Agnes Gooch, I didn't expect to land the film version—if and when it became a film. Broadway actresses usually don't. Angela didn't. Warner Brothers wasn't really interested in making the movie; musicals had been failing and had become so expensive. But Lucille Ball wanted to star, and when she offered to put a lot of money into the production, they capitulated. Madeline Kahn, who was hot then, was signed to play my role, Gooch. They rehearsed for two weeks when, I was told, Lucy suddenly looked at Madeline and said, "When am I going to see

ABOUT FACE (Warner Brothers, 1952), with Dick Wesson, Virginia Gibson, Aileen Stanley, Jr., Gordon MacRae, Eddie Bracken, Phyllis Kirk. Director: Roy Del Ruth.

SO THIS IS LOVE (Warner Brothers, 1953), with Kathryn Grayson, Merv Griffin. Director: Gordon Douglas.

Gooch?" Gene Saks, director of our stage version and now directing the picture, was horrified.

I think that Lucy, then in her sixties, was frightened by the contrast with the youthful Madeline and furthermore didn't understand the younger actress' new wave, oddball comedy style. Lucy belonged to the old school where technique carried you through.

"Get me Gooch!", hollered Lucy, who had the final say on everything. Madeline was paid off and made more money *not* doing *Mame* than I made *doing* it. But I didn't care: I was glad to be in such a big, important movie. Lucy had seen me as Agnes Gooch when *Mame* played the Dorothy Chandler Pavilion in Los Angeles in 1968 and asked for me. While Madeline was maybe a little young for the role, for the closeness of the big screen I might have been a tad too old—after all, the character had to get pregnant and everything. But we got around it.

Lucy didn't trust Gene Saks. She had wanted George Cukor to direct, but he had a previous commitment or something. So she fell back on Gene. He didn't know as much about film as she did, and she didn't know as much about this piece as he did, and they sort of clashed somewhere in the middle of the thing. There was a lot of tension.

Lucy was also unhappy with the costume designer, Theadora Van Runkle. Theadora was a new person with modern ideas, whereas rich, successful, beautiful Lucy was, incredibly, a victim of her own insecurity. She had an unnecessary sense of allegiance to her fans, always thinking that she should be the old Lucy for them. Her hair was as orange as ever and while I don't think she'd had a facelift, she did use some kind of hooks under her wigs to pull up and tighten her jawline. All this, plus the soft focus photography she insisted on hampered her portrayal. Remember, Mame was a character whose credo was "Live, live, live!"—she wasn't so concerned about her appearance or being just so. The familiar freedom seemed to disappear now that Lucy was older. She couldn't throw her body around like she used to for fear of losing a wig or a muscle hook or getting a bad angle.

My relationship with Lucy was different from the others on the picture. I have nothing but affection and gratitude for her. She had chosen me. She had to show her best side to me because of the trouble she'd caused getting me. But I could see where she could be difficult. A lot of her money was sunk into the thing. Sometimes, after a scene, she'd say, "Let's face it, honey. If this doesn't work, that lamp's mine and that and that."

Once, she invited me to dinner at her home. When they brought out a big, steaming lobster dinner, I exclaimed, "Oh, boy!" Lucy said, "Oh, that's for Gary [Morton, her husband]. We're just having leftovers." I thought, "Here I am, in a mansion in Beverly Hills with one of the richest women in show business—having leftovers." Maybe it was some kind of omen.

Lucy was too proud to allow the studio to use someone else's singing

DOWN AMONG THE SHELTERING PALMS (20th Century-Fox, 1953), with William Lundigan, Alvin Greenman, David Wayne, Jane Greer. Director: Edmund Goulding.

THE MEMBER OF THE WEDDING (Columbia, 1953), with Julie Harris, Ethel Waters, Brandon De Wilde. Director: Fred Zinnemann.

voice in *Mame*. She insisted on doing it herself, and this was a big mistake. They had to piece the numbers together.

Occasionally, she would invite me to her trailer to rat on people in the company. I'd tell her what I thought was appropriate—no more. But Lucy could be very loyal to those who were loyal to her. She was devoted to her mother, DeDe, who had been so supportive when Lucy was trying to break into show business many years before. DeDe was around a lot and was present when we filmed the big "Mame" number out at the Disney Ranch in the Valley, watching everything, as always. After the number was done, Lucy (who was always on) joked, "I don't know. DeDe didn't smile when we did that."

One time she got very angry with Theadora over a tight-fitting costume she had made for me as Agnes Gooch. It was the scene where Mame is supposed to pull me by one of my loose-fitting sweaters, and in doing so tightens it to reveal my bustline. "Agnes," she cries, "you *do* have a bosom!" But since Theadora had made the sweater snug to begin with, the bustline already had been well in view. Lucy called me to her house to ask if Theadora was intentionally trying to make her lose the joke. A loose sweater was used.

Of course, to add to our woes Lucy had begun this strenuous role not long after she had broken her leg in a skiing accident. Nevertheless, Onna White, our choreographer, rehearsed her individually and worked her tail off, with no complaints from our star. Lucy was a compulsive "doer"—whether it was working on scenes, figuring puzzles or playing backgammon.

As we were nearing completion, one of our film editors came over and predicted an Academy Award for me. It didn't happen. After the less than earth-shaking preview, I whispered to my old pal Bea Arthur (who was re-creating her role of Mame's "bosom buddy" and was married to Gene Saks), "I wish Angela had done it." Bea gave me one of her famous withering looks. I realized that *she* had always wanted to play the role.

Recently, I went to my local video store to rent *Mame* but was told they didn't have it. "You don't want that one, anyway," advised the proprietor. "It's lousy. You should get the earlier, non-musical version with Rosalind Russell, *Auntie Mame*, which we have." I told him that I was *in* the video I'd requested, and that there on the Upper West Side of New York he should be careful what he says about the movies because he could be talking to someone in them!

❑

MARLENE DIETRICH:

All our friends who had fled Europe had too much self-respect to want to remain in America without working. We helped them find work, and [producer Joe] Pasternak also did his part. It was his idea that I should make a film with René Clair.

At first I resisted, but finally out of loyalty to my old principle that doing your duty was all that mattered, I yielded. *The Flame of New Orleans*, under the direction of René Clair, featured Bruce Cabot, an awfully stupid actor, unable to remember his lines or cues. Nor could Clair, who didn't speak a word of English, lend him a helping hand. Besides, Cabot was very conceited. He wouldn't accept any help. I finally resigned myself to paying for his lessons, so that he would at least know his lines.

The crew loathed Clair (surely because of the language barrier) to such an extent that the technicians almost pushed me off the set the moment they heard the order: "Pack up your things."

The Flame of New Orleans was a flop. I played a double role (sisters) and, as always, wore lavish costumes, but that wasn't enough. I didn't particularly like René Clair, but I didn't hate him as much as the rest did.

❑

HENRY FONDA:

I stormed into Darryl Zanuck's office, furious at the latest lousy script he'd sent me and wanting out. He asked me what kind of pictures I did want to make, and I said, "*The Grapes of Wrath* was a good one. And *The Ox-Bow Incident*, which you didn't want to make but didn't mind taking bows for." He motioned to me, saying, "Come here and see how well *Ox-Bow Incident* did." He flipped through a ledger he kept on his desk. Every number relating to *Ox-Bow Incident* was in red ink. Now I wanted out more than ever.

❑

JOAN FONTAINE:

Henry Weinstein was the nominal producer of *Tender is the Night*, but David Selznick masterminded the production by long distance. He was married to Jennifer Jones, of course, and one day my telephone was tapped into hers by accident and I heard her talking to him about retakes, close-ups, etc. I think poor Jennifer was frightened of the role.

When old Henry King, the director, vetoed a crucial scene that would have had the two leads, unwed, sharing a bed, someone argued that they had made love that way in the F. Scott Fitzgerald novel. "Nobody makes love until they're married in my films," King replied.

I knew the film was doomed.

❑

CLARK GABLE:

The Misfits couldn't be better named. None of us should be in the same goddam room together. [Arthur] Miller, Marilyn [Monroe], Monty Clift—they're all loonies. It's a fucking mess!

THE EDDIE CANTOR STORY (Warner Brothers, 1954), with Marilyn Erskine, Jackie Barnett, Keefe Brasselle. Director: Alfred E. Green.

JANE GREER:

Down Among the Sheltering Palms—oh my God!

That was one of the unhappiest productions I've ever been on, doomed from the start. It was shot at 20th Century-Fox, where I'd just done a pleasant film with Gary Cooper called *You're in the Navy Now*. They sent me the script for *Palms*, saying, "Darryl Zanuck loves you. Please do this." I read it and detested it. Lousy story, lousy everything. June Haver had been set for my role first, but June was a very religious Catholic girl who soon after even became a nun for a while. At the last minute she had pulled out of the picture on religious grounds: she decided she didn't want to play a missionary's niece embroiled in a story of South Sea island Army fraternization. Anyway, that's what I was told. I always wondered if it weren't simply that she was a "pro" who recognized impending disaster when she saw it.

"*Please* do the picture," pleaded the Fox people. "Darryl loves you. As a favor to him. We're ready to start. He'll use you in other pictures if you'll do this for him." Like a fool, I believed them and signed.

Well, there wasn't time to get up new costumes for me, so I had to wear what they had designed for June, who was a cute little blonde, quite different from dark, rangy me. There were full skirts, boat-neck dresses—everything I never wore, everything that just wasn't *me*.

One song I sang was all right, "When You're in Love," but otherwise *nothing* was right with this movie. Our director, Edmund Goulding, who was known for his heavy dramatic productions, had been fighting with Zanuck for some time, and when they gave him the script for this light musical, they hoped he would turn it down so they could lay him off. (I think it was the last picture under his contract and they wanted to get rid of him.) But Goulding had nothing else scheduled, so he said, "I'll do it." They were livid; he was disgruntled throughout the shooting. His battles with Zanuck grew worse. Goulding had his own Dr. Feelgood on the set to give him shots to get him through the thing. He had a reputation for being a painstaking director with women in particular, but every time I'd ask him a question about my role he'd bark back something like, "Oh, what do you care! This is an atrocity! Don't bother me!"

Well, *Darryl* loved me.

We filmed *Palms* in 29 days, which was some kind of speed record for a Technicolor musical from a major studio like Fox. Then came 17 days of retakes!

It was called *Friendly Island* during production, but later on it was changed to *Down Among the Sheltering Palms* because there recently had been a hit song of that title. They tried everything to save their turkey!

It was on the shelf for about two years amid rumors that it might never be released. Finally, in 1953, it sneaked out. Such reviews as there were read like the plot synopses the studio handed out to the media—meaning many critics probably didn't even bother to actually see the film. You couldn't even get people in to see it for free! It was around for about a week, then was pulled.

I recall that the wife of a Fox executive came up to me one day then and said, "Oh, I just saw *Down Among the Sheltering Palms*."

So I asked, "How was it?"

And she replied, "Your hair looked very pretty. I didn't realize it had so much red in it."

Zanuck proceeded to fire all of the principals in the picture who were under contract there—William Lundigan, Gloria De Haven, Mitzi Gaynor, Jack Paar. "AND AS FOR THAT OTHER WOMAN WHO WAS BROUGHT OVER HERE . . .", he ranted—meaning me. Darryl didn't love me anymore. The "other pictures" I'd been promised did not materialize. I never made another movie at Fox.

□

BEAT THE DEVIL (United Artists, 1954), with Humphrey Bogart, Jennifer Jones. Director: John Huston.

SUSAN HAYWARD:

I was filming something called *The Lost Moment*, with Bob Cummings and Agnes Moorehead. I played a schizophrenic, and the director [Martin Gabel] went around telling everybody not to talk to me. Yes, even warned the crew not to speak to me because he said I had to maintain a mood for the part. At one point, I lost my temper and crashed a lamp over his head, and to this day I've never felt sorry.

Well, it was a disastrous film. As miserable a failure as you've ever seen. Their name for it may have been *The Lost Moment*, but after I saw it, I called it "The Lost Hour and Thirty-Five Minutes."

❑

EDITH HEAD:

Myra Breckinridge? Gore Vidal's story was worse than pornographic; it was unpleasant, unreal and contrived. I did Mae West's clothes and saw her costume tests, but I did not view one foot of the film. I hear it was pretty horrendous—but it could not have been as bad as all the goings-on on the set.

Mae had written into her contract that she was the only one who would appear on screen dressed in black, white or black and white—whoever wears black and white in a Technicolor film immediately gets the audience's eye. When Raquel Welch found out, she was furious. Raquel was the star, but Mae was getting special attention because everyone at the studio loved her.

140

❏

PAUL HENREID:

I didn't find out until I arrived in Nice that John Huston had had a fight with the producer, who wanted to rewrite the script, and Huston had walked out on *The Madwoman of Chaillot*. They had then hired Bryan Forbes, an English director who had been an actor and a scriptwriter. He did a good deal of rewriting on what had been a very fine original script, and to make matters worse, when he directed the film he gave Katharine Hepburn her head. When you let Hepburn do what she wants to do, you are in trouble. I kept remembering what Spencer Tracy was always telling her: "Say your lines clearly and don't make any silly faces."

❏

JOHN HUSTON:

The Barbarian and the Geisha turned out to be a bad picture, but it was a good picture before it became a bad picture. I've made pictures that were not good, for which I was responsible, but this was not one of them.

When I brought it to Hollywood, the picture, including the music, was finished, a sensitive, well balanced work. I turned it over to the studio and hurried on to Africa to work on *The Roots of Heaven*. John Wayne apparently took over after I left. He pulled a lot of weight at Fox, so the studio went along with his demands for changes. The picture was released before I got back, and when I finally saw it, I was aghast. A number of scenes had been reshot, at Wayne's insistence, simply because he didn't like the way he looked in the original version. By the time the studio finished hacking up the picture according to Wayne's instructions, it was a complete mess.

I would have taken legal steps to have my name removed from the picture, but learned that [studio chief Buddy] Adler was terminally ill with a brain tumor. Bringing suit under such circumstances was unthinkable.

❏

HENRY KOSTER:

The Naked Maja, an Italian production, was one of the most torturing experiences I had. The star was Tony Franciosa [as the painter Goya], and he was very hard to work with. We fought all day long. He used dirty language against me on the set. When I told him what to do he said, "Why don't you so-and-so." I walked off and said, "I will not come back until he apologizes in public." He finally did. Later, other directors told me they had the same trouble with him.

Ava Gardner was also a young lady who wasn't very happy with her part. The producer wasn't happy with the picture and the writer didn't like what was on the screen. I never saw the picture. I was not allowed to show a little of my own style in the picture. It came out here, but not too successfully.

❏

STANLEY KRAMER:

Frank Sinatra [who hated the Spanish location] left *The Pride and the Passion* six weeks before completion. He simply told me, "I have a lawyer and you have a lawyer," and that he had to go. I pleaded with him, but to no avail. Finally, I made a deal with his attorney, Martin Gang, to finish the film in California on a stage with fake palm trees. Cary Grant made superb efforts to fill the gap. Nothing was too difficult: he played close-ups that were supposed to be with Frank with coats on hangers, put himself out no end and acted as a professional from beginning to end. But he couldn't save the picture.

❏

WILLIAM LUDWIG:

We were all crushed by the failure of *An American Romance*. It was called *America* during production, and we were sure we had a film worthy of that title. We did, too, before it was chopped up in the cutting room.

Originally, it was to star Spencer Tracy, one of the biggest stars of the day, of course. King Vidor, the director and the person who came up with the plot concept of making the refinement of metal ore and immigrant man analogous, was an individual of considerable ego—with good reason. He had a formidable list of films to his credit. One day while he was walking around the lot at MGM he bumped into Spencer Tracy, whom he had recently directed in *Northwest Passage*.

King said, "Spence, we're working on an important story that would be perfect for you. We'd love to have you star in our picture." And he explained what the film was about to Tracy. When he was through, Tracy replied, "As soon as the script is ready, I'll look at it."

I was writing the screenplay, and King came bellowing up to me, "Who the hell does that son-of-a-bitch Tracy think he is, wanting to okay a script of mine?!" So he gave the male lead of this Walter B. Chrysler prototype to Brian Donlevy, who was more of a character actor than a boxoffice star. And for the role of his wife, he cast a new Australian contractee at Metro named Ann Richards.

American Romance was in production for 18 months, shooting all around the country. At one point, King got into an argument with the studio and walked off for a couple of days. I was called in to direct the picture while he was gone. I guess the whole thing was ill-starred right from King's meeting with Tracy.

THE SILVER CHALICE (Warner Brothers, 1955), with Paul Newman, Pier Angeli. Director: Victor Saville.

It was to be a major Technicolor production, with a two-a-day roadshow release planned. The first cut of the film ran over four hours, and it was fabulous. The second cut, about three and a half hours, was even better—the audience ate it up. However, World War II was raging, and just before release the nation went to double daylight savings time to conserve power; we sprang forward two hours instead of one to save energy. The theater owners refused to play anything that long.

At the smaller theaters, where it would eventually go and where double features were still the order of the day, programs were usually shown twice in an evening. People going in to see the long *American Romance* and another feature might not have gotten out till two or three in the morning!

Defense plants also had been very busy for some time with three shifts, posing additional problems for movie people. I remember a year or two before *American Romance* I had written a comedy called *Love Crazy*, starring William Powell and Myrna Loy, which we previewed at Long Beach. The audience laughed hysterically through half of it—then suddenly three-quarters of them just got up and walked out. We couldn't imagine what went wrong; they had seemed to be enjoying the picture enormously. Then someone said, "They just changed shifts at the shipyard." Many moviegoers just weren't able to stay put for long periods at that time.

An American Romance was cut down to its final two hours and seven minutes, which audiences, ironically, thought longer than the first four-hour cut.

❑

MARIE McDONALD:

Nobody saw *Living in a Big Way* but my mother. It was a great script we had. Then it was torn in half and thrown out the window by a genius at Metro. They would hand me a piece of paper on the set and every day it was a different girl I was playing. My big Russian ballet number was out because a certain star [Gene Kelly] wasn't in the scene.

❑

THOMAS McGUANE:

I'd have to say that I'm only *now* getting over *The Missouri Breaks*. I wrote it as something that I could direct, that would star my old buddies—Warren Oates and Harry Dean Stanton and those kind of guys. It was going to be an ensemble movie about a little gang of outlaws who outlived their time. Then, all of a sudden, this star casting [Marlon Brando, Jack Nicholson] came in, and it went from being prospectively a very interesting genre movie to this kind of *monster*.

JUPITER'S DARLING (MGM, 1955), with Marge, Gower Champion. Director: George Sidney.

SINCERELY YOURS (Warner Brothers, 1955), with Dorothy Malone, Liberace, Joanne Dru. Director: Gordon Douglas.

❑

BETTE MIDLER:

I couldn't even think about my work after *Jinxed*. I just felt completely squashed. It undermined my trust in myself. I met with hostility from director Don Siegel and leading man Ken Wahl [who told the press that to get through their love scenes he had to think of his dog]. It was doomed from the start. I thought we were working together. I didn't know it was them against me. Working with people who want you to fail is the most dangerous thing you can do. It broke my heart, and I was depressed.

❑

LEWIS MILESTONE:

I hated *Mutiny on the Bounty*. It didn't represent me at all; after the first two or three weeks I had nothing to say on it.

Everything went fine for the first couple of weeks, and then suddenly we were doing a scene and Marlon [Brando] spoke to the cameraman . . . right past me. He said, "Look, I'll tell you, when I go like this, it means roll it, and this gesture means you stop the camera. You don't stop the camera until I give you the signal."

Well, I was *amazed*, but I didn't say anything about it. He said, "Everybody ready" and the camera started rolling.

I turned my back on it and walked away. I had a magazine stuck in my pocket, and I sat down and started reading it while the scene was going on. The producer came up and said, "Aren't you going to watch it?" I said, "Well, I hate to see movies in pieces, so you let him do this and when it's all finished and cut, for 10 cents I can walk into a theater and see the whole thing at once."

And from then on that's the way we worked. I concentrated my directorial efforts with Trevor Howard and the English cast. Brando is a psychotic man. I don't think the man's responsible for what he's doing.

❑

JEAN NEGULESCO:

Hal Wallis, one of Hollywood's better producers, chose me to direct *The Conspirators*, a story in the vein of *Casablanca*.

He was then replaced by a minor producer. The script was changed. The film that had already been shot under the supervision of Wallis was discarded. Location and the pace of the story were changed. The stars took advantage of the situation, especially Hedy Lamarr. Their demands were granted. My job as a young director became a nightmare. Secretly the film became known as *The Constipators*, with "Headache Lamarr" and "Paul Hemorrhoid" [Henreid].

The just valuation of the film was given by Max Steiner, called in to do the musical score. We saw the finished product together. Hopefully I waited for his comment: just one word, "Ouch!" The critics murdered the film—and me. It seemed a good time to decide to withdraw from cinema and return to painting.

❑

JOE PASTERNAK:

A number of producer friends of mine, in the face of vast public indifference, have insisted on their own judgment against the people's. Darryl Zanuck has his *Wilson*; I have *The Kissing Bandit*. Frank Sinatra and I made *Bandit*, a cataclysm that still jolts my blood pressure when I think of the red ink. Even today I think it's an amusing picture. But my opinion doesn't matter. The nature of the theater art is to please the audience—and they *weren't*.

❑

SIDNEY POITIER:

Paris Blues, in which I played a jazz musician, was all wrong from beginning to end.

The novel on which the movie was ostensibly based really went into the lives of jazz musicians in Paris, but what we did was not that. Also, the original script I read, by a wonderful screenwriter named Irene Kemp, was not the script we wound up with. By the time we were finished, five other writers had been called in, one after another, to change the script according to some idea that one or another of a dozen people connected with the movie had for making it a success. It was a shambles.

I found out once and for all that a bunch of people can't do it. One person has to do it. A group of people engaged in a collaborative creative effort must respond to one person. Mistakes are probably going to be made, but they will be the mistakes of one person, and so they won't be so bad.

❑

MARTIN RACKIN:

Dustin Hoffman, Jesus, the luckiest Jewish midget that ever lived. Makes a couple of great pictures with great directors, and then he goes to an idiot producer that's going to make a picture in New York, and Dustin insists he's going to have complete control. So he hires schmucks, a business manager, a producer, a director whose only credit was a Tampax commercial. The

THAT LADY (20th Century-Fox, 1955), with Olivia de Havilland, Robert Harris. Director: Terence Young.

script was him getting his gun off. The picture was *Who is Harry Kellerman and Why is He Saying Those Terrible Things About Me?* No one went to see it except Dustin Hoffman and four of his friends in Greenwich Village.

❏

BURT REYNOLDS:

At Long Last Love was not as bad as it was reviewed. I mean, *nothing* could be that bad.

What was reviewed was Cybill Shepherd and Peter Bogdanovich's relationship. You see, Peter has done something that all critics will never forgive him for doing. That is, stop being a critic, go make a film and have that film, *The Last Picture Show*, become enormously successful. Well, what he did then was go on talk shows and be rather arrogant and talk about how bad critics are. That was the final straw.

So they were all waiting with their hatchets and knives and whatever. And along came Peter, who finally gave them something they could kill him with. Unfortunately, there I was, between Cybill's broad shoulders and Peter's ego. And I got buried along with them.

❏

DEBBIE REYNOLDS:

Mr. Imperium starred Lana Turner and Ezio Pinza, with Marjorie Main of the "Ma Kettle" series as my aunt.

Marjorie was an older woman who had a real-life bladder problem. She'd be saying her lines on camera, and nature would call. Continuing on with her lines, as if it were part of the movie, she'd walk right off the set into her dressing room. You'd hear the toilet seat go up, the toilet seat go down, the flushing, and Marjorie was still saying her lines. Then she'd come right back on the set, as if we hadn't cut, and finish the scene.

Pinza was fresh from *South Pacific*. I didn't know from Broadway. I didn't know Pinza was the greatest baritone in all the world. To me he was a big, unattractive, over-sexed man, the most conceited egomaniac I'd ever met. Every chance, he'd be groping Lana who was forever maneuvering to keep her body out of his hands. Back in her dressing room she'd be seething with rage. "He's a slime! I can't stand being within 10 feet of him!"

Mr. Imperium bombed at the boxoffice.

❏

FRANK P. ROSENBERG:

I was producing *One-Eyed Jacks*. Brando was the star and we were out on location at Monterrey. Naturally I had my shooting schedule worked out, but before we'd been there two days we were already two weeks behind because our star was acting like a prima donna. We were *bound* to go over budget.

Brando kept insisting on doing expensive scenes which didn't belong in the picture and which weren't even in the script in the first place. Well, there was one particular scene I recall. He wanted a fiesta; I didn't and told him so. But he went over me; complained to the studio head and, because he *had* been a star, Marlon got his way. That particular scene cost over half a million dollars. *One-Eyed Jacks* bombed. Nobody, least of all the younger generation, wants to see Brando anymore.

❏

DON SIEGEL:

I'd let my wife, children and animals starve before I'd subject myself to something like that again. *Jinxed* was the worst experience of my life!

It was absolute torture! I had to shoot some scenes three different ways. It wasn't so much that Bette [Midler] wanted changes. It was that she didn't know *what* she wanted! And to a feisty veteran like me, it's most annoying for someone like her—after making only two pictures—to think she knows everything about editing, directing and acting. It wasn't only me she was unhappy with. It seems that everyone she selected for the picture—actor Ken Wahl, the cameraman—she grew to hate.

And United Artists—the brass there was so in awe of her they let her do anything she wanted. Every time there was an argument—and there must have been 479,000 of them—they sided with Bette. *Jinxed* stinks!

❑

ORSON WELLES:

Macbeth was made in 23 days, including one day of retakes. People who know anything at all about the business of making a film will realize that this is more than fast. I never thought I was making a great film, or even an imitation great film. I thought I was making what might be a good film, and what, if the 23-day shooting schedule came off, might encourage other film-makers to tackle difficult subjects at greater speed. I am not ashamed of the limitations of the picture. *Macbeth*, for better or worse, is a kind of violently sketched charcoal drawing of a great play.

❑

MICHAEL YORK:

Something for Everyone—it came out with no publicity at all, and it died. I don't know *what* they're doing. It was a personal conflict between [director] Hal Prince and Cinema Center. At one point, Hal wanted to buy the print and release it himself. It hasn't even been released in France, and I think it's the kind of film the French would enjoy.

❑

DARRYL F. ZANUCK:

I decided to become a genius. Hollywood was full of "yes men," so I decided to become a "no man." I knocked everything, even Warner pictures. One day Jack Warner said he bet I thought I could run the studio better than he did. I told him I was sure I could. The following Monday morning he made me executive producer.

Now that I had the job of genius, I was going to make the greatest picture of all time. I picked a man who is now [1953] one of the finest directors in the business, Mike Curtiz. I got top stars and I made *Noah's Ark*, one of the biggest flops ever turned out. Now, Jack Warner and his brothers were *certain* that I was a genius.

Image Insults

"I don't think people want to see Stallone with his shirt on."

JUNE ALLYSON:

Even Richard [husband Dick Powell] opposed me violently when I decided to make *The Shrike*. All my advisers said no.

But it was a challenge I could not resist. For years I had been the Perfect Wife: to Jim Stewart, to Alan Ladd, to Van Johnson, to Bill Holden, even on the screen to Dick Powell. And now, in *The Shrike*, in the adaptation of the Broadway play with José Ferrer, I would be far from the perfect wife. I would indeed be a monster of a wife, one of the least attractive in the history of the theater.

As it turned out, the picture was a wonderful flop, but I do not regret deciding to play the vixen, Ann Downs. Other than my personal satisfaction in making my own decision, *The Shrike* was fun, and I even dreamed vaguely of an Academy Award.

❏

JULIE ANDREWS:

I think *Star!* failed because the public wasn't very happy with seeing me in drunken scenes. I wanted to be completely honest in portraying Gertrude Lawrence. I wanted to show that at times she was almost silly. It was very hard for me to play drunk scenes. I had to force myself to do it. I even thought about taking a drink or even a *drug*, but if I did that, I couldn't have played it at all, could I? Finally I got the key: I found that drunken people lose oxygen: when they exhale, they almost collapse. The diaphragm just *goes*. I used that, and I think it worked.

❏

THE PRODIGAL (MGM, 1955), with Lana Turner. Director: Richard Thorpe.

ANN-MARGRET:

Bus Riley's Back in Town was written by William Inge. It was really bru-
tally honest. That was a different era. The powers that be at the studio thought
that particular role, the way I played it, was too much for the young following
I had at that time. A year after completion, they wanted me to redo six scenes.
That would have changed the entire film. I balked. But I wasn't the type to
go to court, so, finally, I agreed to redo three. Inge took his name off the
project. They had mutilated his work.

❏

JOHN BEAL:

I knew in advance that *One Thrilling Night* would not be a big boxoffice
success—Monogram Pictures, where I did it in 1942, was hardly Metro-Goldwyn-Mayer. Nevertheless, I wanted to do it. It was one of my favorite jobs
because it was a happy one and such a funny script. When they clocked it in
theaters, there was more than a laugh a minute. I was Joe Serious in so many
things that I loved being a comic.

It was shot in six days under William Beaudine, who had been a big
director at Paramount. He was so cheerful, such a delightful person to work
with. And so knowledgeable about comedy. He was great. I played a young
man on his honeymoon before being inducted into the Army the next morning. There were gangsters, dead bodies in the bed, chases, and I was doing
pratfalls, double takes, triple takes, everything. It was a very funny picture. I
loved it.

But lowly Monogram was part of what was then called Poverty Row, and
many theaters wouldn't even play Monogram pictures, no matter what they
were.

Years later, *One Thrilling Night* finally became popular—on early television. I wish I had a nickel for every time they showed it.

❏

JACK BENNY:

George Washington Slept Here made a lot of money, so Jack Warner
immediately wanted me to make another picture. He gave me the script of
The Horn Blows at Midnight. I read it and hated it.

I told him, "This is a terrible script. This is going to take months to fix
up. *George Washington* was a good film, so let's make *another* good one."
Warner said, "*The Horn Blows at Midnight* will be great. And if you do it for
me, I'll give you the lead in that picture about George M., *Yankee Doodle
Dandy*." I thought that was a pretty good trade.

I finished *The Horn Blows at Midnight*, this *lousy* picture, and soon found
out they were already making *Yankee Doodle Dandy* with Jimmy Cagney. I

went right to Jack Warner and said, "Wait one minute. You *promised* if I made that crummy picture I could play George M. Cohn!"

"That's Co*han*," Warner said, smiling. "If it was Cohn, you would have gotten it."

◻

INGRID BERGMAN:

Arch of Triumph was one of the few films in my life that I felt "wrong" about. I really didn't want to do it and I told them so, but they persevered and there was Charles Boyer and Charles Laughton, so I decided that it was ridiculous not to do it. But I was always unsure of myself, concerned that I would not be "believable." Then it came out very long and they cut it to pieces, and it didn't make sense.

◻

PANDRO S. BERMAN:

A Damsel in Distress? We had to give Fred Astaire one picture without Ginger Rogers as his partner—that was the deal I made to get him to do a previous picture. And it just turned out that it happens to be Joan Fontaine because she was under contract to our studio [RKO].

The mix of personalities was certainly not as good because there wasn't that energy and pep and comedy that Ginger had. Joan was a quiet girl. But it also turned out to be a bad idea because she couldn't dance. As a result, the picture had no dancing in it to amount to a hill of beans, except what Fred Astaire did by himself. And it was the least successful of all the Astaire pictures.

◻

KAREN BLACK:

After *Five Easy Pieces*, I had a manager who believed you had to do leads in major films only. So I did *Portnoy's Complaint*, because it was meant to be the hit of the year. It was a flop—I think partly because the public couldn't handle dirt, and partly because Dick Benjamin was too intellectual.

◻

HUMPHREY BOGART:

The Return of Dr. X was one of the pictures that made me march in to Jack Warner and ask for more money again. You can't believe what this one was like. I had a part that somebody like Bela Lugosi or Boris Karloff should have played. I was this doctor, brought back to life, and the only thing that

THE GIRL RUSH (Paramount, 1955), with Rosalind Russell. Director: Robert Pirosh.

KISMET (MGM, 1955), with Ann Blyth, Howard Keel. Director: Vincente Minnelli.

nourished this poor bastard was blood. If it'd been Jack Warner's blood, or Harry's, or Pop's, maybe I wouldn't have minded as much. The trouble was, they were drinking mine and I was making this stinking movie.

❏

CHARLES BOYER:

Everyone should have a flop, to know what it's like. Besides, had I not come to Hollywood to make *Caravan*, I would not have found Pat [Paterson, his wife]. As for the picture—well, I suppose they believed they might make capital of a man whose eyes could look as if they mirrored all the sorrow in the world. But really, I wasn't the type to play mad music in cinema moonlight.

❏

MACDONALD CAREY:

Bride of Vengeance was hardly a jewel in my crown, but I enjoyed making it. I *think*. There was a haze over Hollywood then that had nothing to do with smog. In those days—especially immediately pre- and post-World War II—everybody drank in Hollywood. Oh, not during work hours but right afterward. And I drank my share; I don't have the clearest vision of what went on during *Bride of Vengeance*.

I do remember that Mitchell Leisen, the director, was very good to me and frequently gave me roles that other directors wouldn't. You see, I didn't want to be typed in leading man parts. I wanted to be a good character actor. And Mitch gave me a juicy character part in *Bride* as Cesare Borgia. Frankly, though, I was never that happy with what I did with it. Neither was the critic Bosley Crowther in *The New York Times* who wrote, "Macdonald Carey sneers and glowers behind a fringe of black whiskers." I have an oil painting of me in my makeup as a very evil-looking Cesare that was done for the film. After the picture was over, I tracked the portrait down and it now hangs in my library.

Paulette Goddard, with whom I had worked in other films, was the bride of the title, my sweet little sister Lucretia Borgia. And John Lund was the "hero," the Duke of Ferrara. Originally, Ray Milland was supposed to play Johnny's part, but he bolted when he heard that Mitch was personally going to fit the codpieces on the men.

Mitch was great to work with, though. He was marvelous with costume and set design. He was also an interior decorator and had designed costumes and sets for Cecil B. DeMille before going on his own as a director. Visually, the picture was a testament to his designing skill.

Paulette was always wonderful to work with, a no-nonsense, very practical girl. She also took her lumps for *Bride of Vengeance*. While we were shooting, she was sort of preoccupied with her marriage to Burgess Meredith, a union,

MIRACLE IN THE RAIN (Warner Brothers, 1956), with Van Johnson, Jane Wyman. Director: Rudolph Maté.

BUNDLE OF JOY (RKO, 1956), with Eddie Fisher, Debbie Reynolds. Director: Norman Taurog.

as I recall, not on the firmest of legs. She was quite tight with a dollar. If she had to use her own wardrobe in a picture, she'd charge Paramount for the use of it. (She didn't do this on *Bride*, which was a period piece, but on modern things like *Suddenly It's Spring* and *Hazard*, two earlier films we did together.) After a while, Johnny Lund wasn't all that interested in acting. He wanted to write, and, without credit, actually re-wrote some of the weaker scenes in *Bride of Vengeance*.

I'm writing now, too—my third book of poetry, entitled *Beyond That Further Hill*, has just been published. This, and my 25-year continuing role on the TV soap *Days of Our Lives* keeps me plenty busy today.

❏

LINDA CHRISTIAN:

Tyrone [Power] could never forget the dashing of his hopes in his favorite role of the geek in the film *Nightmare Alley*—which he would say had been his only chance of a real performance. He had begged to play the part, and his performance was magnificent. But the film was, for its day [1947], powerfully realistic and violent in its climax. The studio was almost loath to show its most glamorous star in such a role, and the film was slipped out as a second-feature release, unnoticed.

❏

HARRY COHN:

The six people who saw what Orson Welles did to Rita [Hayworth] in *The Lady from Shanghai* wanted to kill him, but they had to get behind me in line.

❏

JEANNE CRAIN:

I may have been in it, but wild horses couldn't drag me to see a movie called *Hot Rods to Hell*. As it turned out, most people felt the same way.

❏

JOAN CRAWFORD:

Reunion in France—oh, god. If there is an afterlife, and I am to be punished for my sins, this is one of the pictures they'll make me see over and over again. John Wayne and I both went down for the count, not just because of a silly script, but because we were so mismatched. Get John out of the saddle and you've got trouble.

THE VAGABOND KING (Paramount, 1956), with Rita Moreno, Oreste, Florence Sundstrom, Billy Vine, Phyllis Newman. Director: Michael Curtiz.

❏

GEORGE CUKOR:

Two-Faced Woman failed because it was anti-Garbo. The World War II loss of the European market meant Garbo had to be Americanized into "the girl next door." They put her in a swim suit, which looked bad, quite bad. She was fairly broad behind and quite flat up front. People had already noticed that she walked like a man, but in those early stunning gowns, it hadn't mattered. It was camouflaged, in fabric and romance.

In *Two-Faced Woman*, her last film, she was supposed to be a modern. But Garbo was at her best in other, more romantic eras. And in highly emotional and glamorous roles. As in *Mata Hari*. Of course, the secret to that film's success was the combination. Garbo played the reluctant seducer, Ramon Novarro the love object. As so often occurs, the homosexual actor excels at playing a romantic hero. Compare him to the male lead in *Two-Faced Woman*, Melvyn Douglas: a dull heterosexual, instead of a handsome, romantic homosexual who makes women in the audience swoon.

MGM got rid of Novarro. Not because of his voice, which wasn't high-pitched, nor because he ever said "What's the matter, Mata?"; he didn't. It was because he was homosexual and refused to marry a woman for publicity. You'll notice that most of Garbo's great leading men were homosexual—and in getting rid of them, MGM tried to make stars of dull men like Melvyn

Douglas, and in the process they hurt Garbo and stripped her of that ethereal romance we loved.

□

BETTE DAVIS:

It had been decided that my work as a tragedian should be temporarily halted for a change of pace. Jimmy Cagney, who had made the gangster artistic—Jimmy, who was one of the fine actors on mine or any lot—Jimmy, with whom I'd always wanted to work in something fine, spent most of his time in the picture removing cactus quills from my behind. This was supposedly hilarious. We romped about the desert and I kept falling into cactus. We both reached bottom with this one. It was called *The Bride Came C.O.D.*

□

IRENE DUNNE:

They felt I made a mistake playing Queen Victoria in *The Mudlark*. I know it was a screen departure for me but it's always nice to get away from routine, and every actor likes to play a character role. It's the public that may not like it.

The makeup was very difficult for Queen Victoria and I don't think I'd ever go through that again. They had to send a makeup man to England and we had a very thin mask that connected below the eyes and went down on either side of the face—so my eyes, nose and mouth were mine. Then it fastened in the back. But it could only be used once—every day there was a new one. It was hard on the face!

Anyway, though I enjoyed making it, they felt it wasn't a picture that did me any good. Maybe if I'd done it earlier in my career when my image wasn't so fixed, it would have been better received.

□

DAN DURYEA:

With the comedy *White Tie and Tails*, I was trying to change my movie character. It was a dismal failure. Since then I've pretty much stuck to being a good heavy and doing fine. After all, we're all heavies at heart sometimes, and most people remember the villain, not the hero, in pictures.

□

CLINT EASTWOOD:

I was terribly disappointed by the way *The Beguiled* was sold. I told the studio before I made it that it was a completely different kind of story, a psychological gothic horror film. Then they sold it as just another Clint East-wood picture, me with a cheroot cigar and stubble beard, which was awfully unfair to both my regular audience and those who wanted something different. That sort of thing can kill you in this business.

❏

GLENN FORD:

I've never played anyone but myself on the screen. I take that back. Once I tried to throw myself into a role playing a Spanish gypsy. The picture was *The Loves of Carmen*, with Rita Hayworth, and it was the biggest bomb in history.

❏

MICHAEL J. FOX:

When I became very successful in comedy, my instinct was to do something else. So I did two dramatic films that didn't do well. I played a coke addict [*Bright Lights, Big City*]; I played a struggling bar musician [*Light of Day*]. Both pictures had such problems. I did *Light of Day* for the wrong reasons. I did it because I wanted to do something that wasn't expected of me, and I wanted to do a dramatic film and goof around and play the guitar for five months. Anyway, I've exorcised a lot of stuff. And I feel comfortable that just because I do a comedy, I'm not taking the easy road.

❏

ARTHUR FREED:

When we did *The Pirate*, Judy [Garland] wasn't feeling well. The last number we shot was "Be a Clown," and Judy rehearsed for that for four hours before we started shooting. I think it's one of the best pictures she's done. It wasn't the success I hoped it would be. I think one of the reasons was the public didn't want to see Judy as a sophisticate. I think today *The Pirate* would be a hit. It was 20 years ahead of its time.

❏

CLARK GABLE:

I really didn't want to play Rhett Butler in *Gone with the Wind*, which was set in the Old South. A couple of years before, I did *Parnell*, another historical drama that was the worst disaster I've ever had. I felt I was strictly a modern type fella.

❏

DIANE (MGM, 1956), with Lana Turner, Roger Moore, Marisa Pavan. Director: David Miller.

BETTY GRABLE:

I have everything in the world I want. The only cloud appeared when I made *The Beautiful Blonde from Bashful Bend.*

I didn't want to do it, but I have never interfered with my studio. I never read a script till it's ready, and I always leave the selection of the story, direction and cast to Darryl Zanuck, for whom I have great respect. But if he ever gives me [producer-director-writer] Preston Sturges again, you'll hear Grable's voice.

However, I don't think Mr. Zanuck will ever make me do a picture again that I am as much opposed to as I was the Sturges atrocity. In fact, I have the studio's promise that I can do the things that my fans like best, and that is musical comedy.

❏

STEWART GRANGER:

None of us really wanted to do *Green Fire*. Grace Kelly was watching us all; she wasn't happy on the film because she knew she was in a potboiler. At the beginning she was rather looking down her nose at us. I felt she was seeing us in this lousy movie. She was very nice to kiss, though. She was always cool and lovely and smelled nice, which is more than can be said for the picture.

❑

CARY GRANT:

I got an Oscar nomination for playing a poor Cockney in *None But the Lonely Heart*, but it wasn't the big acting—what do they say today?—"stretch" that critics seemed to think. I felt closer to that guy than to most of the well turned-out characters I was known for. No one came to see the picture, though, so I got back into my tux *fast*.

❑

LEE GRANT:

When Sophie Portnoy in *Portnoy's Complaint* was offered to me, there were many attractive things about the character. The age range went from 26 to 57, and there were scenes at each age. The progression was very interesting to me. I don't get many opportunities to do a real character, so I really did it as an exercise. But I failed (as did the film). I wasn't the right person for the part. When they edited the picture, they only used Sophie from 47 on, which made me a dumb choice. They really needed an older woman who was a heavyweight.

❑

KATHRYN GRAYSON:

The Kissing Bandit was a real turkey! Frank Sinatra and I co-starred. Although Frank was not yet "the chairman of the board" in 1948, he was a very popular but very skinny singer. I did everything I could to get out of having to kiss him in the film, because he was so thin I thought he had some disease. I was afraid I might catch it!

❑

ALBERT HACKETT:

The Secret of Madame Blanche was an awful picture in which lovely Irene Dunne played a prostitute who always wanted to be a lady. We were always embarrassed when we'd meet Irene after that. Years later she was chosen to present us with a $5,000 award from the Christophers for having written *Father of the Bride*. When she said hello to us, she smiled and said, "I have a friend who thinks the best picture you ever wrote was *The Secret of Madame Blanche*!"

THE FIRST TRAVELING SALESLADY (RKO, 1956), with Carol Channing, Ginger Rogers, David Brian, Dan White. Director: Arthur Lubin.

❑

PAUL HENREID:

Patricia Medina was the leading lady in *Siren of Bagdad*, the director, Richard Quine. He wanted to do the film as a satire, a Chaplinesque burlesque of pirate films. The preview at the Pickwick Theater seemed to justify our expectations. Every situation joke worked; the audience howled. I came out beaming, and producer Sam Katzman, Quine and I congratulated one another on the very funny picture.

The only one who looked unhappy was Katzman's wife who said, "I don't think it will be a success. People who go to pirate pictures want just that, a pirate picture. They aren't as sophisticated as this preview audience. They want their pictures to follow a strict formula. This picture pokes fun at the sacred formula—and I don't think they'll accept that."

She was absolutely right. The picture was a flop!

❑

JOHN HOUSEMAN:

They Live by Night has an odd history. Although it was a small picture by unknown people, a kind of excitement was generated around it under its original title, *Your Red Wagon*. Then, before it could be released, Howard

Hughes bought RKO, and for three years the picture lay in his vaults—together with Robert Wise's *The Set-Up*. Finally, when Hughes was thinking of selling the company, they took these films out of the vaults and dumped them.

They Live by Night was completely ignored on its first native release as a B picture, and was never really seen in America till much later, on television. At the time, one of the few people who saw in it what European critics saw was Iris Barry. She put it on for a special show at the Museum of Modern Art in New York and was criticized by some of her highbrow friends, who wondered what she was doing slipping a "gangster" picture into her series of distinguished films.

❑

BETTY HUTTON:

Dream Girl—I loused that movie up because I didn't understand the girl I was playing. But a Kitty Foyle, that kind of everyday girl, I could understand.

❑

GEORGE JESSEL:

At Darryl Zanuck's request, I tackled *Nightmare Alley* from William Gresham's blood-curdling story about carnival "geeks." No other line producer would touch it. The story and film were years ahead of their time.

The part was played beautifully by Ty Power, and I'll never forget the reaction of an audience in Dallas when the picture was sneaked there. Power, the villain, did everything wrong for a human being. The Dallas (and every other) audience had never seen Ty in anything in which he didn't play the hero or the lover. When an acrobat in the film attacked Power for trying to seduce a sweet, innocent young girl, while also carrying on an affair with a married woman, the kids in the audience yelled, "Knock him down, Ty!"

I knew then the film didn't stand a chance.

❑

ELIA KAZAN:

The only film I ever made that I'm truly ashamed of was a Western called *Sea of Grass* that keeps turning up on *The Late Show*. I was completely intimidated by Spencer Tracy and Katharine Hepburn, and it showed. Every time she went to the toilet she came back in a new gown and he was supposed to be a cowboy born to the saddle, but he took one look at the horse and the horse hated him and the whole thing was a disaster.

❑

THE STORY OF MANKIND (Warner Brothers, 1957), with Marie Windsor, Dennis Hopper. Director: Irwin Allen.

DeFOREST KELLEY:

Where Love Has Gone should have been a success. At least a *commercial* success. It seemed to have all the prerequisites: two stars who even then [1964] were legends, Susan Hayward and Bette Davis; a good director, Edward Dmytryk; a very nice title song sung by Jack Jones; and a story that was based on the sensational Lana Turner-Cheryl Crane-Johnny Stompanato murder case. Its failure is a mystery to me. I have to think that it just wasn't marketed properly, or perhaps the timing was off somehow.

I was delighted to be in it. I had worked with Dmytryk earlier on *Raintree County* and *Warlock* and had been playing heavies in Westerns for years. One day Dmytryk said to me, "I'll find a role for you someday that will get you away from these heavies." And he kept his promise when he cast me in *Where Love Has Gone* as an art critic. A couple of years later I began playing Dr. Leonard "Bones" McCoy on *Star Trek*, and I'm still at it.

By the time of *Where Love Has Gone*, Susan Hayward had left Hollywood, married a car dealer from Georgia and moved there. I recall that we were doing the airport scene in Ontario where it was freezing. While we waited, Susan and I sat for hours in a cold car heated only by the warm rays of the sun. I hadn't seen Susan talking much to any of the others on the picture, but for some reason she seemed to seek me out. She was living an entirely different kind of life now and may not have wanted to get back into all the

THE BUSTER KEATON STORY (Paramount, 1957), with Donald O'Connor, Ann Blyth. Director: Sidney Sheldon.

Hollywood talk. She sensed, I think, that I was living a similar peaceful existence in the San Fernando Valley. The strife of her Hollywood years was behind her; she talked lovingly of her husband and new house in Georgia. Unfortunately, he died very soon afterward. And now she's gone. I'll always cherish those chilly, quiet hours we spent in that car.

I didn't get to see Susan and Bette Davis work together, though there were stories that they didn't get along. I know Bette could be difficult. A day or two after production had started Bette, without telling a soul, took a day off to find (we learned later) the proper wig to wear in her role as Susan's mother. It threw everyone for a loop. No one knew what had happened to her. When she showed up again, she told me, "I like to let everyone know where I stand right at the start." In other words, who was boss.

❑

GENE KELLY:

I had decided on this Fairbanks-Barrymore approach to the role in *The Pirate* at the very start and [director Vincente] Minnelli entirely agreed with it. It didn't occur to us until the picture hit the public that what we had done was indulge in a huge inside joke. The sophisticates probably grasped it— all three of them—but the film died in the hinterlands. It was done tongue-in-cheek but it didn't come off, and that's my fault. But I thought Judy [Garland] was superb—what Minnelli did with color and design in that film is as fine as anything that has ever been done.

❑

FRITZ LANG:

I had only one flop, and it happened when I tried to copy Brecht in *You and Me*. It was the only really lousy picture I ever made precisely because I wasn't being myself.

❑

MITCHELL LEISEN:

Dream Girl—nobody liked that one. All of Betty Hutton's fans were disappointed when she didn't go around screaming "Murder he says" and the rest of the public who couldn't stand her didn't go either.

The day she came in to do the makeup and hair tests, her hair was curled within an inch of her life and her face was absolutely caked with makeup. Her hair was naturally almost white and I had them put a dark blonde rinse on her and style it very simply. Then I gave her a street makeup. She argued all the way through it, but when she saw the tests, she came out of the projection room yelling, "I'm beautiful, I'm beautiful!"

She sincerely believed that she would win the Oscar for *Dream Girl*, and nobody had the heart to tell her otherwise. The day the nominations were announced and she wasn't one of them, she was devastated. I always ducked when I saw her coming on the lot after that.

❑

STEPHEN LONGSTREET:

The First Traveling Saleslady was no one's vessel of glory. I got the idea from a true item: the law that called for the fencing in of the West—no more open range in certain parts of the country. Ranch owners actually killed a few barbwire salesmen, or so the story goes. I invented a smart seller who decided to hire sales*women*. The West respected women, didn't it? Fuck 'em, don't hang 'em.

My agent, Jim Getter, sold the idea to RKO and I wrote the screenplay. The director [Arthur Lubin] wasn't much of a big-timer—his best credits were the Francis the talking mule films. Ginger Rogers, our top-billed star, seemed pleased, but I wasn't sure Carol Channing was for real. The studio seemed to think it needed comedy, and another writer [Devery Freeman] added to my script. Many of us felt that what should have been a bit of Americana and history was turning to slapstick.

I do not think the picture was ever actually released as a major film in

A FAREWELL TO ARMS (20th Century-Fox, 1957), with Rock Hudson, Jennifer Jones. Director: Charles Vidor.

theaters. It may have been shown here and there, but I don't recall any reviews or major advertising.

It sank without a bubble until TV, where it can now be seen on the Late Shows. It has not improved with age.

I would say we can all take group blame: the final overgrown script far from my original, direction, acting, studio-added ideas and casting. All helped with kicks in the ass.

I worked on *Duel in the Sun, The Greatest Show on Earth*, wrote *The Jolson Story, Silver River* and, with William Faulkner, *Stallion Road*, starring Ronald Reagan. The problem with historic screenplays is that the Western myths are mostly tales of a West there never was. The best Westerns by director John Ford are legends—not the real facts. The true West was a mean and dirty place, the cowboy only a hired hand on horseback, the dance hall girls clapped-up whores. Try that in Technicolor!

❑

MYRNA LOY:

Whatever critics and commentators may say against *Parnell*, I like it. I think Clark Gable is wonderful in the title role and I like my Katie O'Hara.

Clark gave a subdued, sustained performance as Parnell, which apparently was the problem. He had been so typed as those red-blooded Blackie

170

Nortons that people didn't want to be reminded he was an actor. They went after the macho stuff. And I was breezy Nora Charles, which prohibited me from donning Adrian's 19th-century finery and creating a more sober characterization. Disgruntled fans wrote to the studio by the thousand. Some of the critics complained that we played against type. We were actors, for God's sake. We couldn't be Blackie Norton and Nora Charles all the time.

I really can't understand the great outcry that persists against *Parnell*.

❑

VIRGINIA MAYO:

Although *A Song is Born* did not do well, it was an interesting picture to make. It was a musical remark of 1941's *Ball of Fire*, which had starred Gary Cooper and Barbara Stanwyck, and most of the people associated with the first version were on it, including some of the supporting cast. Howard Hawks again directed, but this time Danny Kaye and I were the stars.

Danny and I had made several successful films together for Samuel Goldwyn, but our contracts ended with this one. Unfortunately, Danny had none of the famous special material numbers in it that his wife, Sylvia Fine, always wrote for him; critics and audiences missed them. I seem to recall that Danny and Sylvia were briefly separated at the time. Or maybe there were no Kaye numbers because Danny was leaving and Goldwyn decided not to spend any more money on him. I was supposed to be a singer in the story, however, so I got to do several songs. They insisted I watch Stanwyck in the part, and while I was not required to do an imitation of her, I'm a good mimic, so some of Barbara's performance crept into mine.

It was fascinating to observe all the wonderful musicians who were featured in the film—Benny Goodman, Charlie Barnet, Louie Armstrong, Tommy Dorsey and the others. I remember that during the shooting Dorsey got in a public brawl somewhere that made all the papers. When he came on the set, everyone quickly hid them.

Howard Hawks was a very different kind of man, very into himself. He came from a wealthy lumber family and I think he just felt he didn't have to take anything from anyone. On the set, he seemed to take a lot more time than he should have, sometimes just sitting around listening to the musicians. I think he was planning to do another musical and was studying them. He was a fine, highly respected director, but I don't think he was shown to advantage in *A Song is Born*. Goldwyn was on his neck about speeding things up; when Goldwyn would come down and visit the set, Hawks would quickly begin preparing a scene—bluffing.

Goldwyn, unlike most of the other movie moguls, was on the set quite a bit. At the other studios, they were using the stockholders' money, but Goldwyn was using his own. He also only made about one film a year then, so he was able to keep track.

Hawks had a peculiarity: he liked his leading ladies to sound and look like Lauren Bacall, whom he'd discovered and who had been a sensation with her slender appearance and husky voice. He would request that I go into an empty sound stage and scream, so that my voice would become throaty like Bacall's. I did it, but it didn't work. He even had me wear clothes and hairstyles off-camera like his wife, "Slim" Hawks (an ex-model), to make me into this feminine ideal of his. But I'm afraid that no matter what, I just wasn't his type. You could say that I was too well rounded. I never worked with Howard Hawks again. By the time the picture came out in 1948, I was already at Warner Brothers where I stayed 10 years.

❏

DOROTHY McGUIRE:

I was always the good woman. I did make one picture called *Till the End of Time* in which I played an older woman who seduced Guy Madison, and everyone was shocked; the film was a failure. Today, that is quite fashionable. I went right back into playing nice girls and faithful wives, which today wouldn't be considered very appealing.

❏

MICHELE MORGAN:

I made five films in Hollywood—*Joan of Paris, Higher and Higher, Two Tickets to London, Passage to Marseilles* and *The Chase*—and all of them were bad. They just don't seem to know what to do with French actresses in Hollywood. It has happened to many others besides me.

I think it is because Americans have a definite idea of what a French girl should be. She should be the sexy, ooh-la-la type. Cute and funny. Americans don't seem to accept a French girl as a serious dramatic actress.

Maybe that's why I lost *Casablanca*, which I was up for.

❏

PAUL NEWMAN:

The Mexican bandit in *The Outrage* is my best work. I don't know if it is my best movie—that you've got to separate. I can only look at it and speculate, really, but I hope that there is no residual element of anything that I have done before in the picture. Unfortunately, *The Outrage* was a picture that never got any attention or real circulation at all.

❏

BELOVED INFIDEL (20th Century-Fox, 1959), with Gregory Peck, Deborah Kerr. Director: Henry King.

DAVID NIVEN:

Goldwyn loaned me to Universal to make a historical film, *Magnificent Doll*, with Ginger Rogers. Ginger was to play Dolly Madison and I was to portray Aaron Burr—the two most unlikely bits of casting of the century. The script was gibberish.

❑

DOLLY PARTON:

I thought Sylvester Stallone and I would be good together [in the failed *Rhinestone*], the way I thought Burt Reynolds and I would be good together [in *The Best Little Whorehouse in Texas*]. In *Rhinestone*, I didn't finish singing a song in the whole movie, and I don't think people want to see Stallone with his shirt on.

❑

THE AMAZING TRANSPARENT MAN (American-International, 1960), with Ivan Triesault, Douglas Kennedy, James Griffith, Marguerite Chapman. Director credited: Edgar G. Ulmer. Director uncredited (according to Marguerite Chapman): Lester Guthrie.

LUCIANO PAVAROTTI:

The failure of *Yes, Giorgio* taught me one thing: I am a singer not a lover—at least not in public.

❑

GREGORY PECK:

In *The Gunfighter*, the idea of the handlebar mustache and the soup-bowl haircut—and the quaint-looking clothes, with my pants tucked into my high boots—all came from our research of old photos of the West. We saw that they didn't dress like movie cowboys at all. There were no stores when they arrived from the East. And 80 percent of the men wore mustaches. Spyros Skouras was in Europe when we started. When he came back and saw the rushes, he screamed bloody murder. For years, Skouras would torment me: "Gregory, you cost me a million dollars with that goddam mustache!"

❑

MARY PICKFORD:

My first taste of ill luck came when I brought Ernst Lubitsch from Germany to direct me. The power and originality of his work had already spread far and wide.

The result was *Rosita*—the worst picture, bar none, that I ever made. In Europe, Lubitsch's reputation had been built on sophisticated comedies, more than slightly on the risqué side. In line with this I tried to make Rosita very correct but a little naughty, too, and the result was disastrous. *Rosita*— my first punishment for wanting to grow up on the screen.

❑

JANE POWELL:

I was absolutely thrilled when asked to do *Enchanted Island*. I didn't have to sing. I was to do something different, and, even more important, I got to die at the end! If anything was going to establish me as a serious actress, I thought, dying ought to do it.

But by the time *Enchanted Island* appeared, I didn't die after all. My fans wouldn't allow it, the producer said, so they rewrote the script. I played a dark-haired, supposedly dark-skinned native princess of a South Sea island. My blue eyes were explained away by mentioning a Swede who years before had visited the tribe. *Enchanted Island* was, as you can imagine, a really terrible movie. My co-star, Dana Andrews, had a problem with alcohol and neither he nor the director, Allan Dwan, demonstrated any interest in the project.

❑

OTTO PREMINGER:

A Royal Scandal was really prepared for Ernst Lubitsch, whom I admired and loved and who was already sick at the time. He directed again, but his doctor told him not to direct at this time. He chose me. I directed the story from a script by him.

If people felt that Lubitsch would have done the picture better, that is their opinion. However, I learned something from it. We went to a preview and it was very successful. People roared with laughter; still, when we left, I felt something was wrong. I didn't say anything, and Zanuck turned to me and said, "What's the matter with you? Aren't you happy? We have a big hit!"

I said, "Darryl, I feel that people didn't like the picture." He said, "You're crazy!" I said, "No, they laughed, but did you notice how they walked out? I felt somehow a let-down."

The picture was never a tremendous success and I'll tell you why. This was the borderline situation comedy that Lubitsch was so great at, where he took situations and twisted them. He could make everything funny, but he did it at the expense of character. He never worried about the character, and it was, after all, the Empress of Russia, and she didn't always act like the Empress of Russia.

In the end there were laughs, but I found then, and have learned since,

TALL STORY (Warner Brothers, 1960), with Jane Fonda, Anthony Perkins. Director: Joshua Logan.

ONE-EYED JACKS (Paramount, 1961), with Karl Malden, Marlon Brando. Director: Marlon Brando.

that the public doesn't accept it. They like the integrity of the character to remain intact. Even if they laugh less.

❑

RONALD REAGAN:

Every so often *That Hagen Girl* [co-starring Shirley Temple] pops up on *The Late Show*, and I'm reminded of how right my first actor's instinct was and how wrong I was to go against that instinct and do the picture.

When Jack Warner called me in and laid it on the line regarding the big investment they had tied up in the screenplay and then asked me for my help as a personal favor, I was all out of arguments. Even after I'd agreed to do the picture I tried to talk the director into a sixth rewrite that would have put Shirley in the arms of her schoolboy romance, Rory Calhoun, and matched me with a schoolteacher in the story.

Trying to put this over, I spoke one sentence too many to Peter Godfrey, our director: "You know, people sort of frown on men marrying girls young enough to be their daughters." He answered quietly, "I'm old enough to be my wife's father."

At the finish, we climb on a train—Shirley carrying a bouquet—and leave town. You are left to guess whether we are married, just traveling together or did I adopt her.

❑

CESAR ROMERO:

I've been in pictures more than 50 years, so I've had my share of flops.

That Lady in Ermine was a particularly momentous one, though. It was to be produced and directed by the great Ernst Lubitsch, so everyone—Betty Grable, Doug Fairbanks, Jr., Walter Abel, Reggie Gardner and myself—was excited going into it. We hoped it would have that famous "Lubitsch touch." Then, about halfway through, Lubitsch suddenly dropped dead of heart failure. There was no warning; he didn't seem to be ailing while we were working. We all showed up at the studio one day to shoot and were told that he had died. We were stunned! Later, I heard that he'd had a half-dozen heart attacks over the years.

Otto Preminger took over the directorial reins and finished the picture, though Lubitsch still got credit as co-director. Possibly because he knew this was going to be, Preminger didn't exert himself on *That Lady in Ermine*. My most vivid memory of him at the time is of him sitting around on the set endlessly playing with a gold yo-yo. He had a reputation for being difficult, but as I say he seemed to take it easy on this picture. Many years later I worked on an even worse flop he directed called *Skidoo*, and he was very rough. He didn't pick on me or any of the several name actors in that film, but on the little people in the troupe.

I don't even remember seeing *That Lady in Ermine*. I don't think I did see it. All I remember is that I had plenty of company.

It was a period piece based, I believe, on an operetta, and people just didn't want to see Betty Grable—with her bright blonde hair, somewhat brassy manner and beautiful legs—in that setting.

I loved working with Betty, though; she was a great gal. We did several successful films together, including *Springtime in the Rockies* and *Coney Island*, but *That Lady in Ermine* and one that came about a year later, *The Beautiful Blonde from Bashful Bend*, were not among them. *Bashful Bend* was produced, written and directed by Preston Sturges, whose message Betty did not get at all. At *all*! It was a shambles. Betty could be wonderful at the kind of thing she did best—singing and dancing—but in *Bashful Bend* she only had one number at the end. The rest of the time, Sturges turned her into a gun-toting girl of the old West. He didn't give the audience what they expected, and wanted, of her. When the last scene for this film was wrapped, Betty just stormed off the set without saying a word to anyone. I didn't blame her. She knew what was right for her, and she knew that Preston Sturges and *The Beautiful Blonde from Bashful Bend* were all wrong for her.

They didn't do me any good, either.

❑

JANE RUSSELL:

Right after *The Paleface*, I was put into a film about which the less said the better. I was loaned to Republic Pictures for *Montana Belle*, another Western. I played Belle Starr. I ran a dance hall and George Brent was my lover. As the leader of the gang, I robbed trains and banks by night, with *me* masquerading as one of the guys! This epic was over so fast that I barely remember making it, which is just as well.

❑

DORE SCHARY:

The Red Badge of Courage was released in 1951 and remains a film surrounded by swirls of debate. Two facts are unassailable: It received wonderful reviews and it was a mournful disappointment at the boxoffice.

When director John Huston and his producer, Gottfried Reinhardt, assembled their final cut, I had misgivings regarding its length, but none concerning its merits. Sad to say, the preview was disastrous. At the conclusion, approximately one-third of the audience remaining gave the screening a polite, short hand of applause and slowly straggled out to write preview cards that were painful to read. Huston, Reinhardt and I were stunned.

CLEOPATRA (20th Century-Fox, 1963), with Elizabeth Taylor. Director: Joseph L. Mankiewicz.

My phone rang early the next morning. It was Huston. He said he had received a call from London offering him an important assignment and was on his way to the airport. He asked me to take over the film. Reinhardt and director Albert Lewin suggested a narration from the book to clarify the progression of the story, and we consulted with the film editors to make sure there was film for the segues that would be needed. I suggested that Reinhardt use James Whitmore for the narrator.

We previewed the shortened picture a second time, and, quite obviously, had improved the vitality, but it was clear that we were not going to have a boxoffice picture. It was too simple a story, and how could American's greatest war hero [star Audie Murphy] be a coward?

❑

GEORGE SEATON:

The Shocking Miss Pilgrim was one of the big mistakes of my life, and [producer William] Perlberg's. It was with Betty Grable and we were so stupid that we put her in a long dress—it was a period piece—and covered those magnificent legs. That was the only thing that people really went to see her for.

❑

DON SIEGEL:

As a neophyte director under a term contract, I had to take what Warner Brothers gave me. *Night unto Night* is one of my least favorite films. I fell in love with the leading lady, Viveca Lindfors, which affected my direction, and I did very little work on the script—a mistake. I didn't battle with the producer, Owen Crump, a very charming man who charmed me into accepting the script as it was. And the picture was miscast. Ronald Reagan, looking enormously healthy, was cast as an epileptic. Brod Crawford, looking burly and tough, was a delicate, philosophical artist and Viveca couldn't have been more miscast. She is a fine actress and I don't blame her for what went wrong with the picture. It wasn't a success.

❑

ROBERT STACK:

Bombs? How about *The Phantom Pirate*? I literally had to pay not to have that one seen. One of my advisors suggested that I try doing a Doug Fairbanks sort of adventure picture, so I took on *Phantom Pirate*. They gussied me up with a long, flowing scarf, and I was leaping about. After it was finished, someone said, "They ought to call it *The Phantom Fairy*." That did it. I asked the producer not to release it, and he said he wouldn't if I would return my salary. So I gave back the money—all $10—and they never released it.

❑

SYLVESTER STALLONE:

I did try to break out of the Rocky mold. Right after I did the first *Rocky*, I did *Paradise Alley* and *F.I.S.T.*, which were not action pictures. And I'll never forget walking into a theater on the opening day of *Paradise Alley*. There were about 30 people—you could hunt fucking *deer* in there. I was on a down-bound train. So I did the sequel to *Rocky*, and—I make no equivocations about it—it resuscitated me.

❑

JOHN TRAVOLTA:

Every time I did an interview after *Moment by Moment*, those writers went right into the negative things first.

❑

CLAIRE TREVOR:

Edward Dmytryk directed *The Mountain*, which was a horrible picture. Oh, God, that was a terrible picture! It goes on forever and it's bad. Spencer Tracy plays the older brother of Robert Wagner who was then a beanpole, he was so skinny. He looked like he was 12 years old, and Spence had already gotten heavy and old-looking. It was ludicrous.

❑

LIV ULLMAN:

I loved the script [of *Pope Joan*], the working, everything. We really felt what we were doing. Olivia de Havilland played the Mother Superior and she was sitting and reading the Bible all day and lighting candles. Then the producer [Kurt Unger] took over and for half a year he sat and cut it with his friends. Now it's not my picture anymore. I don't recognize it. Even the writer laughed when he saw it. He couldn't help it because it is so funny now. Someone said it's just the story of me looking like George Peppard.

❑

ROBERT WAGNER:

Dean Martin was walking around the Fox lot one day and bumped into me while I was wearing full regalia for *Prince Valiant*, my worst bomb.

Observing the black wig and bangs, he talked to me for 10 minutes before he realized I wasn't Jane Wyman.

❑

TERESA WRIGHT:

I chose to do *The Men* with Marlon Brando for only $25,000. From then, that's what my salary was listed as in Hollywood. I became a $25,000 actress and after that I never got the quality films again. I know that sounds crazy but that's the way it worked in those days in Hollywood. Your importance was determined by how much money you made. *The Men* was a flop and I never again achieved the kind of status I had with my first few films.

❑

LORETTA YOUNG:

Born to Be Bad [1934] was written for Jean Harlow. Then I was signed and it passed on to me. But I was absolutely disastrous as a man-chaser. I didn't know how to act like that and Cary Grant was equally embarrassed. I still remember one review which read, *"Born to Be Bad.* It is."

❑

ROBERT YOUNG:

The fans just couldn't get used to my new image as a Nazi [in *Three Comrades*]. There was a similar problem in the forties when I made a picture called *They Won't Believe Me*, in which I was cast as a heel. The picture was correctly named. The public *didn't* believe me. I went right back to playing good guys after the boxoffice results came in. Fate, I guess.

❑

DARRYL F. ZANUCK:

Preston Sturges crucified Betty Grable in *The Beautiful Blonde from Bashful Bend*! We previewed it in Pomona and I walked around the block 10 times. God, I didn't know what to do!

Stage Strife

"The audience left the theater humming the sets."

LUCILLE BALL:

Do you have to bring that picture [*Mame*] up? I wish to God *I* could bring it up! It was the worst mistake of my professional life. I wasn't completely well when I took it on, and, looking back, I may not have been right for it in the first place. But Mame was a great character and I wanted to play her. As it happened, no one wanted to see her—at least not with Lucy.

❏

CAROL BURNETT:

I was partly responsible for a bomb on a plane once. On a flight I was taking I discovered they were going to show *The Front Page*, which I did for Billy Wilder. Before it went on, I stood up and apologized to everyone for what they were about to see.

❏

JAMES CAGNEY:

In 1946, I played Joe, the champagne-tippling philosopher in William Saroyan's *The Time of Your Life*. Cagney Productions lost half a million dollars on it.

The cameraman and the director had two weeks of rehearsal without turning a crank. They wanted to block it all out and plot exactly where they were going, shot for shot. This was laudable enough. Then when we finally got going, they decided they were going to do something else. Thus we lost two very expensive weeks of shooting time. The lack of decision on both their parts was, let me say, unhelpful.

Notwithstanding the terrific money loss, the picture was beautifully done. We received a lovely letter of thanks from Saroyan saying that when he watched the film he forgot he had written the play. "I was too busy enjoying it," he said.

◻

LEN CARIOU:

They had the late Peter Finch to play my [stage] role opposite Elizabeth Taylor in *A Little Night Music*. But for some reason, he backed out. Almost at the 11th hour. So I called the composer, Stephen Sondheim, because I knew he was going over to Vienna to shoot the film, and said, "Say hello to everybody for me and good luck." Then I got the famous phone call in the middle of the night. They were trying to get movie stars to appear opposite Elizabeth, but director Hal Prince didn't want any of them.

He called me from Vienna and said, "Can you come over?"

I said, "You're goddam right I can!"

We did *Night Music* in 11 weeks. Not even the crew thought we could do it. Working with Elizabeth was wonderful. Some people were shocked to see her as heavy as she was, and I think that put a lot of people off. It got good notices on the West Coast, but in New York everybody shot it down. The critics really took a shot at Prince saying that he didn't change it from the stage to screen. I think it's quite a cinematic film. You have to remember it came from the screen in the first place—*Smiles of a Summer Night*, by [Ingmar] Bergman. I got the feeling that everybody wanted to see *Smiles of a Summer Night* with music. But Prince retained most of the musical theatricality.

Elizabeth Taylor needed help with "Send in the Clowns." Wherever there was any intonation problem, she was dubbed. I don't think that was detrimental to the piece. I suppose it would have been nice all the way around if she had looked better, if she wasn't as chunky as she was. It would be nice to shoot the film now, after she's lost 30 pounds.

◻

JANIS CARTER:

I Married an Angel was a wonderful musical—on the stage. I was in the Broadway show for the full New York run, 14 months; we played to standing room only for much of the time. Then I went on the road with it for six months. It has always been one of my favorite shows, but then I adore Rodgers and Hart. It had a fine cast and was simply done, with an ethereal, lovely, soft sense of mystery and—most of all—wonder.

The film version, which I did at MGM in the early forties, was a vulgarized botch and died at the boxoffice. It was the last time the team of Jeanette MacDonald and Nelson Eddy appeared together on the screen.

As so often happens when stage works are transferred to celluloid, they

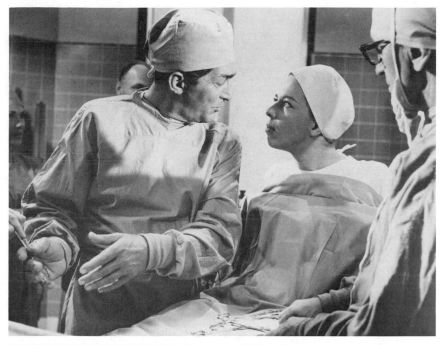

WHO'S BEEN SLEEPING IN MY BED? (Paramount, 1963), with Dean Martin, Carol Burnett. Director: Daniel Mann.

went on and on, lost all the charm, extended the story, added characters and a bunch of goop that had nothing to do with the original plot. Also, the feminine lead should have remained a dancer; on Broadway it was Vera Zorina, who was great. Turning the character into a singer [MacDonald] instead just did not work.

On the stage, there were terrific performances, too, by Walter Slezak, Vivienne Segal, Audrey Christie and Charles Walters, who went on to become dance head of MGM. It was an experience I'll always cherish, whereas the film version was something *everyone* wanted to forget as quickly as possible.

❑

NANCY COLEMAN:

I enjoyed doing RKO's *Mourning Becomes Electra*, although it was not successful and my part wasn't that big. I had recently left Warner Brothers, where I'd had good roles with Ronald Reagan, Errol Flynn and John Garfield. But it was an important picture.

They had wanted a blonde and I was a natural redhead which, in black and white, always photographed dark. So I got a blonde wig, took some photos and gave them to the casting people. I got the part, then dyed my hair blonde.

It was all filmed indoors, even the outdoor scenes, but the great lawn

185

of the family's mansion was made up of real grass. After a few days, though, it all went sour and they kept having to replace it. Kirk Douglas (who was just starting his film career) and I played brother and sister. He called us "the Bobbsey twins," because when we entered together he'd be wearing white and I was in a light blue which photographed white. I remember Michael Redgrave didn't like the smoking jacket they gave him to wear, thought it looked too new, so he threw it on the floor, kicked it around and dropped cigarette ashes on it till it looked worn.

Electra opened on roadshow, but the reviews, I think, were not good. I say "I think" because somehow I never paid too much attention to reviews then. I was more interested in what the producers and directors thought of me. In California I don't think they were quite as aware of reviews as they were in New York. I don't know exactly why it failed. Maybe it was too slow. Maybe it was miscast. Maybe Eugene O'Neill's plays were not fashionable at that point. Maybe it was all of the above.

Anyway, *I* liked it, although I noticed when I saw it on television a while back that my big scene at the end, where I tell off Rosalind Russell, didn't come out quite as I had filmed it. My lines were there, but originally I had had several nice close-ups and now all you could see was my back!

❏

JOAN CRAWFORD:

While *Grand Hotel* was still playing road shows, *Letty Lynton* was released also to big business. And where did I go from there? Down into the fiasco of *Rain*.

I was haunted by my inferiority to famous Sadie Thompsons Jeanne Eagels and Gloria Swanson. I hadn't seen them, but they were constantly held up to me by my co-workers. My director, Lewis Milestone, had worked out blueprints for every scene, precisely what I was to do; but to me, no actress worthy of the name could be a puppet in anyone's hands. I was no Method actress, I was an emotional one—in *Rain*, far too emotional. All you have to do is check the excellent pictures Mr. Milestone has made to see who was right.

Most reviews were written in acid. I grieved over the letters that poured in from fans hating my bold mouth makeup. That's the kind of woman I thought Sadie was, but I hadn't the vaguest idea what she was like inside. I didn't even know then that you could work from the interior to the exterior. I was still working from the exterior.

My fans wouldn't accept her. They would accept me as Letty Lynton who was just as vulgar, but she had style. Cheapness *and* vulgarity they would not accept. Oh, who am I kidding, I just gave a lousy performance!

❏

WHERE LOVE HAS GONE (Paramount, 1964), with DeForest Kelley, Susan Hayward. Director: Edward Dmytryk.

GEORGE CUKOR:

Zaza was a story of adultery, and after we finished it got an absolute turndown by the Hays office. The whole basic plot is that a married man has an affair with a music hall singer, there are these long despairing scenes, and they're all CUT!

I won't be sentimental about something that was a failure and did so badly at the boxoffice—and with a situation that most people today would find comic—but I know the *look* of it. There was a man at Paramount then called Hans Dreier, and he did very atmospheric sets. And it was the only time that Claudette Colbert, who has a very pretty voice, ever sang in a picture. Fanny Brice, a great friend of mine, came and coached her. I remember Fanny telling Claudette how to contact an audience: "You know, kid, when you sing a ballad you'll find it a comfort to touch your own flesh."

The picture was terribly French, of course, and was wonderfully photographed by Charles Lang. Lang could always make the women look ravishing and the sets seem right. I'm really beginning to feel sorry the picture didn't go.

◻

MICHAEL CURTIZ:

The biggest flop I ever had was *The Vagabond King*. Many exhibitors refused to show it. One wrote to Paramount and said, "I wouldn't play *Vagabond King* if it were the last movie ever coming from Hollywood." I cried when I saw the picture.

◻

BETTE DAVIS:

The reason that *Rain* failed with Miss [Joan] Crawford is because Miss Crawford cannot act her way out of a brown paper bag. *I* am an actress.

◻

OLIVIA de HAVILLAND:

As I recall, *That Lady* was important to Spyros Skouras, president of 20th Century-Fox, for some sort of technical reason. I think it was one of the first CinemaScope films made by Fox—perhaps *the* first made entirely in Europe. And there was the problem of persuading theaters to adapt their screens to the new wide image.

The settings in Spain were quite wonderful, and so were the costumes, conceived by a marvelous Catalan costume designer, Mariano Andreu, and executed in Paris by a highly respected Russian emigré, Madame Karinska, at her *atelier* in the rue Washington.

Despite all of these attractive features, from my point of view the film was disappointing and I doubt it did particularly well at the boxoffice. However, I assume that it did achieve whatever Spyros Skouras' objective may have been.

❏

NELSON EDDY:

In our films together, Jeanette MacDonald and I always depicted pure love and we had a lot of trouble with this script [*I Married an Angel*] because religious groups disapproved of an angel going to bed with a man. Everybody on the lot told us that *I Married an Angel* was either going to be the best picture we ever did, or the worst. It was the worst. It took the studio years to figure out how to present it without offending anybody and then they slashed it to pieces. When we finally finished it, it was a horrible mess.

❏

FRITZ FELD:

I saw *Hello, Dolly!* on Broadway, and when the big fat maître d' in it came on, something clicked. I had sort of built my reputation playing maître d's in pictures—I *had* to play this one.

Later, when it was announced that 20th Century-Fox was going to film it, I applied for the job as the maître d' in the famous "Hello, Dolly!" musical sequence. They said I could read for it, and when I got out to Fox there were 14 men sitting there to observe me—Darryl Zanuck's son, Richard; the producer-writer, Ernest Lehman; the director, Gene Kelly; three casting people; musicians. I read, and they all laughed; when I did my trademark popping of my mouth, they howled. Gene Kelly, a charming man, came over and said, "We love you. You're wonderful. You've got the part."

Months passed. I didn't hear from anyone at Fox. I wondered what happened. I called the studio and they said, "Oh, we're looking for a big fat German type. You're too French." I am not French, but I have played many French roles. I was born in Germany. I was out of my mind. This would be the summation of all my maître d' parts in what was expected to be the biggest of big movies. My family had trouble living with me.

Finally, I went directly to Gene Kelly, who told me, "It's been decided you'll play the *assistant* to the maître d'." I was heartbroken. I felt like committing suicide—I was born to play the maître d'. But for some reason they felt that a big fat German type was needed; it had become a tradition for the part, or something.

Time passed, and they got a not very good actor from New York to play the maître d' [David Hurst]. They showed me the role they wanted me to do, a character named Fritz. The salary was very, very good. My family said, "For

BUS RILEY'S BACK IN TOWN (Universal, 1965), with Chet Stratton, Ann-Margret. Director: Harvey Hart.

God's sake, what are you waiting for?" I accepted. I was guaranteed four weeks, but worked eight, while the actor who played the maître d' only worked three. But even to this day, I'm heartbroken over it. On the set, extras and young people who always love me kept coming up and saying, "Why don't you play the maître d'? You're so much better." I don't like to talk against other actors, and I personally got along fine with the man. But there it is.

I got along fine with the male lead, too—Walter Matthau. We played chess on the set.

One day I happened to look into a tall upright mirror that our Dolly, Barbra Streisand, used. Suddenly, her maid came rushing up and screamed, "You can't look in that! That mirror belongs to Barbra Streisand!"

I said, "I don't give a shit."

With that, Barbra appeared and said, "Of course Fritz can look in my mirror. We love him."

In the two months I worked on *Hello, Dolly!*, Barbra only talked to the director, the cameraman and me. She was a little Jewish girl from Brooklyn, and this was only her second picture. Overnight, she had become this big star, but she was still feeling her way. Once, late at night when Barbra and I were shooting, I told her, "You're not only a phenomenal singer, but you're going to be a great actress as well." And time has proved me right. Back in the 1930s, when Judy Garland was just a kid starting out, we had lunch together in the MGM commissary and I told her the same thing.

Another time, I went into a toilet near the *Dolly!* set and found myself standing right next to Darryl Zanuck, the great mogul. I had worked for him many times over the years but never met him before. All of a sudden, he slapped me on the back and exclaimed, "We love you, Fritz!" I almost fell in the urinal.

As to why *Hello, Dolly!* lost money at the boxoffice ... I know it was very successful on the stage, but when the camera got up close to it, despite the $21,000,000 spent there wasn't a great deal there. The story is nothing much, and neither is the score—there's really only one good song in the thing: "Hello, Dolly!"

☐

AVA GARDNER:

I hated *The Little Hut*, that's all. Every minute of it. It was a lousy story. I shouldn't have done it. The director [Mark Robson] was awful. It's not going to be much but what could I do? If I took another suspension they would keep me at Metro the rest of my life.

☐

JUDY GARLAND:

I did almost 30 movies for MGM and they all made money except one: *The Pirate*. So of course when they fired me that one and *Annie Get Your Gun*, which I was too ill to finish, were the only pictures they brought up.

☐

JULIE HARRIS:

The Member of the Wedding was a success on the stage but not on the screen. I liked the picture fine—I don't really know why it didn't attract film audiences. Of course, it was always a very special story and never did appeal to everybody.

☐

HOWARD KEEL:

An efficient director is someone you feel you can talk to or who has a good sense of humor. Most of them stay unapproachable somehow. Vincente Minnelli, for example, on *Kismet*. I just knew it would bomb. As a set decorator Minnelli was fine. In fact he was studying *Lust for Life* set designs while we were shooting *Kismet*. I felt like I shouldn't interrupt him to ask anything.

HARLOW (Paramount, 1965), with Carroll Baker, Fritz Feld. Director: Gordon Douglas.

❏

STANLEY KRAMER:

Who's to blame for the failure of *The Runner Stumbles*? Nobody but myself. I thought it was a pretty good film. It wasn't good enough. Initially, I intended the priest, who falls in love with a nun, to be played by Oskar Werner. But his son had an accident on the ski slopes and Oskar couldn't leave him. So the film ended up with Dick Van Dyke, who was very courageous and a lovely actor and did a fine job. But Oskar Werner had no limits, you see. The range from pathos to murderous power is what the film needed, I think.

❏

WALTER LANG:

The Blue Bird [1940] was a beautiful picture. I think it was ahead of its time. It was not a commercial success. It was a success on the stage and could have been, I guess, on the screen, but it was too difficult for the audience to follow the connections in it. It turned out according to [dramatist] Maurice Maeterlinck's conception but it was not quite the kind of thing audiences went for in that day. It was a little deep. Maybe it was my fault, maybe I shouldn't have done it, but to me it just didn't come off somehow.

❑

ANGELA LANSBURY:

Of course I made pictures with Van [Johnson] and June [Allyson], but the only time we all appeared together was in something called *Remains to Be Seen*. Dreadful movie. I don't think I ever saw it.

The only thing I can remember was coming through a bookcase that swung open. I was wearing a black dress. Mercifully, I have forgotten everything else. Shortly afterward I won my passport to freedom from MGM, and *Remains to Be Seen* may have had something to do with that.

❑

ALAN JAY LERNER:

I signed a three-picture contract with producer Arthur Freed, the first of which was *Brigadoon*, starring Gene Kelly and directed by Vincente Minnelli. It was a picture that should have been made on location in Scotland and was done in the studio. It was a singing show that tried to become a dancing show, and it had an all-American cast which should have been all-Scottish. It was one of those ventures that occur every so often where we all knew we were going down the wrong road but no one could stop. I have always believed that only genuinely talented people can create something that is genuinely bad. As Jean Giraudoux said, "Only the mediocre are always at their best."

❑

SOPHIA LOREN:

I never went into a project with higher expectations than I did with *Man of La Mancha*, my only musical, but it ran into trouble right from the start.

First of all, the indecision of the producer as to just who would direct, and then the indecision as to whether it would be shot on Spanish locations or on sets in Rome. It was ultimately decided to shoot everything in Rome, thereby losing the realistic quality that the magnificent Spanish countryside could have brought. But the film did have its compensations, chiefly the advent of Peter O'Toole into my life. Gay, witty, ribald, outrageous and crazy—but crazy in a lovely way.

Long after *Man of La Mancha* had been completed, I received the album. I had not seen the picture but I knew that it had not been very well received and would not be a commercial success. I put the disc on; what I heard made me burst out in tears. Hearing our songs washed back those five months of hard work, all the anxieties I had endured, all the problems and fears and hopes and frustrations. What I heard sounded so good, so full of life and entertainment, and I cried for the unrewarded efforts of Peter and Jimmy Coco as well as for my own.

The cruelty of our profession, to demand so much from us, to take so much of our enthusiasm and belief, and then cut us down with a few words of dismissal, the most painful of which are "write off." How do you "write off" five months of your life?

❑

VINCENTE MINNELLI:

Producer Arthur Freed had already asked me to direct *Kismet*, but I didn't relate to it, and declined. Now I was being asked again, and the implication was that I wouldn't get the Van Gogh picture [*Lust for Life*] if I didn't direct *Kismet*. I capitulated.

There's an old saw about some theatrical musicals: The audience left the theater humming the sets. Though the Borodin-inspired music was richly melodic, the same could have been said about our picture. Art director Edward Carfagno and set decorator Keogh Gleason again delivered. The cast—Howard Keel, Ann Blyth, Vic Damone and Dolores Gray—tried hard. The whole enterprise sank. The experience taught me never again to accept an assignment I lacked enthusiasm for.

❑

ROGER MOORE:

I made a picture for Warner Brothers that was the worst one I ever did. It was called *The Miracle* and I played the Duke of Wellington's nephew who had an affair with Carroll Baker that turned her into a nun. All I remember was leading a parade of soldiers through the streets of Brussels in Rosalind Russell's corset from *Auntie Mame*. Don't laugh. It's true. I wore her leftover costumes.

❑

ELLIOT NUGENT:

I did one called *Two Alone*, a play that had been done in New York; it was a tragedy, in a way, with melodramatic tones. It was a picture I liked, and the head of the studio [RKO] liked it, but it didn't make any money. If they got their costs back they were lucky; it might have even showed a loss.

Some years later I was doing a picture at Columbia and a fellow from the publicity department came over and told me that there's a famous fellow

THE BIBLE (20th Century-Fox, 1966), with Ava Gardner, Alberto Lucantoni. Director: John Huston.

from South America who has the biggest movie magazine there, like *Pho-toplay*, and he wants to interview me. I said, "Why me?" He said that I had directed a picture that had been chosen in South America as the finest artistic picture in the whole world that year. I said, "You don't mean *Two Alone*, that flop?", and he said yes.

I'd been apologizing for it, but apparently it was better than I thought.

❑

REGIS PHILBIN:

Sextette was a few years ago, although I do remember that Mae West, who was then quite old, looked very fragile but still had a twinkle in her eye. George Raft was very delicate with her. I just had a small scene as a reporter outside a church where they were married. It was a typical shooting scene. It took a few takes to get, and there were supposed to be more, but after a while Mae wasn't up to it anymore so they moved on to the next scene. The movie had a cult following but was not boxoffice.

❑

OTTO PREMINGER:

Ernst Lubitsch had made *The Fan* in 1925, and I admit it was a mistake on my part to have re-made this play. Whatever I did to the film was wrong. It is one of the few pictures I disliked while I was working on it. More than this I don't remember.

❑

ROSALIND RUSSELL:

It was murder [working on *Mourning Becomes Electra*]. Katina Paxinou screaming and yelling all over the set; Michael Redgrave, a hell of a good actor, but nervous, taking pills to calm himself; scenarist-director Dudley Nichols refusing to change a single line because Eugene O'Neill was his idol. We made a five-hour picture, on the sound stages where they'd shot *Gone with the Wind*, and Dudley wouldn't cut an inch, not a frame.

Well, *Electra* had its own style. If you released it today, it might find its audience. But when it came out in 1947, it was an even bigger financial disaster than *Sister Kenny*. Still, as I once told my son Lance, flops are a part of life's menu, and I'm never a girl to miss out on any of the courses.

❑

ROSALIND RUSSELL:

Oh Dad, Poor Dad, Mama's Hung You in the Closet and I'm Feelin' So Sad should have been a fine picture. But what makes a success of anything is the team. It doesn't matter how good an individual might be if everything else doesn't work. There was too much against us in that one.

❑

ANN SHERIDAN:

We worked for five weeks on *The Animal Kingdom*. Then Jack Warner found out that Barney Glazer, the producer, hadn't even had it OK'd by the Johnson Office. So they closed the picture because it had no Johnson Seal and couldn't be released. Irving Rapper was the first director on it. So there was a whole rewrite done. Dane Clark was written out.

I came to New York, stayed six weeks, went back, did *Shine on Harvest Moon*, then went back and finished this with the rewrite. They put Peter Godfrey on as the new director. It was released as *One More Tomorrow*, with Dennis Morgan, Jack Carson, Jane Wyman, Alexis Smith—the Warner stock company. You can tell the difference in the scenes between the things Rapper had done and what Godfrey did. It was one of the most horrible things I've ever seen in my life! They bought Mr. Glazer's contract, paid him $150,000 and sent him for—so they told the papers—a rest in South America.

A COUNTESS FROM HONG KONG (Universal, 1967), with Sydney Chaplin, Marlon Brando. Director: Charles Chaplin.

☐

PHIL SILVERS:

There was so little money that *Top Banana* was shot in a day and a half. [Director] Al Greene just pointed the camera and let it roll. He didn't dare stop. In the final cut, you could see a stagehand walking behind a drop.

The sound quivered and faded, and yet it managed to pick up every off-camera shoe squcak. The 3-D process was obsolete by the time the picture was released, so the 3-D film was projected on regular two-dimension machines. This left all sorts of strange vertical blurs. But the comedy was still there. Somewhere. I made nothing out of the picture.

Top Banana is occasionally shown on the TV too-late shows, which add a little blur of their own. The young film buffs who stay up all night consider it a collector's item. With all its out-of-synch sound, inexplicable noises, scenes that seem to float under water, it's now avant-garde.

☐

NEIL SIMON:

I've had flops. *God's Favorite* was a flop. It ran three months on Broadway. Not all the movies have been successful. *After the Fox* was a flop. *Last of the Red Hot Lovers* was a flop as a film.

❏

BARBARA STANWYCK:

The only time I worked with John Ford turned out to be a disaster. He used the Abbey Players in *The Plough and the Stars*—with a couple of other Irishmen, Preston Foster and me, co-starring. We thought it was a very honest, moving version of the Sean O'Casey play. Sam Briskin, who was running RKO then, ran it and said halfway through, "Nobody's gonna understand those accents!" So they called Preston and me back and we shot scene after scene of "translations"—"Listen, Nora, you hear what they're saying? You know what it means? Why, it means—" and so on for scene after scene. Mr. Ford very wisely was unavailable on his yacht.

❏

GLORIA SWANSON:

Erich Pommer, a producer at Fox, called and offered me the starring role in a screen version of *Music in the Air*, the Broadway hit of 1932 with music by Jerome Kern and book and lyrics by Oscar Hammerstein II. We all felt fairly certain of success during the shooting, but the picture flopped. Hollywood producers learned once again that the taste of New York and Broadway, during the darkest days of the Depression, was no barometer for the taste of the nation at large. The nation at large ignored *Music in the Air* and rushed instead to see *Stand Up and Cheer*, a musical starring a six-year-old Shirley Temple.

❏

JULE STYNE:

Gypsy is the most important thing I've ever written. But after the 1962 film, the show was dead in stock. It took almost 30 years to offset that lousy picture.

❏

GENE TIERNEY:

I don't know that I ever went into a movie more excited, with less cause, than I did for *The Shanghai Gesture*. The picture was to be a comeback for German director Josef von Sternberg, who had launched Marlene Dietrich,

STAR! (20th Century-Fox, 1968), with Daniel Massey, Julie Andrews. Director: Robert Wise.

PAINT YOUR WAGON (Paramount, 1969), with Clint Eastwood, Lee Marvin, Jean Seberg. Director: Joshua Logan.

a taskmaster who came to work in riding clothes with high leather boots. He carried a riding crop and brandished it whenever he got excited, which was a good deal of the time. *Shanghai Gesture* had been a huge success on Broadway. I had the Mary Duncan part as the illegitimate daughter of Mother Gin-Sling, played by Ona Munson.

Shanghai Gesture was released to devastating reviews. Singled out for special mention was one of my unforgettable lines. Just before she shot me, I hissed at Mother Gin-Sling, "You're no more my mother than a toad!"

Years later, in France, strangers would ask me about *The Shanghai Gesture* as though it had been a work of art!

❑

ORSON WELLES:

After all, the film [*Macbeth*] cannot be worthless if people like Jean Cocteau like it. I now see its shortcomings, but I still think it is better Shakespeare than most stage productions of *Macbeth* I have seen.

❑

SHELLEY WINTERS:

Knickerbocker Holiday—we all sensed disaster from the third day. Charles Coburn was a fine actor, but he wasn't Walter Huston. Nelson Eddy had a beautiful voice, but he was self-conscious in this role and took on a *Chocolate Soldier* quality. Also, he didn't want Connie [Dowling] to look into his eyes when they did a scene, insisting she look at his forehead instead. It really threw her.

One evening I was napping in my dressing room when the dignified Nelson stumbled in, quite drunk, still in costume and weeping. He knew this picture wasn't going to do him any good. Suddenly he muttered, "The rushes were lousier today. I think I'd better go back to the Mounties. Move over." I made for the door.

❑

JOANNE WOODWARD:

Signpost to Murder? Oh, my heart. What I remember most about that one is that we were shooting the film the day John Kennedy died. We had an awful director [George Englund] and the last scene was so bad we decided to throw it out and improvise on camera. I think the movie ran 45 minutes, but I liked the way I looked in the main opening shot. I was wearing a bathing suit, a large hat and high heels.

❑

WILLIAM WYLER:

I remade *These Three* under the play's original title of *The Children's Hour* in 1962, but by that time the subject was too strong for the thirties and too mild for the sixties!

The film was criticized because so much tragedy was extracted from the mere rumor of a homosexual relationship between the two teachers in the girls' school [Audrey Hepburn and Shirley MacLaine]: the two women were ruined, one of them committed suicide and the school was closed. It seemed to some critics to be much ado about nothing. But I saw the story as a tragedy about the power of a lie—in this case the lie that one of the students spread about two of her teachers. In any event, the first, milder version of the story made in 1936 was successful, and the more genuine adaptation in 1962 was not.

❑

DARRYL F. ZANUCK:

A Flea in Her Ear—a catastrophe! An absolute bust everywhere.

❑

FRED ZINNEMANN:

The Member of the Wedding is both my favorite film and my biggest flop.

Late Laurels

"A lot of pictures of mine that people thought bad at the time have since been called 'classics.'"

FRED ASTAIRE:

Yolanda and the Thief was a beautiful picture. It was a very well intentioned movie that never got off the ground, was not considered a hit. But it was a very smart thing—by smart, I mean attractive—it could have been a nifty picture. But it was a bit ahead of its time.

❑

ANNE BAXTER:

Sunday Dinner for a Soldier is very special to me because I met my husband, John Hodiak, on it—he was my leading man. The film did no business in the United States, for some reason, but was a smash in London. It's still remembered there.

❑

IRVING BRECHER:

After *Meet Me in St. Louis*, [producer] Arthur Freed began to smile at me. He assigned me to do a screenplay with a man whose work I admired, Ludwig Bemelmans. Freed had bought his story, *Yolanda and the Thief*. The story was nothing. But Freed wanted to make it . . . and to star Lucille Bremer, who had been in *Meet Me in St. Louis*, and, if she was not having an affair with Freed, was at least being coveted by him. I didn't think there was a picture in that.

And then Bemelmans goes away. I go to Sam Katz: "Sam, I don't want to work on this shit." He says, "You know, we made a lot of money with Arthur. This one is for Arthur." I said, "You're going to make a lousy picture and give him a present?" He says, "Yeah. He likes this girl. What can you do? You know, this [tugging his crotch] is stronger than anything. What's your salary?" I said I had a contract for so many months, $1250 a week. He said,

"Four firm years at $2000, with 12 weeks off with pay." I went back to work.

I do *Yolanda* as fast as I can. And they play with it, [director Vincente] Minnelli and the rest, and they do the best they can. But the girl never had it. The film had a couple of good songs, but *Yolanda* turned out, as expected, not profitable. Oddly, now it's become something of a cult picture, and many people think highly of it, for some reason.

❑

LUCILLE BREMER:

Yolanda and the Thief certainly has gotten more attention in 1989 than when it came out in 1945! For years I've received letters from young people who had just discovered it and wanted to tell me how much they had enjoyed it. And now that MGM/UA has released it on home video, we *really* get letters.

When we made the picture, we worked very hard and hoped for a good reception, but the reviews were mixed and nobody seemed to want to go. I think it was too fanciful, too much of a fairy tale for the day. People were still into the war then, too involved in realism. The songs [by producer Arthur Freed and Harry Warren] were beautiful, so were the sets and the Technicolor. And Vincente Minnelli's direction was always sensitive. It was all very imaginative—much *too* imaginative for its time. Audiences nowadays are more sophisticated and seem to appreciate it more.

I was still new at MGM then. My only previous feature film was *Meet Me in St. Louis*, which was a big hit. So of course I was delighted to learn that I next would be co-starring in *Yolanda* with the great Fred Astaire—*any* dancer would have been thrilled at such a prospect. He was a lovely gentleman; you couldn't find anyone who would say an unkind word about him. Yes, he was a perfectionist, but so was I. I didn't really get to know him well socially, though—I know I never met his wife. (We did two films together, *Yolanda* and, a year later, *Ziegfeld Follies.*) I was a very private person and didn't chat with a lot of people on the lot. I had my friends there but I kept pretty much to myself.

Vincente Minnelli, who also directed me in *Meet Me in St. Louis* and *Ziegfeld Follies*, was a genius, a man of immense taste and imagination. Eugene Loring did the choreography for *Yolanda*. The "Coffee Time" number that Fred and I danced near the end was interesting to do. Gene devised this strange thing: we worked to a counter beat—we were dancing to one beat while the music was playing another. And the wavy black and white floor on which we performed gave the routine an almost three-dimensional look. I didn't realize the floor would play such an important part in the number's effectiveness until after I saw the picture.

By the way, in the big dream ballet, "Will You Marry Me?", that wasn't me walking up and out of the lake. This is how things are done in Hollywood: they had a girl covered by veils walk backwards into the water, then for our

HELLO, DOLLY! (20th Century-Fox, 1969), with Walter Matthau, Barbra Streisand. Director: Gene Kelly.

picture they ran the footage backwards to make it appear that *I* was walking out of the lake, veils billowing in the breeze.

People also often ask about the number "Limehouse Blues" which Fred and I danced in *Ziegfeld Follies*. We played a Chinese couple and used fans throughout in an elaborate, very complicated manner. Funny thing is, Bob Alton, the writer-choreographer for this number, originally planned to have us use the fans only at the beginning of the piece—they had figured in the plot prologue to the number. But after we got into the dance, we just couldn't find a graceful way to throw them away!

Fred and I would work on a number for quite a long time. There would be three or four weeks of rehearsal, then we'd shoot it and go on to the next one. Later on, Fred said some very nice things about my work in interviews.

Leon Ames was wonderful in *Yolanda*. He had played my father in *Meet Me in St. Louis*, and in *Yolanda* he was my guardian angel.

A few years later I married Abelardo Rodgriguez, whose father was the President of Mexico. I retired from the screen and moved to Mexico, where I did my own producing—I have four children. I didn't really miss Hollywood. I enjoyed the work while I was there very much, but life moves on along different levels. I was entering a new stage as a wife and mother in a foreign country. I had plenty to keep me busy.

But I'm happy that my films (though there were only eight of them) are remembered. And I have to marvel at *Yolanda*. For a boxoffice wallflower, she certainly has a long line of admirers today!

◻

HUMPHREY BOGART:

Only the phonies think *Beat the Devil* is funny. It's a mess.

◻

ELLEN BURSTYN:

Alex in Wonderland never really got a chance because the critics were so hard on it. It never had time to find its audience—until now, when it's become a kind of cult film on college campuses. It's shown and admired in college courses throughout the country, and wherever I speak to students, I'm always asked about *Alex*. [Director/co-author] Paul Mazursky and I wanted to buy *Alex* from MGM and re-release it, because we feel it has an audience, but the studio wasn't interested.

◻

JOSEPH COTTEN:

When David Selznick gave me the script of *Beyond the Forest* to read, I did not like the part or the story. Also, there was talk that Bette did not want to do the picture. I said to David, "If Bette Davis is not starring in it, there's no point in my doing it." (He was loaning me to Warners.)

Bette decided to do it, but the picture was a low point in her enduring career. King Vidor, who directed, told me that he could not remember a less rewarding moment in his long and historic life behind the camera. The film, however, has become a cult classic for the perverse. It even earned a moment of dubious recognition in Edward Albee's *Who's Afraid of Virginia Woolf?* . . . Bette saying "What a dump!"

As for me, I'll admit to having stumbled into several trashbins here and there, but never into quite such an important trashbin. After all, I did work with one of the all-time great actresses.

◻

GEORGE CUKOR:

Usually, when you make a picture that doesn't turn out well, it's soon happily buried. Except, of course, that television keeps popping up and you may be confronted with your past failures. The funny thing about *Two-Faced Woman* is that because of Garbo it also appears at film festivals. People tell

DARLING LILI (Paramount, 1970), with Rock Hudson, Julie Andrews. Director: Blake Edwards.

LOST HORIZON (Columbia, 1972), with George Kennedy, Bobby Van, Sally Kellerman, John Gielgud, Liv Ullmann, Peter Finch. Director: Charles Jarrott.

me, "It's very interesting." Well, I think it's lousy! The script was bad—not funny. We all knocked ourselves out, but it just wasn't funny.

❏

GLORIA DE HAVEN:

Summer Holiday was one of the great joys—and disappointments—of my life. It was a musical version of Eugene O'Neill's *Ah, Wilderness!* and had a great score by Harry Warren and Ralph Blane. The director [Rouben Mamoulian], script and cast were also the best, but while it was an artistic success it was a commercial flop. In some areas the picture even played the bottom half of double bills.

It was a magnificent production, although maybe a little *too* artistic. It was like a Currier and Ives or Grant Wood painting come to life. The costumes alone were incredible. They were done under the supervision of Irene and designed by Walter Plunkett, who had done the costumes for *Gone with the Wind*. Even the undergarments, all silk and lace and embroidery, were hand-done. I remember that L. B. Mayer, our boss at MGM, used to say, "I don't want anything cheap *anywhere* on our ladies." His feeling was, if his actresses were wearing muslin underneath, *they'd* know it and then so would the audience. The clothes were perfect in every detail for the period and locale—1906 Connecticut.

The picture originally ran almost four hours, which was much too long for the double bill programs of the 1940s. There was an extremely long musical dream sequence called "Omar and the Princess" in which teenager Mickey Rooney, after reading Omar Khayyám, dreamed that I was his princess in a sylvan Persian setting. The whole segment was cut from the picture. My character was always afraid to get too involved with Mickey, so I was given a lovely solo entitled "Wish I Had a Braver Heart." This was cut, too.

Walter Huston, who plays Mickey's father, had a natural successor to his famous "September Song" in a gorgeous number he sang in *Summer Holiday* called "Spring Isn't Everything." This also was cut. Now, when he embraces his wife [Selena Royle] on the balcony at the end and says, "Spring isn't everything," the audience really doesn't know what he's talking about because the number he's just sung has been cut! I do the song in my nightclub act today and explain the story behind it. I also do "The Stanley Steamer," a delightful tune that *was* left in the picture, which, without the cuts, might have been a musical *Gone with the Wind*. It's *still* a beautiful film.

Several years ago, Rex Reed, the movie critic, who is a great fan of *Summer Holiday*, tried to track down the cut musical numbers from it at MGM, but he was told that they had all been lost in a fire.

The film was made in 1946 but not released until 1948. The timing was off, I think. At that time they were doing very dramatic, socially conscious stories like *Gentleman's Agreement, The Snake Pit* and *Pinky*, and a cheerful,

Technicolored slice of Americana like our film may have seemed old-fashioned. Actually, in style it was very advanced and today is recognized as a landmark in movie musicals.

I had never worked with so many legendary actors, artists like Mickey, Walter Huston, Frank Morgan, Agnes Moorehead, Selena Royle, little Butch Jenkins and my good friend, the late Marilyn Maxwell, who was so wonderful in her seduction number with Mickey, "The Sweetest Kid I Ever Met." These people are what really made *Summer Holiday* a joy for me.

❏

MARLENE DIETRICH:

Today, *The Scarlet Empress* is a classic. In 1934, however, it didn't enjoy the hoped-for success. Now we know that this film was ahead of its time; certainly this is the reason why it is shown in film museums and workshops throughout the world.

Young people write me and talk about the costumes—particularly my white boots—and other impressive details they seem to understand thoroughly—much more than the public of that time. They are also fascinated by the artistic direction, which was in [Josef] von Sternberg's hands. But he didn't believe wholeheartedly in *The Scarlet Empress*. He told the cast: "If this film is a flop, it will be a grandiose flop, and the critics will rage. But I prefer to see you in a grandiose flop than in a mediocre film."

Von Sternberg was proved eminently right. The critics' rage was immense.

❏

COLEEN GRAY:

I was just starting in pictures at 20th Century-Fox when I read the novel *Nightmare Alley*, by William Lindsay Gresham, which the studio was planning to film. I knew I was born to play Molly, the loyal wife. I told our boss Darryl Zanuck this, and he said, "If we can get a top star for the male lead, we can afford to float an unknown for Molly."

They put me to work supporting several actors who were testing for *Nightmare Alley*—one was Mark Stevens, I recall—and when their tests were seen, so was I. I was given the feminine lead in *Kiss of Death*. When, in turn, they saw the rushes of *Kiss*, I was offered Molly in *Nightmare Alley* if I would sign a seven-year contract at the same salary. I thought this was wrong and refused. They hired me anyway—it was just a power play.

Tyrone Power ultimately had been signed to play the unscrupulous "hero" who becomes a carnival "geek." I was thrilled to appear opposite him: I'd had a crush on him since high school. We came to the parts very well prepared: he was studying acting then with Elsa Schreiber and I was

MAN OF LA MANCHA (United Artists, 1972), with Peter O'Toole, Sophia Loren. Director: Arthur Hiller.

MAME (Warner Brothers, 1974), with Lucille Ball, Jane Connell. Director: Gene Saks.

studying with her husband, George Shdanoff. It became Ty's favorite (if most uncharacteristic) of all his roles.

He was a joy to be around. His feet never seemed to touch the stage floor—he had such grace and poise and confidence and sweetness. He was a true gentleman, as well as the handsomest man in movies. He was going with Lana Turner at the time, and I remember she visited him on the set once during some night shooting. They sat in director's chairs and I just gawked at them from my trailer—they were so beautiful together.

Our director, Edmund Goulding, was most helpful. There was one long, very critical scene where Ty's character persuades me to go along with this deception, and I say, "You're going against God!" He was after me like a spider with a fly, encircling me around a trunk. It was beautifully staged. I was naturally distraught and Mr. Goulding cried, "Cut!"

He took me to a corner and said, "I want you to think of cabbages." But I just couldn't think of cabbages at such a dramatic time.

So again he said, "You will think of cabbages."

Finally, I thought of cabbages and he said, "Beautiful!" This had been his way of telling me I was doing too much in the scene, and correcting it.

When *Nightmare Alley* was released in 1947, the studio thought it was a bummer, too downbeat, and did nothing, publicity-wise; there was no campaign. Consequently, it came and went without notice. It wasn't until it was re-released 10 years later, when people had begun really to study film, that it was recognized as a remarkable motion picture.

210

❏

RITA HAYWORTH:

I didn't rejoice but I wasn't as upset as everyone else by the failure of *The Lady from Shanghai*. I believed in the picture from day one, or I wouldn't have let Orson [Welles] turn me into a blonde for it. I had a feeling that someday he would be vindicated and it would become a classic.

❏

KATHARINE HEPBURN:

A lot of pictures of mine that people thought bad at the time have since been called "classics," but of those *Sylvia Scarlett* is the most surprising. I remember going home one night from the studio and writing in my diary, "This picture makes no sense at all and I wonder whether George Cukor is aware of the fact, because I certainly don't know what the hell I'm doing."

❏

KATHARINE HEPBURN:

Sylvia Scarlett was a disaster, and the reason why it's a success now [the eighties] is that the audience is also a disaster. At least when it was made the audience had sense enough not to go.

❏

DUSTIN HOFFMAN:

Perhaps one value of home video is that it will give good, unknown little films like *Agatha* another chance to find an audience.

❏

JOHN HOUSEMAN:

Sabotage of my favorite film, *They Live by Night*, left me with *Letter from an Unknown Woman* as my last hope of establishing my reputation as a filmmaker. A San Francisco preview had gone well; so had the Hollywood trade showings.

My euphoria was short-lived. In the latter part of April *Letter from an Unknown Woman* was given a hurried national release. It was praised by a few but clobbered by most of the press, including the *New York Times*. It took several years and three much admired European films to restore *Letter* to its present honored place in the canon of director Max Ophuls' film work. Later still it emerged as one of the first and most successful major films to be shown nationally on American television.

But in 1948 it was an unmitigated disaster—critically and commercially —and a devastating defeat for us all.

□

ROCK HUDSON:

"If only I had a second chance," people say to themselves. That was the theme of *Seconds*, in which I played my favorite role, a 60-year-old man who is remade through plastic surgery to have the face and body of a 35-year-old. The film was certainly depressing, but it was a horror story with certain science fiction elements. Director John Frankenheimer went to great trouble to make each scene or sequence as real as possible. Macabre as the film was in some ways, I had the best time of my career making it; I enjoyed getting a chance to do acting chores so different from any I'd ever done. I feel *Seconds* is a good film, but it was a boxoffice flop, which, of course, means nobody went to see it. However, I've been told that it has become a cult film on college campuses.

□

BURT LANCASTER:

I always tried to do different kinds of pictures. Like *The Leopard*, for example. There's a movie that never made a nickel. I played the part of a Sicilian nobleman. Most people don't care about this business of royalty, but I did it because it was a wonderful role. I got involved in it. I read the book and loved it. Well, in spite of magnificent reviews in Europe, the reviewers here said Lancaster was ridiculous in the picture.

Now, 20 years later, the picture was re-released, and the big cities raved about it. So I tend to have a cynical attitude toward critics. I don't know what changed in *The Leopard*. It's the same movie. As we used to say in the old days, "We make a picture, have a preview in Hollywood, get marvelous reviews. We put it on a train, and when it arrives in New York, it stinks. What happened to it on the train?"

□

BARBARA LAWRENCE:

Today, *Unfaithfully Yours* is admired by film scholars as an original, "fun" movie. It was even remade with Dudley Moore (*terrible!*). But in 1948 it was killed by the advertising—it was way off base.

This was a *comedy*, produced, directed and written by Preston Sturges, but the Fox advertising department tried to sell it as some sort of murder mystery. "Will somebody 'get her' tonite?", said the ad copy, surrounded by spider webs! Consequently, it never hit its mark. I suppose it *was* a flawed

WON TON TON, THE DOG WHO SAVED HOLLYWOOD (Paramount, 1975), with Gloria De Haven, Art Carney, Phil Silvers, Bruce Dern. Director: Michael Winner.

picture, but the ad campaign destroyed any chances it might have had. Why did they take that approach? I don't know—maybe the advertising people never *saw* the movie!

I thoroughly enjoyed working with Preston, Rex Harrison and Linda Darnell. Gene Tierney had been announced to play the Darnell role, with her husband, Oleg Cassini, set to design the costumes. Then, for some reason, she didn't do it and Linda stepped in. At this point, I had done several films, had had some very nice parts, but this was the first time I received star billing above the title. I played Linda's acid-tongued kid sister. To be frank, I really didn't care all that much for the role; the continual one-liners became a little boring after a while. I was always saying things like, "Some men make you think of champagne, others, prune juice."

Preston was quite a character, always passing out 50-cent pieces if you could come up with a line he could use—"so you won't sue me later," he laughed. He was very easy to work with; most qualified people are. I'm writing a screenplay now and was looking at his script just the other day. Like most scripts then, it was very simply written. It would say, ". . . after a good bit of that, we'll do this. . . ." It was almost as if he were writing to himself, which in a sense he was, since he was the director, too.

He was going with a very attractive girl, a model, I think. We were always so overdressed in films then. One day Preston and Bonnie Cashin, who replaced Cassini as designer, went to a furrier to buy a matching leopard skin skirt and top for me to wear in the picture. It cost $2,000, and after I'd filmed the scene wearing it you never saw the skirt on the screen! They had filmed me from the waist up only! Preston then bought the outfit for his girlfriend; I think that's really why he wanted to get it in the first place. I can still hear her saying that she could just see herself walking down a gangplank in it—people still traveled by boat a lot in those days.

Another time, we were shooting in the big concert hall set for a week or so and I was wearing a gown made of tulle and netting. Preston was terrified that cigarette ashes would fall on my highly flammable dress. He got a fireman to follow me around and whenever I stopped to light up, he'd plant a stand with a sign reading, "Please Don't Smoke."

When *Unfaithfully Yours* opened, one New York critic wrote, "I would rather see a Sturges failure than a DeMille success."

❑

JOHN LITHGOW:

Harry and the Hendersons has made me more famous than anything else I've ever done. When it was released theatrically a couple of summers ago, everyone was so sad because it felt like such a failure. And yet, everywhere I go people ask, "Where's Harry?" "How's Harry?" It's like everybody has seen this movie! It must be the number one family video!

❑

FRANCIS LEDERER:

People told me that *The Diary of a Chambermaid* did not turn out to be boxoffice, but I still place it near the top of my favorite pictures. What I always looked for in a film was a solid character to portray, and this warped butler was a *fantastic* character. Jean Renoir, who was to direct, approached me about doing it, and since the story and screenplay also were top-notch, I signed on. I was never sorry.

Renoir and his wife became my close friends. He was a man of extreme sensitivity and humor and warmth—actors could not help but respond to him. And our actors were *divine*—Paulette Goddard, Hurd Hatfield, Judith Anderson, Reginald Owen, Irene Ryan and Paulette's husband, Burgess Meredith, who also wrote the screenplay, co-produced with Benedict Bogeaus and was so funny in his role as the flower-eating old captain. Renoir brought his French set designer, Albert Laurie, with him on the project, and the sets were perfection, very true to the sort of French villages where the action took place.

Although made in Hollywood, the movie had a very foreign flavor. Maybe that's why it didn't do well. In 1946, foreign films were not yet so popular in America. Anyway, I thought *Diary of a Chambermaid* was a gem!

❏

JANET LEIGH:

There was a telegram waiting: "Delighted you are in our picture [*Touch of Evil*] . . . Regards, Orson Welles." *Orson Welles?* What picture?

I called Edd Henry, my agent. "He wasn't supposed to contact you. We don't have a finished script."

"I don't care about a completed script. I would like to work with Orson."

Edd sighed, "That's just what Charlton Heston said."

Orson called upon his friends to do capsule appearances *not* in the script. For him, rules were made to be broken. Marlene Dietrich appeared as a madam. We never knew who might turn up at night or where we might be shooting. Chuck Heston and I were mesmerized.

Not so the studio. I guess they felt they had been "had." After Orson finished his contractual "first cut," they came to us for retakes. They did not understand all of the detours and believed the flow was disjointed. To some extent their argument had validity, but to tamper with the content meant to devitalize what was Orson. We were compelled to acquiesce because of the Screen Actors Guild code. So we did some "linking," explanatory, dull shots. The release of *Touch of Evil* was disappointing. But it warms the cockles of my heart to know that it is now considered a cult classic and honors Orson Welles.

❏

ANITA LOOS:

Recently a young writer asked me, "Miss Loos, could I interview you on that silent film you wrote for Douglas Fairbanks called *The Mystery of the Leaping Fish?*" I could only apologize that I'd forgotten it completely. "That may be a Freudian blackout," she chuckled. "It was a terrible flop." "Then why did you ever dig it up?", I asked. "Because it's one of the few old films that hasn't yet been analyzed in the arts magazines."

❏

STEVE MARTIN:

Pennies from Heaven flopped because the material is extremely sophisticated. It's never going to reach a mass audience because it's very dark. It doesn't have a broad appeal.

Yes, *Batman* is very dark, too, but that's a different kind of dark. It's not literary. *Pennies from Heaven* is very literary and complicated with layers and layers of allusions.

Another film of mine that was not appreciated when it was released but has a following now is *The Man with Two Brains*. In England, it's listed among the top 10 underground flicks.

AT LONG LAST LOVE (20th Century-Fox, 1975), with Cybill Shepherd, Burt Reynolds.
Director: Peter Bogdanovich.

◻

ARTHUR MAYER:

Samuel Goldwyn imported *The Cabinet of Dr. Caligari*. A very unusual [German] film, *Caligari* was, shall we say, a flop.

After he showed the picture in his projection room, Goldwyn wanted to know from his staff, "How was it?" Not a word. My own position was equivalent to assistant office boy. I said, "I like it." "Ha!" he said. "We have one bright young man. I'm going to let you help me on the campaign."

The campaign was a catastrophe. Theaters sued us. We ruined their business for weeks. People wouldn't come back after we played *Caligari*. However, it was and still is a very great picture. It's the daddy of all horror films, but America wasn't ready for anything of that nature. It was surrealistic. Goldwyn was fired; *I* wasn't. My salary was so small nobody paid any attention to me.

◻

RODDY McDOWALL:

I *loved* doing that film [*Lord Love a Duck*]. George Axelrod was a terrific director. It was great working with Tuesday Weld and Lola Albright. Sad that it didn't meet with any commercial success, but I guess it does have a cult following.

◻

BURGESS MEREDITH:

Diary of a Chambermaid was an underestimated film in this country. Jean Renoir directed that. I thought it was a much better film than anybody had any idea of, but for some reason they didn't grasp the notion; then it became a classic, a minor classic, later. It was always appreciated in France, very much so. It was one of my favorites.

◻

DAVID MILLER:

Universal had no confidence in *Lonely Are the Brave*, but I had a track record there so I got to do it. I came in exactly one hour ahead of schedule. At first Kirk Douglas was difficult, trying to see how far he could go. Then he discovered how marvelous Dalton Trumbo's script was. But Universal took one look and showcased it in Brooklyn! A slow build in a Manhattan art cinema would have made all the difference.

◻

GABLE AND LOMBARD (Universal, 1976), with Jill Clayburgh, Alice Backes, James Brolin. Director: Sidney J. Furie.

LIZA MINNELLI:

New York New York—we all thought it was going to be a huge hit, but it wasn't. But the funny thing is that people still watch it and talk about it and love it. It's the movie that won't die.

❏

PETER O'TOOLE:

I'll talk about *The Ruling Class* until the cows come home, because it's a favorite of mine and I love it and I'm *very* pleased that it's having a reissue. It's not a fortune maker but because of its critical acclaim it became top heavy in terms of its commercial audience. It just wasn't for that. It's an immodest subject but designed for a modest audience. Most of the criticism at the time it came out [1972] said that it was 10 years before its time.

❏

GREGORY PECK:

Moby Dick was the most dangerous film I've ever made. Director John Huston liked to test his actors for courage. I wouldn't say uncle and he nearly killed me. The film was not well received when it came out. The critics thought that I was too young for the part, which I was. They fancied Orson Welles, Walter Huston or Fredric March in the role. I didn't know it at the time, but Huston could not get the picture financed with an older character actor. So he persuaded me to play it, with a three-hour makeup job. Now, 35 years later, the picture has been re-evaluated. It plays better now, apparently, than it did in 1956.

❑

ROD STEIGER:

Run of the Arrow—that was one of my capital errors. It's a cult film now and I can't believe it. I was playing a Civil War veteran and so I read up about the South. I found that the South was settled by the Scotch and the English and the Irish. So, idiot me, I go ahead and do the first Irish cowboy. Well, *you* try to say "They went thataway" with an Irish accent in front of an audience.

❑

FRANCES STERNHAGEN:

Although by and large things went smoothly enough during the filming of *Fedora*, there were hints very early that there might be problems with it later.

Billy Wilder, who produced and directed and also wrote the screenplay with I. A. L. Diamond, cast me as Fedora's personal companion, Miss Balfour, after seeing me in *Equus* on Broadway. I flew to Germany (where we were to film part of the time) a few days early for makeup tests and said to Billy, "I'd like to talk to you about my character." In that cute Katzenjammer accent of his, he replied, "Just do vot chew do in da play and dot vill be fine."

So much of the film's desired success depended on Marthe Keller who played the mysterious, ever-youthful, legendary movie star Fedora (who was, in actuality, the deluded girl's mother, played by Hildegard Knef). Billy originally had wanted one actress to play both the old Fedora and the young girl, but there didn't seem to be anyone at the time with the virtuosity to do it. Today, Meryl Streep *might* have been able to pull it off. The role was almost unplayable, really—the girl had to be like Garbo, and what actress could substitute for Garbo? When the film was released, Marthe drew some criticism. But it had been so difficult for her. She had just filmed *Bobby Deerfield*, under the direction of Sydney Pollack who was very actor-oriented and took time with his players. Now she comes to *Fedora* and Billy Wilder, who was under a great deal of pressure to hurry up and come in under budget and whose rehearsals, if you could call them that, were mainly just for camera. Marthe was very unhappy: she had been used to working out her scenes with Syd Pollack.

One day, Bill Holden, one of the stars, and I were talking about his recent film, *Network*, which he had so enjoyed doing. He said that the director, Sidney Lumet, rehearsed every scene as if it were a play. I remarked that it was a shame Billy Wilder didn't do that, and Bill quietly answered, "He used to."

There's no question that Billy's situation was stressful. He had been unable to find an American film company to fund *Fedora*, so he finally made a deal with a German-French company to make it. But costs had to be kept way down. On the set, though, he was a wonderful kind of emcee, always joking with the crew—which, frankly, could be a bit unnerving when you were trying to concentrate on the character you were playing.

There were no great problems while we filmed. In fact, it was lovely fun for the most part, traveling as we did to several delightful European locations. Oh, occasionally airplanes would zoom overhead and ruin a take. And Hildegard Knef was very ill with cancer during the filming. I remember that Stephen Collins, who was cast as the young Bill Holden in a flashback, had to carry in a swan for one scene. Now, swans look beautiful but can be dangerous. No way, said Stephen, would he do this. The trainer had to tranquilize the swan before Stephen would touch him.

The script suffered little change as we filmed. I. A. L. Diamond was always there on the set if needed. In the original Tom Tryon novella, my character had been softer; Billy and I. A. L. made her slightly more menacing in the picture. Still, I can't help wishing that Miss Balfour had had a little more range as a character.

There could be several reasons for the film's failure. Besides the problem of Marthe, maybe the story itself was a little old-fashioned for audiences in 1979. Movies were starting to be made for kids, while older people had sort of retired to television. Also, Bill Holden, our biggest international star name among the principals, didn't have enough dramatic thrust in his part; he was mainly the narrator. The drama was that the daughter had been playing her mother all these years. Bill was narrator, too, in Billy Wilder's great 1950 film *Sunset Blvd.* (to which *Fedora* was compared), but in that Bill was also a major dramatic participant. There may have been too much narration in *Fedora*, and not enough acting out of scenes.

But *Fedora* has its advocates. Some of the reviews were very good and it seems to have acquired a cult following. Recently, while vacationing in London my son and I visited a pub. Whereupon a bearded gentleman of about 40 or so came over and introduced himself as a film critic. "I just have to tell you," he went on, "that *Fedora* is one of my all-time favorite movies."

❑

JAMES STEWART:
It's a Wonderful Life was the first picture I did after getting out of the war.

BOUND FOR GLORY (United Artists, 1976), with James Jeter, David Carradine, Ti-Ju Cumbaka. Director: Hal Ashby.

One afternoon Frank Capra called and said he had an idea for a movie and would I come over. He says to me, "You're a fella in a small town, you see, and you're not doing very well. You want to do something for your wife, you want to help people, but everything is going to pieces. You try to commit suicide and an angel named Clarence, who hasn't won his wings yet, jumps into the water to save you. But he can't swim, and you save him!" Then Frank says, "It doesn't sound too good, does it?" I said, "Frank, if you want to do a movie about an angel who hasn't won his wings named Clarence, I'm your man!"

It didn't do well at all. I don't think it was the type of story people wanted right after the war. They wanted a war-related story or a pure slapstick, Red Skelton-type of comedy. Our movie just got lost. It was television, years later, that made it a classic.

❏

SHIRLEY TEMPLE:

Why did *The Wizard of Oz* succeed and not our *Blue Bird*?

The Wizard of Oz appealed to both young and old, while *The Blue Bird* was principally for children. *Oz* was a glorious, lighthearted musical based on reality, while *Blue Bird* drifted off into obscure fantasy.

Dorothy of Oz was a naive Kansas farm girl knocked unconscious by a tornado, but her dream remained linked with the dust-bowl realities of home and a noble wish to help others. Our blue bird went flapping off in a different direction. Like *Oz*, its takeoff point was reality, followed by a dream. However, there we got stuck, wallowing midway between vaudeville and a ponderous, barely intelligible spirituality.

Another major contrast was between selfless Dorothy and hateful me. I remained nasty until far too late in the film.

Just as Europe had hostilities, Hollywood had its own 1939 warfare, a highly personalized battle between MGM and 20th Century-Fox. Their wizard against our blue bird. In the end, it was more a battle between their cannon and our cap pistol. Summarized *Time* magazine: "*The Blue Bird* laid an egg."

Thirty years later our *Blue Bird* would receive critical acclaim, but in the increasingly realistic time of 1940 it had to wait.

❑

KING VIDOR:

One night we were showing *The Crowd* to Ryan O'Neal and his agent, Sue Mengers, with the thought of doing a remake of the picture. Ryan said, "We've got to do this story!" He came up and put his arm around me, and Sue Mengers piped up and asked, "When *The Crowd* was made, was it a big success?" I said, "No." They dropped out of the deal.

❑

ORSON WELLES:

Touch of Evil never had a first-run, never had the usual presentation to the press and was not the object of any critical writing in either the weeklies, the reviews or the daily papers. It was considered to be too bad. When the representative from Universal wanted to exhibit it at the Brussels Fair in 1958, he was told that it wasn't a good enough film for a festival. He answered that, in any case, it must be put on the program. It went unnoticed and was sent back. The film took the *grand prix*, but it was no less sent back.

❑

WILLIAM A. WELLMAN:

The Ox-Bow Incident didn't make money, but they finally got hold of it in Europe [under the title *Strange Incident*], and it was a great success. One of the great critics of the time in the States—he was the biggest voice of them all—went against the mainstream at that time. He said it had less merit than the smallest B Western. I've still got that review. I have it in my safe deposit box—it's reading something like that that can still turn an artist's insides into knots. But mostly the reaction was favorable. I'm proud of it.

❏

BRUCE WILLIS:

A lot of people gave *Sunset* a hard time. I think in a couple of years, however long it takes, it's going to be rediscovered. I'm not sure if I had the choice again I would choose to play a famous person like Tom Mix.

❏

ROBERT WISE:

I was a boy editor, but a damned good one. On *The Magnificent Ambersons* I found myself in a position not unusual under the studio system— caught in the middle between the director and the front office. The editor had to mediate.

Ambersons was an extreme case because the director-writer, Orson Welles, was in Rio doing a never-finished film at this crucial time. The previews were disastrous, and it was up to me to cut. Problem was, it was long and kind of slow and a victim of its timing. We were shooting when Pearl Harbor hit. When the film was released we were six months into the war, the country was all revved up, its mood against a long, elegant film about turn-of-the-century rich people.

I'd be the first to admit that Welles' original *Ambersons* was better than what was on the screen. But there's no way of reconstituting it, as happened recently with *Lawrence of Arabia*, because it was the custom then that when you lifted a sequence from a film you put it in a vault, kept it for six months after release and then junked it for the silver in it. That's what happened to *The Magnificent Ambersons*, so I'm afraid we'll never see it as Orson shot it.

Turkey Time

"Having started with a sow's ear,
we wound up with a silk sow's ear."

ROBERT ALDRICH:
I'm sorry to say that *The Legend of Lylah Clare*, about a film director played by Peter Finch who tries to recreate a star he once loved in the image of Kim Novak, was a disaster, and none of it was Kim's fault. Audiences didn't understand the picture. I tried to make everything explicit, but it wasn't clear enough.

❏

WOODY ALLEN:
The best film I ever did, really, was *Stardust Memories*. It was my least popular film. That may automatically mean it was my best film.

❏

EVE ARDEN:
Warner Brothers decided to make a movie of *Our Miss Brooks*, and Al Lewis and I were co-producers. We used the original TV cast and added a millionaire with a yacht, played by Don Porter, who hired Miss Brooks to tutor his "rich brat son," whom she tamed completely, of course. Unfortunately, the movie was released after one the studio had done with Liberace [*Sincerely Yours*] to cash in on *his* popular TV show. That turned out to be a disaster and Warners promptly tossed us right after him, giving us no publicity or support of any kind.

❏

RICHARD ARLEN:
Early in my career I was offered the lead in *Vengeance of the Deep*. The only reason was the thing was going to be shot in Hawaii and it called for

the hero to do several scenes swimming in shark-infested waters. No stunt man was assigned to the picture, and I grabbed the job because here right away I figured was my chance to become a star. There were sharks in the water, all right, but I was a good and lucky swimmer.

Vengeance was an awful picture. One critic said the water scenes were interesting, but when the actors got on dry land, they emitted an odor worse than the sharks killed in the picture. He intimated that the actors, not the sharks, should have been shot. The thing played in St. Paul, and my father saw it. He came running out to Hollywood to see me, and he said, "Is this going to be your vocation?"

❑

FRED ASTAIRE:

I found that my next [film] would be *Belle of New York*, the one I had avoided back in 1946 by retiring (briefly). It never did get off the ground although plenty of money and pains were spent on it.

For some reason, I liked making it, probably because Vera-Ellen and I had some interesting dance ideas to keep us busy. One trick we hoped would prove effective was dancing on air and this above all failed to register. Phyllis [his wife] went to the sneak preview and overheard a remark from some lady seated behind her, as she watched me walking on air: "Well, how silly can you get?" I knew then how we stood. The critics loathed the film.

I was on *Belle* for eight months, beating my brains out, and all I got out of it was—a fortune. There's one thing about having a flop movie at a major studio that has it all over a stage flop. You do get paid.

❑

KIM BASINGER:

I needed, and this is a pun on itself, the exposure [in *Playboy*]. As soon as the layout appeared, three very big directors checked in. Blake Edwards came back with a firm offer first, so I took it. *The Man Who Loved Women* didn't make a dime, and it was a pretty sorry movie, but it was amazing to get the comedic aspect of my life on the map. I'd do *Playboy* over tomorrow morning.

❑

RALPH BELLAMY:

Oh, that was unfortunate. *Lady in a Jam*. I liked [director] Gregory La Cava, but he only had about half a script, with a big cast including Irene Dunne and Patric Knowles. We went on location to Phoenix, Arizona, and shot a couple of things that didn't make a lot of sense. We were told not to pay too much attention to the script. We wandered around Phoenix for over two weeks while Greg, a writer and a cutter tried to put a story together. He was trying to do what Leo McCarey had done with *The Awful Truth* but didn't do very well with it.

❑

PANDRO S. BERMAN:

I remember the night Katharine Hepburn, George Cukor and I attended the preview of a picture we made together called *Sylvia Scarlett*. The film was actually responsible for the emergence of Cary Grant as a comedy star —he was wonderful.

The picture itself was completely wrong for audiences. They didn't know what it was all about. The preview in Huntington Park was such a disaster I think there were about 12 or 14 people left in the theater when it ended! We went up to George Cukor's house and sat around and moaned and groaned, not knowing what to do. And I'll never forget this, because George will never let me forget about it: He says that he and Katharine said to me, "Now don't you worry, because we're going to make up to you for this. We're going to make another picture for you for free!"

George says I replied, "Oh, my God, no! Anything but that!"

❑

KAREN BLACK:

The Day of the Locust: I had the worst time on that movie that I've ever had. It was a film made without a compassionate eye, and that's why it wasn't a success. You tend to move away from a film like that.

❑

HENRY BLANKE:

Satan Met a Lady was the worst picture I ever made. Jack Warner ribbed me about it for years afterward. We decided that we could redo the story so soon after the original [1931's *The Maltese Falcon*] by switching certain elements around and turning the whole thing into a comedy. But, as I later found out, the director [William Dieterle] had no flair for that kind of film and it failed.

❑

CHARLES BRONSON:

Guns for San Sebastian? One of the worst films I ever made. I got along well with [director] Henri Verneuil and the failure of the film was not his

THE BLUE BIRD (20th Century-Fox, 1976), with Ava Gardner. Director: George Cukor.

fault. The script was difficult—there were six scriptwriters, each different from the others. With [Anthony] Quinn, they were responsible for the failure.

❏

ELLEN BURSTYN:

Every time a movie fails, the studios want to blame the movie instead of themselves.

Because *Resurrection* is a film about a contemporary faith healer, Universal had the bright idea that the film would appeal to the Midwest and the Bible belt, so they decided to test-market it in the rural areas before exposing it to the cynical New York critics. They designed an ad campaign that made it look like a horror film, so they got the horror film buffs instead of the people who would like to have a beautiful spiritual experience. The picture died.

Meanwhile, the national magazine critics were raving. So they took a chance on New York and Los Angeles and got great reviews. But instead of taking out full-page quote ads, they printed black squares with one-word quotes that revealed nothing about the movie and people in cities like Seattle and Boston still don't know what the film was about. Now Universal has gotten discouraged and given up. I feel devastated. If the film got bad reviews or people didn't like it, I'd fold my tent and go away. But everyone who sees the film seems to love it. I've had people come up to me and say, "This movie changed my life!"

The studio says it's not working. When the critics love it and the public loves it, what's not working? It's their stupid ad campaign that's not working. It's that commercial Hollywood mentality that's not working. And they'd rather drag a good film down with them than be proved wrong.

❏

TRUMAN CAPOTE:

Bogart thought *Beat the Devil* would flop. Oh, he said he thought it was funny, but he claimed it was too esoteric. And I guess he was right. Besides, John Huston and I were the only ones who really liked it.

When he and Bogart first called me, wanting me to rewrite the wreck of a screenplay for a mystery film, I was in Cannes. I'd just finished a screenplay for an Italian film, and when I saw what they had, I thought that instead of a straight melodrama, it should be sort of a takeoff on all those movies Bogart and Sydney Greenstreet used to make.

When we were shooting, I would write the next day's script the night before. It was typed the next morning by the secretaries, and nobody knew what was going on except me. Sometimes, not even me. I did it that way because I didn't think they'd like my ideas or go along with them.

❏

JOHN CASSAVETES:

I like *The Killing of a Chinese Bookie*. It's obviously a picture you don't easily relate to your own life. The difference between this film and my previous ones is that they were more along the theme of family existence. But it's interesting to me to see how other people live in our society, to look at them and ask myself: Why do they do it? And how do they do it? Without trying to explain. The picture says something to me: that we might sell anything mindlessly—even our own lives.

We only played five or six theaters, and it did not do well in any of them. I suppose that audiences generally disliked the film and didn't want to see it. That doesn't disappoint me. The nice thing about a film is that it's *there*. This one is a section of life that I think there's a place for.

❏

JOANNA CASSIDY:

I loved *1969*, but it just came and went. It didn't bother me. I knew it was a small movie that would pick up a small following, develop a cult, or not. I've had films that I thought would be huge successes and they haven't been.

❏

CYD CHARISSE:

I tore all the ligaments in my knee. It took me two tough months to recover. From the immobilizing, my leg muscles had virtually atrophied, and I'd have to sit there, swinging my legs with weights attached to them. But Joe Pasternak wanted me in *The Kissing Bandit*, so I swung those weighted legs as hard as I could.

I shouldn't have bothered, because the picture was a disaster. It started with a bad script and went downhill fast. Strangely, Tony [Martin, her husband] was supposed to do that film, but he left the studio about then and Frank Sinatra was hired. I did a number called "Dance of Fire" with Ricardo Montalban and Ann Miller. They inserted it in the film after the shooting was finished to help save it. It was the only decent thing in it—but it still didn't save it.

❏

JAMES COCO:

In *Tell Me That You Love Me, Junie Moon*, I played a character who was maybe gay, maybe not. It was a mixed-up movie! They had Liza Minnelli

NEW YORK NEW YORK (United Artists, 1977), with Liza Minnelli, Larry Kert. Director: Martin Scorsese.

playing a girl who lost her looks through scarring. Now, Liza's a talent, but next to Streisand she's homely . . . so she didn't lose much. Then Ken Howard played a dumb blond jock who's losing his mind or something—and very convincingly. Robert Moore was the gay guy. Only, they had him somehow "convert" to being a heterosexual, and Bobby could not make it believable.

And Otto Preminger, our director, was lording it over everyone; I think he felt the script was nowhere as interesting as the characters. Only thing, the characters never had anything to *do*. I don't even think *Junie Moon* did well in Poland.

❑

PAT COLBERT:

I think Bill Cosby's disapproval of *Leonard Part 6* was with the editing. The script was very, very funny, and while shooting the movie everyone was very happy and elated when it came to the dailies. The discontent came later. Somehow, something got lost between the script and the screen. I noticed some things got cut out that would have been hilarious . . . but I guess they had reasons for that.

As far as Bill supposedly saying he'd pay to have the film destroyed, if he said anything at all, it may have been that he'd like to get it back and re-edit it.

❑

JOAN COLLINS:

I was finally playing a role I really liked and had fun with: witty, outrageous Angela in *Rally 'Round the Flag, Boys*.

Fox had originally wanted Jayne Mansfield to play the sexy young vamp who tries to seduce Paul Newman away from Joanne Woodward. Joanne and Paul insisted to director Leo McCarey that Mansfield was far too tarty and obvious, and that the character should have a touch of class and an impish sense of humor; they persuaded him to cast me.

The picture was a happy experience—although, like most of my movies, neither a critical nor financial success. McCarey was a famous and beloved director. But now he was old, seemingly feeble and had lost the zest and comic flair which had flourished in the thirties. Why did I always seem to work with famed directors who were on their last legs careerwise?

❑

JACKIE COOPER:

I did two things for Mike Frankovich at Columbia that nobody saw. I acted in a six-million-dollar-picture, *The Love Machine*, and I directed a two-million-dollar-picture, *Stand Up and Be Counted*, and nobody saw either one of them.

☐

BILL COSBY:

Leonard Part 6: I don't want [fans] to go see this movie thinking that I'm saying to them this is a great picture or that this is even a good picture.

☐

JOAN CRAWFORD:

Everyone was out of their collective minds when they made *Ice Follies of 1939*. Me, Jimmy Stewart and Lew Ayres as skaters—preposterous. A dancer I am, a skater I'm not; whenever I couldn't fake it or use a double I skated on my ankles. Nice music and costumes, and the Shipstad Ice Follies people helped, but it was a catastrophe. The public thought so, too.

☐

BING CROSBY:

Top O' the Morning did nothing. I don't really know why. I had Barry Fitzgerald again, the tunes were by Jimmy Van Heusen and Johnny Burke and Ann Blyth couldn't have been a more appealing leading lady. I began to worry a bit.

☐

BETTE DAVIS:

I'd like to burn all the movies made during my first five years in Hollywood. They were such terrible scripts—with such terribly written dialogue—with the exception of the [George] Arliss films and one or two others. But such nonsense as *Parachute Jumper* and *Housewife* and *Front Page Woman*, thank God they're not too often shown. And yet I can't say I really regret those five years of trash. Those years helped me to learn my business.

☐

BETTE DAVIS:

I had been off the screen for one year before I returned and made *Winter Meeting*. The director, Bretaigne Windust, had the idea that he would introduce a brand-new Bette Davis to the screen. He would have been smarter to leave the old one alone. The story of a New England poetess and a naval

THE WIZ (Universal, 1978), with Diana Ross. Director: Sidney Lumet.

officer who plans to become a priest was a badly drawn triangle in which the church spire was the apex. It was a dreary film and hardly a triumphant return.

❏

BETTE DAVIS:

Oh, that was a terrible movie—*Beyond the Forest*. It didn't have to be; primarily it was terrible because they insisted on putting me in it. I was too old for the part, and I was temperamentally wrong. I mean, I don't think you can believe for a moment that if I was so determined to get to Chicago I wouldn't just have upped and gone years ago. I told them they should have put Virginia Mayo in the part—she would have been great.

It was all a great pity, because the book is very good and could have made a marvelous movie. But they turned it all inside out. The husband, for instance, is supposed to look like Eugene Pallette and be an absolute monster. So what do they do? They cast Joseph Cotten, who is so nice and sweet why should any wife be so desperate to get away from him? And then the lover —that big boring blond actor, what's he called? [David Brian]—was so dull you could understand it even less.

The one interesting thing [director King] Vidor did in the film was to make the train into her lover; that bit was good. But all the rest was just crazy.

❑

DORIS DAY:

Marty [Melcher, her husband] became terribly concerned over the box-office failures of *Tunnel of Love* and *It Happened to Jane*. I had dropped out of the top 10, which meant nothing to me but everything to Marty, primarily because it would have an effect on my earnings. I pointed out to Marty that if he hadn't hustled me into doing these films, if he had waited, I might have found good scripts that would have produced better results.

❑

GLORIA DE HAVEN:

Bog was never finished. I was never paid. They released it incomplete and then disappeared—like a floating crap game. I have a copy of it. The monster looks like a huge chicken.

❑

MYRNA DELL:

I've done 60 movies but if you want to talk turkey, two that I made more than 30 years apart stand out—for very different reasons.

After my five years at RKO, one of the first pictures I did was a little gem over at Republic in 1949 called *Rose of the Yukon*. I had the lead—the saloon owner, as usual—but it's a film I never saw and never want to see.

The script wasn't bad, and the people on it were fun. Steve Brodie, who had been at RKO with me, was my leading man. But I looked so terrible in it that I've tried to block it out ever since. I was about 20 pounds overweight, my hair was badly cut; I was just miserable on it.

We shot the whole thing in seven days. Our director, George Blair, said, "I think this is going to be a seven-bottle picture"—meaning that's how many bottles of booze it would take us to get through it. We were working in parkas in the San Fernando Valley in 100-degree weather. I was bathed in perspiration.

My only consolation is that, as it turned out, I was far from alone in not wanting to see the picture. Recently, though, at a film festival I attended someone thrust a poster at me from *Rose of the Yukon*. There was that puffy face, that hair and even, I swear, that sweat. I shrieked, "How revolting!"

I'd rather be old and thin than young and fat!

Buddy Buddy came out in 1982. This is how it came about. I was at a party in Hollywood and talking to the great director Billy Wilder. Jokingly, I said, "I've worked with just about everyone in Hollywood except Billy Wilder."

So he said, "I'm getting this picture *Buddy Buddy* together for Jack Lemmon and Walter Matthau. I have a part in it that you could do, Myrna.

Frankly, it isn't a great part, but if you want it, it's yours." I accepted on the spot.

I hadn't been working much by then, and I soon learned that my Screen Actors Guild membership had lapsed. They wanted five or six hundred dollars for me to rejoin. It wouldn't have paid me, so regretfully I phoned Billy's office and told his secretary I wouldn't be able to do the picture, and why. In a little while, she called me back and said, "They've just raised your salary. You're in."

I told her, "You just tell Billy I love him."

When the film was completed, it ran a little long, so my already smallish role was cut quite a bit. Mostly, what you wound up seeing was the back of my head. Still, my columnist friend Robert Osborne of *The Hollywood Reporter* gave me a very nice write-up, though *Buddy Buddy* was a turkey— "Cruddy Cruddy" quipped one critic.

I bumped into Billy Wilder again right after this and, very surprised, he exclaimed, "Everyone hated my movie but they loved you!"

❑

CECIL B. DeMILLE:

Four Frightened People was one of my few spectacular failures at the boxoffice. It fell about $500 short of returning its cost. It comforts me to think that this was due in part to the final [insensitive] editing; but perhaps it should also confirm me in sticking to my own last and leaving whimsical stories to directors like Preston Sturges or Leo McCarey or Billy Wilder who are so good at that type of picture.

❑

JONATHAN DEMME:

When did I realize *Citizens Band* was in trouble at the boxoffice? The day it opened, in a 700-theater regional break. Nobody went. It hadn't been tested at all. The studio, the producers, *everybody* was so convinced that it was going to be an unqualified success because of the CB mania of the day that their attitude was: "Get it together and get it out there and get ready to count the receipts." And nobody went.

❑

WILLIAM DIETERLE:

The work on the film *Concealment* [released as *The Secret Bride*] was not very pleasant. The script was bad. I could not refuse it for contractual reasons. Why Barbara Stanwyck did not reject the script, as Bette Davis would have done, I can only guess. She was not happy at Warners and wanted to

MOMENT BY MOMENT (Universal, 1978), with Lily Tomlin, John Travolta. Director: Jane Wagner.

get out of her contract as quickly as possible. Of all the films I directed, *Concealment* is the picture I don't like to think about any more.

❏

BARRY DILLER:

What movies am I most proud of [as Paramount Pictures' chairman and C.E.O.]? Of course, *Won Ton Ton, the Dog Who Saved Hollywood.*

You know, when Diane Von Furstenberg and I got together, she used that awful movie as the symbol of our lives. We really began going out when we went to the preview of *Won Ton Ton* together. We were on our way to the country, so we dropped by this theater in the suburbs of New Jersey. It was in some mall somewhere. Just awful. The audience was full of motion picture exhibitor types and their fur-clad wives. And there was Diane, watching *Won Ton Ton* with all these *furs*. She survived it, but she still says to me, "Well, you know, you can always go back to *Won Ton Ton*."

It was the lowest. To watch that movie in that huge theater with those people was an awful experience.

❏

STANLEY DONEN:

Surprise Package. The critics sat on their hands. The audience stayed home. The film's very poor because it's a bad script. It does have a lot of wonderful jokes by Harry Kurnitz, though, and Noel Coward's terrific in it.

Noel accompanied me to the preview, which went miserably except for his scenes. As we were walking out of the theater, a lady came right up to him and said, "Mr. Coward, you were absolutely wonderful; you stole the movie." He turned to her and very dryly replied, "My dear, believe me, it was petty larceny."

❏

KIRK DOUGLAS:

I think *Ace in the Hole* is one of Billy Wilder's best pictures. It was a hit in the rest of the world, but it wasn't doing well in the United States, so they changed the title to *The Big Carnival.*

I think the reason it wasn't successful here was the newspapers. The unfavorable reviews of this movie about an unscrupulous newspaper reporter—based on a true incident, the Floyd Collins case, where a reporter actually kept a man down in a mine—were written by newspaper reporters. Critics love to criticize, but they don't like being criticized. Also, Billy Wilder was saying to Mr. and Mrs. Average, "This is you, the people who stop and stare at accidents."

❏

RICHARD DREYFUSS:

The Big Fix, The Competition and *Whose Life Is It Anyway?*—I felt humiliated. I felt that, after three failures, *I* was a failure.

❏

DAPHNE du MAURIER:

I felt the performances of both Alec Guinness and Bette Davis were bad [in *The Scapegoat*]. I wanted her to play the role I had devised with zest and vitality but she had neither. I was so disappointed with her I can't even remember if I met her. I've just blanked the whole thing out. It was a disaster.

❏

PHILIP DUNNE:

I didn't like the assignment—to write the screenplay of *Forever Amber.* I thought the book was trash. Even the name "Amber" would have been an

SEXTETTE (Crown International, 1978), with George Raft, Mae West. Director: Ken Hughes.

impossibility in the 17th century—and probably that of her lover, "Bruce," too. I wrote the script—or rather re-wrote it (they already had a script as trashy as the book)—as a favor to Darryl Zanuck, our boss. My heart was never in it, and that may be one reason why the picture didn't make a fortune.

Originally, I wanted to take a satirical approach to the material, kid the pants off it, which seemed to me the only way we might avoid disaster. But Darryl said no, he didn't buy a comedy.

Amber had suffered from a false start, with a wooden director from silent days, John M. Stahl, and a miscast Peggy Cummins as Amber and Vincent Price as Charles II. This added much to the cost. I thought the new version I wrote with Ring Lardner, Jr., much better, and director Otto Preminger a great improvement on Stahl, ditto Linda Darnell on Cummins and George Sanders on Price (it wasn't Vincent's fault—he was just miscast).

The book was worthless. Its success was based on its supposed gaminess, and that meant we were doubly vulnerable to censorship. I had no objections to the final casting, even though Linda Darnell was not too convincing as an Englishwoman, nor Cornel Wilde as an Englishman. I got along poorly with Stahl, and very well with Preminger. The trick with Otto, who was generally reputed to have been a writer-eating monster, was not to let him get the upper hand. Neither Ring nor I ever did.

The finished film? I didn't bother to see it for nearly a year, when my wife, out of sheer curiosity, finally twisted my arm. Afterward, she felt as I did: so what? Not really worth the effort. I'd go as far as to say that, having started with a sow's ear, we wound up with a *silk* sow's ear; the best that could be done with the damn thing. I haven't seen it since, which classes it with the two other pictures of mine I've never bothered to see. Why didn't it make money? Because it promised sex and didn't deliver. The censors saw to that.

It was a chore. I did my best. I was glad to be free of it and go to work on something I liked: *The Late George Apley* and *The Ghost and Mrs. Muir*.

❑

ALLAN DWAN:

Surrender—oh, boy. That's another one with those two great actors in it—John Carroll and Vera Hruba Ralston. I can't tell you what I think about it—it should be buried some place! Republic Pictures President Herbert J. Yates loaned Carroll some money and that was one way of getting it back— give him a lot of work.

❑

HECTOR ELIZONDO:

Private Resort I'd like to see burned to ashes, never to rise again. I don't think it was ever released to theaters, only to videocassette, cable and local TV.

It has not one redeeming value. It's exploitive, cut badly, says nothing about the human condition. It speaks to cucumber-heads, to the lowest common denominator, and was nothing like what I expected it to be. My role, a debonair jewel thief, was supposed to be a wonderful character, but it never evolved that way. All the producer wanted to do was make money and he didn't care how.

There was a script that was to be totally rewritten, but the director involved with the rewrites was fired just before I started the movie. The producer promised up and down that the picture would be shaped the way he originally talked about. Of course, it never happened.

I prefer to think I never did it, that the movie never happened. That fantasy soothes my aching soul about that lousy picture. I never saw it, but I did see enough of it when I was dubbing some dialogue afterward.

I've been told that my crazy scenes were the best part of the movie. Maybe one day I'll suffer through it to watch myself get beaten up, but I doubt it. Except for your book, I hope never to mention IT ever again!

❑

A LITTLE NIGHT MUSIC (New World, 1978), with Len Cariou, Elizabeth Taylor, Laurence Guittard, Diana Rigg. Director: Harold Prince.

ROBERT EVANS:

Players—the film was not only a disappointment but a disaster on every level.

DOUGLAS FAIRBANKS, JR.:

Green Hell is better forgotten. At the time, the students of Harvard University voted it the worst picture of the year [1940]. I was inclined to agree with them. It was a bad picture, an absolute turkey!

SALLY FIELD:

I'm going door-to-door selling this movie [*Kiss Me Goodbye*], and literally nobody has known it was out there. I'd go out to promote—on talk shows, in interviews—and I'd come up empty-handed. Because nobody knew anything about the movie. The studio hadn't really screened it early enough for the press. There's some sort of psychology to that, but it beats me.

See, I thought we had a nice little movie; I thought I could hold my head up, stick my face out there, and I tried, God knows. I tried talking to

Fox, but maybe I don't have enough power. Maybe I still play "the girl" too much. Maybe I couldn't put my feet down. All I know is, they just didn't want to screen the movie. They told me it wasn't a critics' picture, that early negative reviews would hurt us. I don't buy that. I believe in not hedging your bets. I say, "Don't play games, don't manipulate. You got a movie, let 'em see it. Let 'em throw a pie at it, or love it, but don't hide it from them." The folks at Fox weren't real happy with me.

Whatever their plan, it obviously wasn't good for the movie.

❏

HENRY FONDA:

The pictures I've loved, others—save for a very small club—haven't. *The Ox-Bow Incident*, for instance, was, in my opinion, one of the finer pictures, but at the boxoffice one of the finer fade-outs.

❏

JANE FONDA:

After *Rollover* flopped in 1981, I spent three and a half years trying to sort things out. I've always sort of played on the edge in my personal life, but careerwise I don't take risks. When I pour my heart into something and it fails, it hurts. I kept asking myself, where did I go wrong? What happened, and why?

❏

HARRISON FORD:

Hanover Street? Look, at that stage in my career I'd made *American Graffiti, Star Wars, Heroes* and *Force Ten from Navarone* and I'd yet to kiss a girl or be involved romantically. Then along came this love story and I agreed to do it, expecting that the script, which I didn't have total faith in, would be changed as we went along.

Well, it wasn't. And making that film was not a happy experience for me. I haven't seen it so I don't like talking about it. I keep saying that if 50 people tell me they liked it, then I may change my mind and see it. But so far I'm just up to 18 so there's no immediate danger of that happening.

❏

JOHN FORD:

The Fugitive, with Henry Fonda, came out the way I wanted it—that's why it's one of my favorite pictures—to me, it was perfect. It wasn't popular. The critics got at it, and evidently it had no appeal to the public, but I was very proud of my work. There are some things in it that I've seen repeated a million times in other pictures and on television—so at least it had that effect. It had a lot of damn good photography—with those black and white shadows. We had a good cameraman, Gabriel Figueroa, and we'd *wait* for the light—instead of the way it is nowadays where regardless of the light, you shoot.

❏

SALLY FORREST:

Although Howard Hughes was running RKO at the time, he had little to do with the film *Son of Sinbad* except for ordering the women's costumes to be cut down or up—anything for a scantier style.

The only problems I recall while we were shooting were caused by Dale Robertson's pronounced Oklahoma accent, which was thought incongruous in our Old Bagdad setting. In the long run, it turned out to be a great plus, adding to the satirical approach of the production. The film could have been much better, though. It was shot for the 3-D process which might have been fun, but by the time it came out the craze was over.

Son of Sinbad was not a success because Mr. Hughes held it back from release. There was a great censorship outcry over the film—this was the mid-1950s, remember. Strangely enough, despite everything going on elsewhere in the picture (which featured Lili St. Cyr, the top stripper of the day), my relatively mild little dance number was the one the censors wanted cut. But Mr. Hughes refused to do it. Finally, about a year later, *Sinbad* was released—too late. At any rate, it was fun to make. Vincent Price and Dale were joys to work with.

❏

CLARK GABLE:

Adventure is lousy. I could tell because I had to work so hard. A picture that is going to turn out well is easy to do. It just seems to flow along by itself. Everybody on it has a swell time. Nobody strains because he doesn't have to. And it all comes out fine. When you are on a bad picture you find everybody working like hell, and nothing comes of it.

❏

BEVERLY GARLAND:

Stark Fear? Oh, Christ! That was the worst picture I ever made in my life! We made that in Oklahoma. The head of the drama department of a college there wanted to do a movie. So he and his wife wrote this script, and they directed it, and it was a disaster. I went to see it in Westwood, and when

I asked someone how long it was going to run, he said, "It's been here two days, and there've been three people in the theater. It'll never run again." It was just abominable.

❑

TAY GARNETT:

My marriage was followed by two additional catastrophes: a pair of highly forgettable films entitled *Bad Company*, which it was, and *Prestige*, which it wasn't.

❑

TERI GARR:

The Escape Artist played in theaters for two minutes before going directly into airplanes. You have to pay $500 to see it now.

❑

GREER GARSON:

I don't mean that I am ungrateful to MGM. They couldn't help *Adventure* any more than I could. They, too, were disappointed that it didn't come out the way everyone hoped. I would be ungrateful indeed if I didn't appreciate the fine pictures Louis B. Mayer has given me. I have had *Madame Curie, Random Harvest, Blossoms in the Dust, Mrs. Miniver, Goodbye, Mr. Chips* and *Valley of Decision*—all fine and successful pictures.

So let's forget *Adventure*—it wasn't any better for Clark Gable than it was for me. It was as bad for him as *Parnell*.

The rumors that we did not hit it off? Nonsense. I like Clark very much. If the right story came along for both of us, of course we would make another film together.

❑

RICHARD GERE:

No one can say how well a film will do. At the preview of *Yanks*, everyone said it would be a smash. It bombed. At the preview of *An Officer and a Gentleman*, everyone said it was a nice little program movie but nothing much. It went through the roof.

❑

MENAHEM GOLAN:

Bolero with Bo Derek—completely insufferable and a total embarrassment.

FEDORA (United Artists, 1979), with Frances Sternhagen, Marthe Keller. Director: Billy Wilder.

❑

SAMUEL GOLDWYN:

Dodsworth—f'Chrissake. Don't talk to me about *Dodsworth*. I lost my goddamn shirt. I'm not saying it wasn't a fine picture. It was a *great* picture, but nobody wanted to see it. In *droves*.

❑

SAMUEL GOLDWYN:

We Live Again with Anna Sten—the public stayed away in droves.

❑

ELLIOTT GOULD:

I'm really crazy about *The Long Goodbye*, and I'm really upset it didn't do well. We wanted a big, big hit, and I needed that to re-establish myself as a commercial entity. They made the mistake of opening it in Los Angeles and it was destroyed in the papers. It's an art film that should have been opened in New York. [Director Robert] Altman pulled it, redesigned it and reopened it in New York, and we got something back for it.

❏

BETTY GRABLE:

That Lady in Ermine—audiences stayed away like it was *That Lady with Leprosy*. I thought, "Well, there's one consolation. It can't possibly get any worse than this." Then along came *The Beautiful Blonde from Bashful Bend* which was even rottener.

❏

LEE GRANT:

I called my agent and said I needed to make some money—and do you know what they got for me? *The Swarm*, where my big line was "The bees are coming!"

❏

GRAHAM GREENE:

The only film made from one of my books that I really liked was one very few other people seemed to have liked, *Confidential Agent*.

❏

JOAN HACKETT:

I was in this tacky movie in Zurich called *The Assignment* [release title: *Assignment to Kill*] after I finished *The Group* and nobody ever saw it but I got a trip to Zurich. I drowned in a bathtub in it and the ads read "Dominique was always in hot water—but now she was in over her head!"

❏

GENE HACKMAN:

When *Conversation* and *Scarecrow* did poorly at the boxoffice, I got depressed. I just said the hell with it, and decided to take whatever was offered. So I did things like *Domino Principle* and *March or Die*. Now they haunt you when you do interviews.

❏

ARSENIO HALL:

Eddie [Murphy] had this one movie [*Best Defense*] that bombed and which he really wasn't responsible for, but everybody blamed him anyway. And he was saying to me, "I don't know how to deal with this, a flop. I don't want to go back to where I'm from." That's how I get to feeling sometimes. You have a couple shows in a row where you're not funny or a couple bad monologues and you start thinking, "I've lost it." I don't want to go back to where I started.

❏

ED HARRIS:

I know films like *A Flash of Green* and *Walker* mean absolutely nothing to the industry. They think, "Why is the guy doing these films?" Well, because they are important both as films and for me to do as a person.

❏

REX HARRISON:

An instance of sloppy professional judgment came when I weakly agreed with my agent to go to Madrid to make a film called *The Happy Thieves*, with Rita Hayworth. My agent said something about "getting the money while I could," and instead of sacking him, as I would have done in other years, I fell in with his suggestion. Rita was an old-time friend, desperately shy and uncertain of herself, although she had worked for Columbia for many years and kept that studio going. Rita was absolutely beautiful, the film was absolute rubbish, so bad that the press was asked to stay away and not to review it— a fairly unusual request. I don't think anyone did see it, luckily.

❏

HENRY HATHAWAY:

We shot a bit of *Woman Obsessed* up at Big Bear Lake and I even found the tree where Henry Fonda and Sylvia Sidney had carved their initials [in *The Trail of the Lonesome Pine*]. But management dictated we shoot mostly on the stages because they were practically empty by now [1959]. And Susie Hayward, always feisty, turned to me one day and yelled, "I can't think of a single reason why I'm making this damned thing, can you?" I couldn't either except to finish off my contract.

❏

HOWARD HAWKS:

Sam Goldwyn said, "There has to be some way you would remake *Ball of Fire*." I said, "Probably could. For $25,000 a week I probably could." He said, "You made a deal." Then he wouldn't let me do anything. One of the things that I said was, "I don't have to use that—what's her name?—Mayo." Not only did I have to use Virginia Mayo, but he had her go to work and run all the scenes that Barbara Stanwyck did [in the first version]. Well, she wasn't

Stanwyck. It was completely awful. *A Song is Born* was the most unpleasant picture I've ever known.

◻

GOLDIE HAWN:

Making *Swing Shift* was a major disappointment. Nothing ever happens in that movie. I expected the movie to be funny and it didn't turn out that way. But oh my gosh, I met Kurt [Russell, her boyfriend] on that picture. Are you kidding, I'd do that again!

◻

GOLDIE HAWN:

Overboard was the biggest disappointment I've ever had. It's like having a big fish on the end of your line and then you bring it up and it just kind of wiggles off your hook.

◻

KATHARINE HEPBURN:

Grace Quigley, which I thought was a brilliant idea, was really a very poor idea. You can't make people have any sense about death. It really depresses them. But that film's failure was not discouraging. When you've lived as long as I have you've had a lot of flops, many of which were your own fault. And I suppose that to make sympathetic a woman who bumps off a taxi driver and his two children because he asked for her shoe is not accepted. The critics roasted it. I've never been a critics favorite.

◻

JOHN MICHAEL HAYES:

I had moved to Metro and they were going to cast *It's a Dog's Life* with all the top stars in cameo roles. But then it was decided in New York they should put all young people in it—because they had an acting school. We had, finally, just two old character actors, Edmund Gwenn and Dean Jagger.

It got fantastic reviews when it opened. The dog narrates the whole thing with a wry, wonderful sense of humor. But they put it out on a double feature with a picture which was not a good one, *King's Thief*, with Edmund Purdom. When that died, mine went down with it. I think, probably, the two pictures I've gotten the finest reviews on were *Dog's Life* and *Rear Window*—*Peyton Place* maybe third.

◻

HEAVEN'S GATE (United Artists, 1980), with Isabelle Huppert, Kris Kristofferson. Director: Michael Cimino.

ALFRED HITCHCOCK:

The Trouble with Harry needed special handling. It wouldn't have failed commercially if the people in the distribution organization had known what to do with the picture; but it got into the assembly line and that was that. It was shot in autumn for the contrapuntal use of beauty against the sordidness and muddiness of death.

Harry is very personal to me because it involves my own sense of humor about the macabre. It has in it my favorite line of all the pictures I ever made: when Teddy Gwenn is pulling the body by the legs like a wheelbarrow, and the spinster comes up and says, "What seems to be the trouble, Captain?"

❑

BOB HOPE:

Some Like It Hot [called *Rhythm Romance* on television] was the rock-bottom point in my movie career. After that one, there was no place to go but up. For years afterward, Bing [Crosby] wouldn't let me forget it. Whenever I started to give him the needle about something, he came back with something like, "By the way, can you come over to the house tonight, Bob? We're going to barbecue some steaks and then all sit down and watch *Some Like It Hot*." That shut me up in a hurry.

❑

DENNIS HOPPER:

It was unbelievable to win the Venice Film Festival with *The Last Movie* and come back and have [Universal] tell you they're not going to distribute the movie. Why? Because I made fun of the audience and I didn't end the picture with a dramatic ending. They wanted me to kill him at the end and make a linear film out of it, and I refused.

And [Lew] Wasserman, head of MCA and Universal Pictures, said, "O.K., if you're not going to re-edit it, then we're going to distribute it for two weeks in New York, two weeks in L.A. and two days in San Francisco and then we'll shelve it." And they did what they said they were going to do.

❑

A. E. HOTCHNER:

A screenplay of mine that did get made into a film was *Adventures of a Young Man*, from Ernest Hemingway's short stories.

He died while we were making it, and I wish for the sake of his memory it had been better but it was produced by Jerry Wald, a 20th Century-Fox hustler whose benchmark was expediency. Robert Redford, relatively unknown, was dying to do the part [of Nick Adams], and I strenuously urged

Jerry to test him, but instead he cast Richard Beymer who was tied to a cheap 20th contract and was as wrong as wrong could be.

Marty Ritt is a friend, a very gifted director, but this was simply not his kind of film, especially the large segment that had to be shot in Verona, Italy. Marty's life is centered around attending Santa Anita racetrack, and he likes to eat dinner at six-thirty, neither of which he could do in Verona. He also had no patience for auditioning Italian actresses for a pivotal role, and instead accommodatingly cast Susan Strasberg whose contrived Italian accent fell somewhere between Sophia Loren and Goldie Hawn.

❑

JOHN HOUSEMAN:

At RKO, *The Company She Keeps* had made its sleazy way onto the sound stages under the direction of John Cromwell, who despised the project almost as much as I did. Of the two dozen films I have produced this is the only one of which I am totally ashamed—it is silly and bad—absurd soap opera.

❑

ROCK HUDSON:

The failure of *Avalanche* and *Darling Lili*? Well, one movie had a glacier, the other had Julie Andrews. I guess the audience couldn't tell the difference.

❑

JOHN HUSTON:

Some of my pictures I don't care for, but *The Unforgiven* is the only one I actually dislike. Despite some good performances, the overall tone is bombastic and over-inflated. Everybody in it is larger than life. I watched it on television one night recently, and after about half a reel I had to turn the damned thing off. I couldn't bear it.

❑

JOHN HUSTON:

The Red Badge of Courage got beautiful reviews, but nobody went to see it, not a soul. And then some critic in London had seen the picture at a suburban theater where it was running on a double bill and said this is a masterpiece and why haven't we been allowed to see this great picture? So he had a showing with all the London critics. Metro took an ad out with all the critics signing it and it opened in the West End . . . and nobody came.

❑

MARTHA HYER:

I was in Hawaii on vacation when a call came through from the producer of *War, Italian Style* in Rome, who said it would be perfect for me. Only one catch: he couldn't send me a script. *That* should have warned me to have no part of it; but, when I learned that Buster Keaton, always one of my idols, would be in it, I decided to take a chance.

But it was a horrible mistake! I flew to Los Angeles, long enough to pack. Then I flew off to Rome. They gave me the script at my hotel. I read it through and—well, I cried! Yes, I really wept to think I'd gone to all that trouble and had travelled so far to do something so ghastly. Naturally, I wanted out. I told them, "I can't play this girl. I don't want to be a Nazi!"

So they told me not to worry, they'd doctor the script. But, of course, they never did. You know, I've never seen that picture and I never will.

❏

ELIA KAZAN:

America, America, in my opinion the best film I ever made, was a total flop—total catastrophe. Nobody went to see the goddamn thing, and I think it's a beautiful film. *A Face in the Crowd* was a flop. *Baby Doll* was a flop. *Viva Zapata!* was a total financial catastrophe.

❏

HOWARD KEEL:

Jupiter's Darling—that was a perfect example of my problem at MGM. I'd do very well in pictures like *Annie Get Your Gun, Show Boat* and *Seven Brides for Seven Brothers*, but between those good vehicles I'd be stuck in lemons which would kill all the momentum I had going for me.

❏

MARTHE KELLER:

The failure of *Fedora* didn't touch my professional life at all. It was a Billy Wilder movie—his responsibility, not mine. I tried the best I could. If a film is not a success, it hurts; but I do not take it serious. My son [nine-year-old Alexandre] and my work I take serious.

❏

GENE KELLY:

Living in a Big Way was not supposed to have any musical numbers in it.

I came out of the service and they had nothing for me to make. L. B.

PENNIES FROM HEAVEN (MGM, 1981), with Steve Martin. Director: Herbert Ross.

Mayer said, "I have a girl here at the studio who is going to be a great star, Marie McDonald. We have some great writers, Charlie Lederer and Harry Kurnitz, and a great director, Gregory La Cava. They are coming to New York to meet you."

I was working out dancing in the Charles Weidman Studio to get back in shape after the service. "They can't wait. They are going to fly in and tell you the idea of the story because it is not written." So they came to New York. And we all looked blankly at each other. This array of talent. We had no story but we went out and started to make a picture.

To be as kind as possible, it was a bomb. When Metro saw it, they said to me, "Could you do a few numbers to sort of pep it up?" I did three, one of them with Marie McDonald even. Since we built a house in the story, I thought we should do a number with the kids in the park. Then I did one where I danced with a big statue and a dog. We sneaked them in with the retakes and that's how they come to be in the picture. The picture still bombed.

Those last two numbers are among my favorites. About three people have seen them, and two of us are in this room now.

◻

EVELYN KEYES:

I made a picture with David Niven, *Enchantment*, for Sam Goldwyn. Columbia had actually loaned me to him—to justify the salary I was getting,

252

I suspect. Sam had tried to borrow me before without success. He professed to be one of my greatest fans, booming out every time he saw me anyplace, "Ahhh! My favorite actress!"

David was under contract to him. So was Teresa Wright, also in the picture. It covered a wide time span, ranging from David as a very young man to a very old one. I played the niece of his former young love. Farley Granger played my paramour. The picture flopped. Sam stopped calling me his favorite actress. He had to blame somebody, and he owned all the other players.

❑

KRIS KRISTOFFERSON:

I chose to do *Convoy* right after completing *A Star is Born*, though everyone advised me not to. Sue Mengers, my agent, told me I was a dummy if I accepted the role. But [director] Sam Peckinpah called to say he had a good script and was on the wagon. Since I was on the wagon, too, I thought we'd be a good influence on one another.

I really love working with Sam, but even my wife warned me: "It won't be easy with him in charge." Rita was right. It was hard work, and it seemed everything went wrong on the picture. I must have had brain damage to get involved with *Convoy*.

❑

JESSICA LANGE:

I'd rather forget *King Kong*. It made its money back but it wasn't well received, partly, I think, because it was over-publicized. I hate to see any movie fail, but really they should be left to word of mouth instead of being hyped up so much.

❑

REGINALD LeBORG:

The Flight That Disappeared was a quickie for [producer] Eddie Small that came out very good, but it had no stars. I liked the film because it had an idea. It was against war, you know, and against the atomic bomb, a fantasy about a flight from Los Angeles to Washington. During the flight, something happened and we didn't know whether it was a dream or real. Suddenly, the plane was higher and opened and everybody was out in the clouds. The film was an appeal against the atomic bomb and when the plane landed, the fellow who had the idea to bring some new test device threw it away and didn't go through with it. If the film had been on a big budget with stars and so forth, it would have been a fairly interesting picture. But it was a quickie and the second half of a bill and never did anything. It had a few good reviews, but that's about all.

◻

JANET LEIGH:

Safari was a stinker and I was lonely out there [in Kenya]. Vic Mature was such a scaredy cat. One day I was in the river and he was supposed to dive in and rescue me. The assistant director told him the natives had been firing shots up and down the river to scare the crocodiles off. Vic merely said, "What if one of them is deaf?" and that got me out of the water in a hurry.

◻

JACK LEMMON:

We were sitting together at a screening of *Alex and the Gypsy*. After it was over, Walter [Matthau] said something I'd never heard anyone say to someone about a movie. I'd heard the remark made to an actor in a bad play. He turned to me and said, "Get out of it."

◻

MERVYN LeROY:

In 1946, I stepped in to reshoot much of *Desire Me*, which had been started by George Cukor. It starred Greer Garson and Robert Mitchum. They had a good cast but a rotten script that made absolutely no sense. I tried my best to make something out of it, but I failed, just as Cukor had failed. Both of us insisted that our names not appear on the screen, and so the picture came out without any director listed at all. It was a botch, and Cukor and I have always been happy we were anonymous when it was released. It was the only major film ever issued without a director's credit.

◻

JOAN LESLIE:

Born to Be Bad [1950] was not a hit with audiences but it was with me. I had a very good part and enjoyed doing it. During production, it was called *Bed of Roses* and was shot at RKO, which Howard Hughes had recently purchased.

In the story Joan Fontaine was after every man in sight, and as it opened I was engaged to rich flyer Zachary Scott. She eventually stole him from me, and in the ending we did first everything was sort of left up in the air. About two months after we shut down, we came back and shot the ending that went

JINXED (MGM/United Artists, 1982), with Bette Midler. Director: Don Siegel.

out to theaters in which Zachary returned to me. This was probably Mr. Hughes' doing. He was known for changing the endings of his films—sometimes several times!

Nicholas Ray, a very dramatic, dictatorial sort of fellow, directed. An example of his astute direction occurred when it came time for me to tell Joan off. Now, much of the time my character was not supposed to be aware that Joan was stealing my man. Joan was very insidious—oh, she'd advise him how to handle me, and to me she'd say things like, "Wear this veil, dear. It'll soften your face." Now comes our confrontation. I am to give it to her at last and feel that I should be the one to come off with total sympathy. But our director wants tears streaming down *Joan's* face as I berate her.

At first I told him, "I don't know if it should be done this way," and he replied, "Well, this is how we're doing it." He insisted I coarsen my voice and play the scene very strongly. I had always played gently spoken, sweet little girls, so I loved doing it. And it seemed to work.

Off camera, I wasn't quite sure what to expect with Joan. I mean, she was a big star and there was the well publicized feud with her sister, Olivia de Havilland. Then there was her role in *Born to Be Bad*—actresses have been known to live their parts. But she turned out to be fun and we got along fine. She had me to her house where I recall that I was Artur Rubinstein's dinner partner.

Howard Hughes never came near the studio while we were filming, but stayed in his office at the Samuel Goldwyn Studio. Not long after we finished the picture, he asked me to meet him there alone. He then told me he wanted me to sign an exclusive contract with RKO. But I had recently gotten free of my contract with Warner Brothers and didn't want to tie myself up again.

I can't help wondering what course my career would have taken if I had signed with Howard Hughes.

❑

VIVECA LINDFORS:

To the Victor opened and was a flop, in spite of all the money spent and all the fuss made. It was worthless that I was good in it, that my reviews were brilliant. It was still a flop. I went to an afternoon performance on Hollywood Boulevard. I sat among the audience in the balcony. I didn't understand the film. I hadn't understood it when I read the manuscript, either. At that time I had figured that "they" knew better than I. Now I knew that "they" did not. What was I doing in Hollywood?

❑

JOHN LITHGOW:

As for *Harry and the Hendersons*, I dislike talking about it in any way that portrays it as a failure. To me it's a wonderfully successful film; to hell with this phrase "box office."

❏

SIDNEY LUMET:

After I brought *The Hill* back from England, I sat down with Metro's head of sales and he told me, "I don't know what to do with your fucking picture"!

❏

SHIRLEY MacLAINE:

I don't make calculated career decisions. I do things I enjoy doing. God, *Cannonball Run II* was hardly even a movie. But I did it to work with all those guys again [Frank Sinatra, Dean Martin, etc.]. The process is one thing and the outcome another.

❏

GEORGE MAHARIS:

I made a movie called *Quick, Before It Melts*. You had to catch it quick, before it disappeared.

❏

JOHN LEE MAHIN:

I don't think [director] John Ford ever liked *The Horse Soldiers*. He never really got into the script. He never really applied himself to it. One day we were sitting around on his boat the Araner, and he said to me, "You know where we ought to make this picture?" "No," I said, "where?" "In Lourdes. It's going to take a miracle to pull it off." *The Horse Soldiers* wasn't a good picture. We barely got our costs back.

❏

NORMAN MAILER:

The Naked and the Dead was one of the worst movies ever made. If it had been just a little worse it would have come out the other end and been extraordinarily funny, a sort of pioneer classic of pop art, and film critics might have decided that it had a profound influence on the James Bonds. But the picture was finally not bad enough. Here and there the vestige of a serious

SWING SHIFT (Warner Brothers, 1984), with Goldie Hawn, Kurt Russell. Director: Jonathan Demme.

THE RAZOR'S EDGE (Columbia, 1984), with Bill Murray. Director: John Byrum.

attempt manifested itself, and so the picture never got through the tunnel at
all, it just expired in its own glop.

◻

DOROTHY MALONE:

I remember one called *Quantez*, with Fred MacMurray, that I did because
we were old friends and I thought it would be nice for auld lang syne. I
hated the script, but I knew he wanted me to do it, so I said O.K. The night
we previewed it, he said to me, "Why did you want to do a dog like this?"
So I confessed. I told him I did it just because he was keen on it. He roared.
"I hated it!" he said. "I did it just because I thought *you* wanted to do it!"

◻

ROUBEN MAMOULIAN:

I had just finished *The Gay Desperado* and was tired. My agent sent me
the script for *High, Wide and Handsome*, even after I had told him I was
against it. But they sent it anyway, asking me to read it—hoping that it would
interest me.

The stars were to be Gary Cooper and Irene Dunne. That appealed to
me; I'd never worked with them before. It was an interesting idea, but I knew
I had to rewrite the script. And then the combination of oil and music isn't
an easy one, as you can appreciate. To find a way in which I could get out
of doing it, I set them impossible conditions. Three days later, my agent called
me in New York to tell me that they'd agreed to everything I'd wanted!

It was a very rough picture to make, half dream, half reality. Some things
in it are good, but I don't feel that I succeeded. I don't think it is an organic
whole. [Randolph Scott wound up playing the male lead.]

◻

JAMES MASON:

One Way Street—I never encountered anyone who saw this film, other
than studio personnel. It must have been a left-over project from some previous régime, for you'd think that Universal would no longer have afforded
the floor space for this sort of pretentious melodrama, having recently struck
a rich seam of boxoffice gold which included Donald O'Connor and that
talking donkey, Ma and Pa Kettle and acres of "Tits and Sand." Not to mention
Abbott and Costello.

◻

WALTER MATTHAU:

Years ago I wrote, produced, directed and starred in an $80,000 movie titled *The Gangster Story*. It was so bad the world premiere was held at Loew's Newark with an admission price of 85 cents. The guys who put their money in it never got a cent back. But I'll say one thing for that movie. I co-starred with the world's greatest living actress. Her name is Carol Grace. She also happens to be my wife.

❏

MARILYN MAXWELL:

Paris Model—wasn't it dreadful? I owed Columbia a picture and that was the script they sent. I read it and told my agent no way! So I told him to hike my price up to some truly astronomical figure, thinking the studio would say forget it. So you can imagine how shocked I was when they said instead, okay. Well, I hated every moment the damn thing was in production and I always swore I'd never go to see it, but I got money for it like you would *not believe*. They never got it back in the theaters.

❏

JOEL McCREA:

I once had a picture called *Ramrod*, with a good story, and I tried to get Raoul Walsh to direct it. We couldn't get him from Warner Brothers. So Harry Sherman came up with André de Toth. Well, de Toth did the picture; there were long, stalling scenes where I'd stand there for a while, and Donald Crisp would say, "Well, what do you think, boy?" And I'd say, "Well, I'm gonna get Frank Ivy if it's the last thing I ever do ..." There was nothing I could do; the direction had to be more fluid.

Veronica Lake was the girl and she wasn't any good in it, either; they were married and de Toth loved her so. That was another difficult thing; when you work with the director's wife, this is for the birds. Because he's not gonna be tough with her, you know, or she'll kick his ass when he gets home at night. So you suffer through it with him. What are you gonna say? "Get me a new girl ...?" "What, my wife ...!" So *Ramrod* turned out to be a lousy picture.

❏

RODDY McDOWALL:

I was petrified when I made a film after being away from the screen for eight years. I came back to Hollywood in 1960 to make *The Subterraneans*. And I was only in my early thirties. *The Subterraneans* was supposedly going to be a big movie, but it bit the dust. It was wide screen and in color, and [cameraman] Joe Ruttenberg said, "CinemaScope is only good for photo-graphing snakes and cathedrals."

❑

ETHEL MERMAN:

Since I had a month with nothing to do before marrying [Ernest] Borg-nine, I accepted an offer from Ross Hunter who was producing *The Art of Love*. It was a featherweight comedy that sank like lead.

I played a madam. I had lots of gowns and some outrageous wigs, including a pistachio-colored one. On the wall of my office there was a photo of me in a feathered headpiece. That photo is about all that remains of that picture—except for an occasional disinterment for TV. When my friend Morty Sussman, who designs my clothes, was furnishing his new apartment, I de-cided it was just the touch his guest bathroom needed.

❑

RAY MILLAND:

I was once inveigled into a remake of *The Awful Truth* [*Let's Do It Again*, co-starring Jane Wyman], which turned out to be a fizzle of the worst kind, for which I still haven't been paid, and rightly so.

❑

VINCENTE MINNELLI:

I was very pleased the way *The Pirate* turned out. Judy [Garland] gave one of her best performances and the Cole Porter songs were excellent. Unfortunately, the merchandising on the film was bad, and it failed to go over when it was released.

❑

ROBERT MITCHUM:

After the preview of *Desire Me*, I sneaked out with my coat collar turned up. I didn't want to be recognized—angry ticket-buyers might have stoned me!

❑

DUDLEY MOORE:

I have had several films that may not have succeeded at the boxoffice or with critics, but *Six Weeks* was the one that really had no chance at all. I think it's really quite wonderful, and some of my music is in it, so it has rather a soft spot for me. We probably marketed the film rather irresponsibly.

THE HOTEL NEW HAMPSHIRE (Orion, 1984), with Nastassja Kinski, Rob Lowe, Jodie Foster.
Director: Tony Richardson.

RHINESTONE (20th Century-Fox, 1984), with Sylvester Stallone, Dolly Parton. Director: Bob
Clark.

We released it at Christmastime and never stopped to consider that people wouldn't want to spend the holidays going to films about a little girl having six weeks to live.

❑

MARY TYLER MOORE:

At Universal, they kept putting me in after-thought productions. "Oh, yes, let's do that movie."

One was a little disaster with Elvis Presley called *Change of Habit*. I played a nun. Elvis I found to be a teddy bear of a man, a very physical, loving person who hugged a lot. Also, a perfect gentleman. If you didn't watch yourself, he'd call you "ma'am." And I was in something they billed as an "optimistic comedy" [*What's So Bad About Feeling Good?*], with George Peppard, all about a bird with the miraculous ability to make everybody love everybody.

❑

BILL MURRAY:

Scrooged was a miserable gig. I had much more fun on *The Razor's Edge*, which made *no* money. But I got to go around the world and meet all kinds of people. On *Scrooged*, I was trapped on a dusty, smelly and smokey set in Hollywood for three-and-a-half months, having a lousy time by myself, and just coughing up blood from this fake snow that was falling all the time.

❑

JEAN NEGULESCO:

We made a picture in England which was quite bad, *The Forbidden Street*. The critics crucified us, so I wrote Darryl Zanuck: "I'm sorry, Darryl. I liked the cast, I liked the story, I thought I did my best. I promise I'll make it up to you somehow."

He replied: "Who the hell do you think you are, playing the hero like that? I okayed the picture, I bought the book, I okayed the cast, I saw the rushes and approved them. Sure, you made a mistake, but so did we. Don't try to be a hero, just don't do it again, that's all."

❑

PAUL NEWMAN:

On the fiasco of *A New Kind of Love* ... Joanne [Woodward, his wife] read the script and said, "Hey, this would be fun to do together. Read it." I read it and said, "Joanne, it's just a bunch of one-liners." And she said, "You son of a bitch. I've been carting your children around, taking care of them at the expense of my career, taking care of you and your house." And I said, "That is what I said. It's a terrific script. I can't think of anything I'd rather do." This is what is known as reciprocal trade agreement.

❏

OLIVIA NEWTON-JOHN:

Xanadu? I thought the musical numbers were great, but the dialogue left something to be desired. I knew that while we were shooting, but there wasn't much I could do. Then they changed the whole story midway through production, and that didn't help. Although *Xanadu* didn't do well in this country, it was very successful abroad.

❏

JACK NICHOLSON:

I co-wrote *Head*. Nobody ever saw that, man, but I saw it 158 million times. I loved it. Filmically, it's the best rock and roll movie ever made. I mean, it's anti-rock and roll. Has no form. Unique in structure, which is very hard to do in movies.

❏

DAVID NIVEN:

Soldiers Three, which I made at MGM in 1951, was a costume adventure picture. But it was so laughably bad that the very sparse audience thought it was a comedy. Humphrey Bogart told me, "Get outta town, kid. They gotta have time to forget that one."

❏

AL PACINO:

The flop of *Revolution*—I'm not wary about that sort of thing. I've made other movies that weren't successful and made as loud a noise on the way down.

❏

HERMES PAN:

There's a wonderful number in *Excuse My Dust*, a Red Skelton film. It's the turn of the century. In his mind, he sees a girl in a very old-fashioned dress. As she moves, the skirt comes off, the blouse comes off and she has on a completely different outfit. The music goes from rinky-tink to heavy blues and then it goes into reverse and the clothes come back and she ends as the demure little girl he was looking at to begin with. All this happens in his mind. Unfortunately, the film was a flop.

❑

GREGORY PECK:
I'm not sure it [*Moby Dick*] can be done at all. I saw both previous versions with John Barrymore, and they were perfectly awful, too.

❑

GREGORY PECK:
[Producer David O. Selznick] came up with a cash shortage. He had a commitment with me for $60,000, and he sold me to Warner Brothers for $150,000 for an independent William Cagney production called *Only the Valiant*, the worst picture I ever made. Also, I knew that it was a low-budget picture, and I had been doing fairly high-toned things. This was definitely a step in the wrong direction. What rankled me more than anything was that I played a cavalry man, and they didn't even make me a new cavalry suit. When I got into costume, I discovered Rod Cameron's name in my cavalry pants.

❑

ANTHONY PERKINS:
I've made more than my share of flops. The most frustrating one was probably *Green Mansions*. They sent two doubles to Brazil for Audrey Hepburn and me. Mine was bitten by a poisonous insect as he stepped off the plane and he was replaced by an assistant director. The whole thing was shot on Stage 24 at MGM. They even imported a South American tribe to Culver City to live on the backlot, that's how realistic *that* film was. Did you see it? It was pretty horrible.

❑

WALTER PIDGEON:
Years later, we brought the old girl [Mrs. Miniver] back to kill her off in *The Miniver Story*. She died at the boxoffice, too.

❑

VINCENT PRICE:
Green Hell is one of the 50 worst pictures ever made! There are lines in it that people still come up to me and quote. Joan Bennett played my

wife—and we never met! There was a scene where Alan Hale—playing a doctor—finds Joan on the floor of the jungle. In the story, she's been missing three weeks and she's wearing a beautiful gown and has two little smudges. Alan Hale leans over, listens to her breathing and announces: "It's all right, fellas, it's just a coma!" To top it all off, I get killed by being shot with 12 poisoned arrows!

❑

VERA RALSTON:

My worst film has to be *Angel on the Amazon*. It was unreal. I played a woman frozen in a state of eternal youth. I played my daughter who killed herself, and finally I was a doddering old woman of 70 after a shock released my aging process. I told them "It's unreal!" every chance I got, but they ignored me. And audiences ignored the film.

❑

BURT REYNOLDS:

I spent six months on *At Long Last Love*, a picture nobody saw. I enjoyed making it, I learned from it. I grew, but that's too much time out of my life.

❑

MARTIN RITT:

I saw a good, well made, serious movie last year [1988]. *Orphans*. It was really good. Know what it did? *Nothing*. I don't think it stayed open two weeks. Know what *Cocktail* did? Eighty million dollars. I'll settle for that.

❑

MARK ROBSON:

I made what I think is a very good film, *Bright Victory*. It was interesting because it provided a confrontation with the Negro problem. It was the story of a boy from the South, with the normal intolerance of people from that part of the United States, who acquired human perception after he was blinded. While I believe it was a disaster financially, it won the New York Critics' Award for Arthur Kennedy in the main role, and a lot of awards all around the world.

❑

HAROLD ROSSON:

I Take This Woman was with Spencer Tracy and Hedy Lamarr. So much footage was shot and thrown out and shot again before it finally hit theaters

A CHORUS LINE (Columbia, 1985), with Blane Savage, Jan Gan Boyd, Gregg Burge, Michelle Johnston, Audrey Landers, Vicki Frederick, Matt West, Yamil Borges, Pat McNamara, Nicole Fosse, Charles McGowan. Director: Richard Attenborough.

HOWARD THE DUCK (Universal, 1985), with Lea Thompson. Director: Willard Huyck.

that wags were calling it *I Re-Take This Woman*. As far as audiences were concerned, though, it was strictly *I Forsake This Woman*.

❏

MICKEY ROONEY:

I made *Quicksand* for $10,000. As a few hundred critics wrote, I sank in the stuff.

❏

MICKEY ROURKE:

The problem was, *Barfly* was released by Cannon. Those guys ought to go into the auto repair business. But everybody knew that going in. The irony was, only Cannon had the nerve to make the picture, but they didn't know how to release it. You get what you get.

I also think another problem was that *Barfly* was made for an intelligent audience, and that's where you cross the line, especially in this country, because everybody is so geared to watching a certain type of film, they're all getting brainwashed to a certain level of shit. I get a lot of scripts to read that are sure-thing big moneymakers, but I just couldn't get out of my trailer to do them.

❏

KURT RUSSELL:

The best thing that came out of *Swing Shift*, as far as I'm concerned, was my relationship with Goldie. I never felt it would be a great movie, and I didn't think it would do much business. But I did think it would be good to work with Goldie Hawn.

I didn't like *Swing Shift*. I didn't think it worked. I think I was largely responsible for that because I couldn't do anything with the role. It was a fun movie to do—it was funny—but it was not an earth-shattering experience workwise. So I was not surprised when *Swing Shift* did not do too well.

I'm glad I did the picture because there were a lot of people who did like it. But if I were to do it over again, and if I were to produce the picture, I'd hire a different actor.

❏

ROSALIND RUSSELL:

I'll match my flops with anyone's. For instance, *Mourning Becomes Electra* won me many awards, but not at the boxoffice. *The Guilt of Janet Ames* I rarely mention except in an inaudible whisper. And *The Casino Murder Case*

I don't mention even in a whisper. These pictures showed me not so much what to do, but what *not* to do. Failure has taught me more than successes.

❏

NATALIE SCHAFER:

I had a lovely time making *Forever Darling*, which starred Lucille Ball, Desi Arnaz and James Mason. I never knew it was a failure until recently— I thought all MGM pictures were successful then. Someone told me that James Mason called it the worst film he ever made. He made worse.

The shooting was very Noel Coward (even if the script wasn't). Lucy and our director, Alexander Hall, were ex-lovers and Louis Calhern, from whom I had been divorced for years, was also in the picture. We all used to lunch together and reminisce.

Now, just about everyone connected with *Forever Darling* is dead except me.

I always loved working with Lucy. I worked with her on television several times, including one of her classic half-hours in which I played a charm school proprietress who taught Lucy how to walk. I knew Lucy before she owned the studio [RKO], and when you know someone before they owned the studio that always gives you more in common to chat about.

Forever Darling was done at Hollywood's Motion Picture Center, where they shot *I Love Lucy*, and was distributed by Metro. Desi was the producer. Actors were treated so divinely then, everyone waiting on you, seeing that you rested. It was like that, really, at *all* the Hollywood studios in those years [the 1950s]. I just did an independent film, a little horror called *Beverley Hills Brats*. They picked me up at noon and brought me home at eight the next morning—I worked continuously. For our scenes we'd go to people's homes and I'd change costumes in their bathrooms. I even had to rewrite some of my part.

Forever Darling may not have been big at the boxoffice, but the company was delightful and, believe me, we actors were treated differently then.

❏

JOHN SCHLESINGER:

I've never been able to gauge the public's reaction to my films. The ones that were hits (*Midnight Cowboy, Darling*) took me totally by surprise as did the ones that were disasters (*The Day of the Locust, Honky Tonk Freeway*).

❏

MARTHA SCOTT:

When I Grow Up was made by Horizon Pictures, the company owned by John Huston and Sam Spiegel whose *African Queen* was released the same

ISHTAR (Columbia, 1986), with Dustin Hoffman, Warren Beatty. Director: Elaine May.

year [1952]. *When I Grow Up* is never mentioned in any of the articles or books on John Huston, and he was on the set often. It was a little gem, made in about four weeks, but it was put out with a batch of B pictures and got lost. Hardly anybody even bothered to review it. Now it seems to have disappeared altogether. It doesn't even turn up on TV.

❏

TOM SELLECK:
Three Men and a Baby tested well, but I had made other pictures that tested well and then didn't perform at the boxoffice. Preview audiences loved *High Road to China* but it didn't go through the roof. *Lassiter* opened strong, but it didn't have legs.

❏

DAVID O. SELZNICK:
There was at MGM in 1933 a horror that I produced called *Meet the Baron*, starring Jack Pearl. MGM had decided to capitalize on the popularity of radio stars, and at the suggestion of [producer] Harry Rapf, signed Ed Wynn and Jack Pearl. I have never been a devotee of radio comics. I had never heard either Wynn or Pearl on the radio. Rapf had been my benefactor in the early days at Metro, and so, when he appealed to me to take one of them over (he felt he could only handle one at a time), I agreed and he gave me Pearl. I made the picture with a loathing for it, and it was a terrible flop. I

learned then what I should have learned long before: never tackle a picture for which I had no enthusiasm.

❏

ROBERT SHAW:

All the good films I've been in have pretty well failed—*The Caretaker, The Birthday Party, The Luck of Ginger Coffey, The Hireling.* Whereas *Jaws* went through the roof, and now there's *Black Sunday* and *The Deep.*

❏

JOAN SHAWLEE:

The "audition" for *Prehistoric Women* was like a Marine obstacle course. First you had to grab a rope and swing through the outer office into the producer's office—and that broke me up to begin with. So I swung on the rope and fell into his office and picked myself up.

"Terrific," he said. "Now we have these hurdles over here." So I did that and passed the tests.

"Where's the script?" I asked. *Panting!* "What do I say?"

He said, "This is *prehistoric* times. They didn't even have the alphabet yet."

So he had me improvise a scene eating meat before a campfire and saying "Unga-chunga-lunga." Later on I got the script. Guess what the dialogue was like? "Unga-chunga-lunga."

They picked a gorgeous girl named Laurette Luez to play the leader of the women. Couldn't act to save herself. How is she going to do it, I thought. She can't even get by with "Unga-chunga-lunga." Well, she married the director, Gregg Tallas, the day before the picture started. So there was *no way* to be thrown off the thing. And the day it was completed she filed for divorce.

When I played Morey Amsterdam's wife, Pickles, on Dick Van Dyke's old TV show, Dick found out I had made this movie. And his favorite thing was to come running up to me. "Joan! Joan! Tonight! At nine o'clock! *Prehistoric Women!*" He knew it would just absolutely destroy me. Because I figured it would be gone, buried, no one would ever remind me.

❏

DON SIEGEL:

My greatest concern is what the public thinks about my films, and that's why I'm still so bitter about the way Universal sold *The Beguiled*, or rather threw it away. It's the best picture I ever made and Clint [Eastwood] ever made, and because it didn't do what we wanted it to do, Clint and I had to make *Dirty Harry* and I had to make *Charley Varrick.*

That's the way it's gone, and I suppose I shouldn't grumble. I'm doing far better than I ever thought I would, but before I die, I would like to do two things. I would like to make a hilarious comedy that knocks people out of their seats with laughter, and an enduring love story that brings tears to everybody's eyes. I would like to do that and go on making more failures like *The Beguiled*.

❑

FRANK SINATRA:

I used to joke with Jack Benny about it. He had *The Horn Blows at Midnight* and I had *The Kissing Bandit*. Was *Kissing Bandit* the nadir of my career? Hell, it was the nadir of *anybody's* career.

❑

SYLVESTER STALLONE:

I'm not intellectual about it. I'm very emotional. When I see a script, I just jump right into it. I thought I was doing *Romancing the Stone*, not *Rhinestone*!

❑

BARBARA STANWYCK:

Cattle Queen of Montana? Dreadful! Awful! You wonder how such a thing could happen. The answer is simply that I made a horrible mistake. One gets taken in by what seems like a good idea and a sort of rough, temporary screenplay, and you sign to do the picture without ever having seen a completed script. Within one week after the start of shooting, everybody on the set knows that the thing is just not jelling. But by that time, you're hooked. So you do your best and you privately hope that nobody goes to see it.

❑

MARY STEENBURGEN:

Of course I was disappointed by the failure of *Sex Comedy*. But I still think that it's a sweet little movie. I really believe that the critics were gunning for Woody Allen at the time. They compared *Sex Comedy* to his earlier films and decided that it was lacking. If the film had been made by an unknown, it would have been very well received, I think. It's just a shame that the critics have tried to stereotype Woody.

❑

HARRY AND THE HENDERSONS (Universal, 1987), with John Lithgow, Melinda Dillon, Margaret Langrick, Joshua Ruddy. Director: William Dear.

FRANCES STERNHAGEN:

I loved *Outland*, with Sean Connery, but it was overlooked, mostly because it came out at just about the same time as *Raiders of the Lost Ark*.

❏

PAUL SYLBERT:

The effort to pacify and enravish the addicted public led the panicked *savoir mourir* Joseph E. Levine to save *The Steagle* by removing all that was Jewish, "bizarre, subjective, etc.", from it, and the effect, as usual, was the extinguishing of the film's few lights. He would have been well advised to heed Arnold Schoenberg's warning to the traveler in art: "The middle road is the only one that does not lead to Rome."

The reviews were, to say the least, mixed. Finally, even loyal Dick Benjamin made the public admission that he thought the film flopped because it was "too intelligent." He was wrong. It flopped because neither the film as it was, nor the producers, as it were, were intelligent enough. What would have resulted from the film being released as it was made will never be known; but there is no doubt whatever about the results in the case of Levine's version.

❏

SPENCER TRACY:

My worst film? There are several candidates. But I remember that when I saw a little doozey I did called *Malaya*, I thought, "Well, the jig's up. I wonder if I'm too old to get back in the Navy?"

Fortunately, very few others saw it. At the time, someone told me about a story in one of the trade publications concerning a theater somewhere that booked it, and one night nobody, absolutely *nobody*, showed up to see it! Yep, *Malaya* had to be the bottom of the barrel.

❏

JOHN TRAVOLTA:

Suddenly it's very hard for me to do just any play or movie. [The much publicized failure of] *Moment by Moment* proved that. I thought I was going to get away with doing a little art film that wouldn't cost very much, that no one would pay much attention to. Then I slowly realized, "God, if I get this much focus on a film I couldn't get away with doing a play somewhere!"

❏

KATHLEEN TURNER:

Was I disappointed about the failure of *The Man with Two Brains*? No, because there isn't much that I can do about it. Essentially, my work is done when my last scene is shot. If I thought there were scenes I'd copped out on, then I would be anxious when the film opened. I've had my satisfaction.

❑

LANA TURNER:

I used to go on bended knee to the front office and say, *please* give me a decent story. I'll work for nothing! So what happens? Last time I begged for a good story they gave me *The Prodigal*.

Why is it that after so many turkeys I still maintained my position at the boxoffice and people will still pay to see me? What could I be if I had decent pictures?

❑

LANA TURNER:

The Prodigal played two weeks in Pomona. It shoulda played Disneyland.

❑

LIV ULLMANN:

I did *Lost Horizon* and they gave me a fantastic [Hollywood] house to live in, but you couldn't even see the toilets because they were discreetly disguised as chairs. As soon as the film was over, I went back to Sweden to make another film for [Ingmar] Bergman on a deserted island with no drinking water, where you had to walk almost a mile to an outside toilet. It was more fulfilling than doing *Lost Horizon*.

❑

TRISH VAN DEVERE:

I liked *One is a Lonely Number* because it was a simple, truthful movie, an attempt to explore a young woman's life and how she copes. I was in every frame of that movie and I was scared to death and I worked my fanny off because I was so aware of the responsibility. But MGM put it out and took it back so fast that practically no one saw it. My friend Elaine called me up one day and said, "Oh, it got super reviews" and then she called up and said, "I can't find the damn movie anywhere!"

❑

LEONARD PART 6 (Columbia, 1987), with Bill Cosby. Director: Paul Weiland.

GREAT BALLS OF FIRE (Orion, 1989), with Dennis Quaid, Alec Baldwin. Director: Jim McBride.

HAL WALLIS:

About Mrs. Leslie starred Shirley Booth and that very fine actor Robert Ryan. It was the story of a middle-aged woman who gives up on life until she meets and falls in love with the right middle-aged man. Bob and Shirley played their roles very sensitively under Daniel Mann's direction, but for some reason the public didn't buy it. It failed at the boxoffice and Shirley did little film work after that.

❏

JACK L. WARNER:

Once and only once I was a guest on one of Jack Benny's CBS shows several years after we starred him in one of our worst turkeys, *The Horn Blows at Midnight*. Although our bookkeepers were still in shock after their red-ink bath, Benny saw some humor in his flopperoo, and suggested talking about it on the show, like this:

> BENNY: Mr. Warner, you yourself told me that the theater made money when *The Horn Blows at Midnight* was shown in Hollywood.
>
> WARNER: That's because we rented out the balcony as a trailer camp.
>
> BENNY: Mr. Warner, you can't put all the blame on me. When you did that picture, you made one mistake.
>
> WARNER: I know. We put film in the camera.

❏

HARRY WARREN:

Ever since I'd been in Hollywood I'd been deploring the feeble scripts of most of the musicals I had done, even though they had resulted in lots of hit songs. I loved the script of *Yolanda and the Thief*, and we all thought we would come up with a winner.

But fantasy is the hardest thing to put on the screen; seeing it in your mind's eye when you read it and then making it come alive is terribly difficult. The end result was less than what we aimed for, but I still think the picture is charming, and it's the kind of project that really interests me as a composer.

❏

WILLIAM A. WELLMAN:

Track of the Cat is a picture I wish to God I'd never made. For seven years I'd looked for a story that I could do — and this sounds silly—in black and white in color.

And I found it in *Track of the Cat*. The cattle were either black or black and white. The snow was white, the house was sort of white. If I shot a scene with the fir trees, I'd shoot the shadowy side so they were black. The only color in the whole picture was the red hunting coat that Robert Mitchum had and a yellow scarf that one of the girls had. Now, I didn't tell it to anybody. I didn't tell it to my wife. I told it to Bill Clothier, who was my cameraman.

After, Bill and I went in to see the thing. And when it was all over, we both cried. It was so beautiful and so unusual. Jack Warner saw it—the whole gang. They never noticed it. It was released. Nobody saw it. No one paid any attention to it. It was just a dream that went up like a bubble had burst. It just broke my heart. And Bill did a great job on it—got no mention as a photographer, nothing. It was a big flop.

❑

GEORGE WELLS:

When we previewed *Angels in the Outfield* in Westwood one night we had the best sneak preview in history. A real smash. The studio was getting ready to do a sequel of some kind, as I remember. Then the picture was released and fell flat on its face. It might have been the combination of fantasy and baseball—two subjects which have never been boxoffice.

❑

RICHARD WIDMARK:

Oh, God! *Slattery's Hurricane*—that's one we made three times. We were constantly doing retakes. It was so bad that [Darryl F.] Zanuck couldn't figure out what to do with it. He finally decided to *flip* it. He did a very complicated cutting thing. He started it at the end and we wound up at the beginning.

❑

BILLY WILDER:

Fedora only cost $4,000,000, a B movie price today [1979], and it did extremely well in France and quite well in Germany. The thing that makes me miserable is that a picture that shows a small profit is regarded as a washout. A picture that makes its money back, keeps people employed, adds to the stature of the studio, is of no interest to them. In their eyes, it's a failure.

❑

BILLY WILDER:

I should have been more daring [on *The Private Life of Sherlock Holmes*], but, unfortunately, the son of Conan Doyle was there. I wanted to make Holmes a homosexual. That's why he is on dope.

Look, we have been freed now from the Breen Office or the Johnson Office or that stupid thing. In many respects, it's terrifying because now any idiot and any pornographer can do anything. But for the ones who are a little bit discriminating, who do it delicately, a grand new thing has opened. But that was after *Private Life*. The saddest thing about the film is that it was a waste of a year and a half of my life.

When you get to be my age, you say, "Shit, if I just had the time back that I wasted on pictures that were failures." But I'm not ashamed of it. There are many pictures I wish I could scratch out, but this I'm not ashamed of. It was just a failure. It just did not work.

❑

TREAT WILLIAMS:

I don't really have much to say [to interviewers]. It's not that I'm secretive or shy or anything like that, but I just don't see the point in talking to lots of people about myself. It doesn't help the film. And if you don't believe me, remember that Jack Nicholson was on the cover of dozens of magazines and did scores of interviews but still people didn't go to see *The Postman Always Rings Twice*.

❑

JANE WYMAN:

I made two pictures but I had bad luck because they both came at the end of cycles.

Stage Fright, which I did in England for Hitchcock, came at the end of the suspense-drama cycle. We had to re-dub everything because Michael Wilding mumbled all the way through it and you couldn't understand a word he said. By the time it came out, that kind of movie was dead.

Then I did *Miracle in the Rain*. I hate to bring up my own work, honey, but what a wonderful movie! By the time we got that one out, Van Johnson and I weren't so big, and Warners was already spending all its money promoting *Giant* so it never got any attention.

Bibliography/Additional Sources

Books

Adamson, Joe. *Byron Haskin*. Metuchen, N.J.: Scarecrow Press, 1984

Agan, Patrick. *Robert De Niro: The Man, the Myth and the Movies*. London: Robert Hale, 1989

Aherne, Brian. *A Proper Job*. Boston: Houghton, Mifflin, 1969

Arden, Eve. *Three Phases of Eve*. New York: St. Martin's Press, 1985

Arnaz, Desi. *A Book*. New York: William Morrow, 1976

Astaire, Fred. *Steps in Time*. New York: Harper & Brothers, 1959

Atkins, Irene Kahn. *Henry Koster*. Metuchen, N.J.: Scarecrow Press, 1987

Baker, Carroll. *Baby Doll*. New York: Arbor House, 1983

Baker, Fred, with Ross Firestone. *Movie People*. New York: Lancer, 1973

Bankhead, Tallulah. *Tallulah*. New York: Harper & Brothers, 1952

Barris, Chuck. *Confessions of a Dangerous Mind*. New York: St. Martin's Press, 1984

Basinger, Jeanine. *The It's a Wonderful Life Book*. New York: Alfred A. Knopf, 1986

Behlmer, Rudy, ed. *Memo from David O. Selznick*. New York: Viking Press, 1972

Bennett, Joan, and Lois Kibbee. *The Bennett Playbill*. New York: Holt, Rinehart and Winston, 1970

Berg, A. Scott. *Goldwyn*. New York: Alfred A. Knopf, 1989

Bergman, Ingrid, and Alan Burgess. *Ingrid Bergman: My Story*. New York: Delacorte, 1980

Black, Shirley Temple. *Child Star*. New York: McGraw-Hill, 1988

Bogdanovich, Peter. *Allan Dwan: The Last Pioneer*. New York: Praeger, 1971

Bogdanovich, Peter. *The Cinema of Alfred Hitchcock*. New York: The Museum of Modern Art Film Library/Doubleday, 1963

Bowers, Ronald. *The Selznick Players*. South Brunswick, N.J.: A.S. Barnes, 1976

Bradford, Sarah. *Princess Grace*. New York: Stein and Day, 1984

Brady, John. *The Craft of the Screenwriter*. New York: Touchstone, 1982

Braun, Eric. *Deborah Kerr*. London: W.H. Allen, 1977

Capra, Frank. *The Name Above the Title*. New York: Macmillan, 1971

Carpozi, Jr., George. *Vince Edwards*. New York: Belmont Books, 1962

Carey, Gary. *Cukor & Co*. New York: The Museum of Modern Art, 1971

Casper, Joseph Andrew. *Stanley Donen*. Metuchen, N.J.: Scarecrow Press, 1983

Cassini, Oleg. *In My Own Fashion*. New York: Simon and Schuster, 1987

Castle, William. *Step Right Up!* New York: G.P. Putnam's Sons, 1976

Chaplin, Charles. *My Autobiography*. New York: Simon and Schuster, 1964

Chierichetti, David. *Hollywood Director*. New York: Curtis Books, 1973

Christian, Linda. *Linda*. New York: Dell, 1962

Collins, Joan. *Past Imperfect*. New York: Simon and Schuster, 1984

Cooper, Jackie, with Dick Kleiner. *Please Don't Eat My Dog*. New York: William Morrow, 1981

Coslow, Sam. *Cocktails for Two*. New Rochelle, N.Y.: Arlington House, 1977

Cotten, Joseph. *Vanity Will Get You Somewhere*. San Francisco: Mercury House, 1987

Crawford, Joan, with Jane Kesner Ardmore. *A Portrait of Joan*. Garden City, N.Y.: Doubleday, 1962

Davis, Bette. *The Lonely Life*. New York: G.P. Putnam's Sons, 1962

Davis, Bette, with Michael Herskowitz. *This 'n That*. New York: G.P. Putnam's Sons, 1987
DeMille, Cecil B. *The Autobiography of Cecil B. DeMille*. Englewood Cliffs, N.J.: Prentice-Hall, 1959
Dietrich, Marlene. *Marlene*. New York: Grove Press, 1989
Dmytryk, Edward. *It's a Hell of a Life But Not a Bad Living*. New York: Times Books, 1978
Douglas, Kirk. *The Ragman's Son*. New York: Simon and Schuster, 1988
Druxman, Michael B. *Make It Again, Sam*. Cranbury, N.J.: A.S. Barnes, 1975
Druxman, Michael B. *Merv*. New York: Award Books, 1976
Dunne, Philip. *Take Two*. New York: McGraw-Hill, 1980
Durgnat, Raymond. *Jean Renoir*. Berkeley-Los Angeles: University of California Press, 1974
Fairbanks, Jr., Douglas. *The Salad Days*. New York: Doubleday, 1988
Fisher, Eddie. *Eddie: My Life, My Loves*. New York: Harper & Row, 1981
Fonda, Henry, with Howard Teichmann. *Fonda: My Life*. New York: New American Library, 1981
Ford, Dan. *Pappy: The Life of John Ford*. Englewood Cliffs, N.J.: Prentice-Hall, 1979
Fontaine, Joan. *No Bed of Roses*. New York: William Morrow, 1978
Freedland, Michael. *Gregory Peck*. New York: William Morrow, 1980
Garnett, Tay, with Fredda Dudley Balling. *Light Your Torches and Pull Up Your Tights*. New Rochelle, N.Y.: Arlington House, 1973
Gehman, Richard. *Bogart*. New York: Fawcett Gold Medal, 1965
Geist, Kenneth L. *Pictures Will Talk*. New York: Scribner's, 1978
Gish, Lillian, with Ann Pinchot. *Lillian Gish: The Movies, Mr. Griffith and Me*. Englewood Cliffs, N.J.: Prentice-Hall, 1969
Goodman, Ezra. *The Fifty-Year Decline and Fall of Hollywood*. New York: Simon and Schuster, 1961
Gottesman, Ronald, ed. *Focus on Citizen Kane*. Englewood Cliffs, N.J.: Prentice-Hall, 1971
Graham, Sheilah. *Hollywood Revisited*. New York: St. Martin's Press, 1984
Griffin, Merv, with Peter Barsocchini. *From Where I Sit: Merv Griffin's Book of People*. New York: Arbor House, 1982
Gussow, Mel. *Don't Say Yes Until I Finish Talking*. Garden City, N.Y.: Doubleday, 1971
Hanna, David. *Ava: A Portrait of a Star*. New York: G.P. Putnam's Sons, 1960
Harrison, Rex. *Rex*. New York: William Morrow, 1975
Head, Edith, and Paddy Calistro. *Edith Head's Hollywood*. New York: E.P. Dutton, 1983
Henreid, Paul, with Julius Fast. *Ladies' Man*. New York: St. Martin's Press, 1984
Higham, Charles, and Joel Greenberg. *The Celluloid Muse*. London: Angus and Robertson, 1969
Higham, Charles. *Celebrity Circus*. New York: Delacorte, 1979
Higham, Charles, and Roy Moseley. *Cary Grant: The Lonely Heart*. San Diego, Calif.: Harcourt Brace Jovanovich, 1989
Hill, James. *Rita Hayworth: A Memoir*. New York: Simon and Schuster, 1983
Hirschhorn, Clive. *The Films of James Mason*. Secaucus, N.J.: Citadel Press, 1977
Hope, Bob, and Bob Thomas. *The Road to Hollywood*. Garden City, N.Y.: Doubleday, 1977
Hotchner, A.E. *Choice People*. New York: William Morrow, 1984
Hotchner, A.E. *Doris Day: Her Story*. New York: William Morrow, 1976
Hotchner, A.E. *Sophia: Living and Loving*. New York: William Morrow, 1979
Houseman, John. *Front & Center*. New York: Simon and Schuster, 1979
Huston, John. *An Open Book*. New York: Alfred A. Knopf, 1980
Jessel, George, with John Austin. *The World I Live In*. Chicago: Henry Regnery, 1975
Josefsberg, Milt. *The Jack Benny Show*. New Rochelle, N.Y.: Arlington House, 1977
Kaminsky, Stuart M. *Don Siegel: Director*. New York: Curtis Books, 1974
Kazan, Elia. *Elia Kazan: A Life*. New York: Alfred A. Knopf, 1988
Keyes, Evelyn. *Scarlett O'Hara's Younger Sister*. Secaucus, N.J.: Lyle Stuart, 1977
Kobal, John. *Gotta Sing Gotta Dance*. London: Hamlyn, 1970
Kobal, John. *People Will Talk*. New York: Alfred A. Knopf, 1985
Kotsilibas-Davis, James, and Myrna Loy. *Myrna Loy: Being and Becoming*. New York: Alfred A. Knopf, 1987
Lahr, John. *Notes on a Cowardly Lion*. New York: Alfred A. Knopf, 1969
Lake, Veronica, with Donald Bain. *Veronica*. London: W.H. Allen, 1969
Lambert, Gavin. *On Cukor*. New York: G.P. Putnam's Sons, 1972
Leigh, Janet. *There Really Was a Hollywood*. Garden City, N.Y.: Doubleday, 1984

Lerner, Alan Jay. *The Street Where I Live*. New York: Norton, 1978

LeRoy, Mervyn, with Dick Kleiner. *Mervyn LeRoy: Take One*. New York: Hawthorn, 1974

Lewis, Arthur H. *It Was Fun While It Lasted*. New York: Trident Press, 1973

Lewis, Robert. *Slings and Arrows*. New York: Stein and Day, 1984

Lillie, Beatrice. *Every Other Inch a Lady*. Garden City, N.Y.: Doubleday, 1972

Lindfors, Viveca. *Viveka . . . Viveca*. New York: Everest House, 1981

Linet, Beverly. *Star-Crossed*. New York: G.P. Putnam's Sons, 1986

Logan, Joshua. *Movie Stars, Real People and Me*. New York: Delacorte, 1978

Loos, Anita. *Kiss Hollywood Good-by*. New York: Viking Press, 1974

Madsen, Axel. *William Wyler*. New York: Thomas Y. Crowell, 1973

Maltin, Leonard, ed. *The Real Stars*. New York: Curtis Books, n.d.

Marshall, J.D. *Blueprint on Babylon*. Tempe, Ariz.: Phoenix House, 1978

Martin, Tony, and Cyd Charisse. *The Two of Us*. New York: Mason/Charter, 1976

Marx, Groucho. *The Groucho Phile*. New York: Bobbs-Merrill, 1976

Marx, Samuel. *Mayer and Thalberg*. New York: Random House, 1975

Mast, Gerald. *Howard Hawks, Storyteller*. New York: Oxford University Press, 1982

McClelland, Doug. *Blackface to Blacklist*. Metuchen, N.J.: Scarecrow Press, 1987

McClelland, Doug. *The Unkindest Cuts*. South Brunswick, N.J.: A.S. Barnes, 1972

Merman, Ethel, with George Eells. *Merman*. New York: Simon and Schuster, 1978

Merrill, Robert, with Robert Saffron. *Between Acts*. New York: McGraw-Hill, 1976

Meyer, William R. *Warner Brothers Directors*. New Rochelle, N.Y.: Arlington House, 1978

Milland, Ray. *Wide-Eyed in Babylon*. New York: William Morrow, 1974

Miller, Ann, with Norma Lee Browning. *Miller's High Life*. Garden City, N.Y.: Doubleday, 1972

Minnelli, Vincente, with Hector Arce. *I Remember It Well*. Garden City, N.Y.: Doubleday, 1974

Morley, Sheridan. *Katharine Hepburn*. London: Pavilion Books, 1984

Morley, Sheridan. *Tales from the Hollywood Raj*. New York: Viking Press, 1983

Murphy, George, with Victor Lasky. *"Say . . . Didn't You Used to Be George Murphy?"* New York: Bartholomew House, 1970

Neal, Patricia, with Richard DeNeut. *As I Am*. New York: Simon and Schuster, 1988

Negulesco, Jean. *Things I Did . . . and Things I Think I Did*. New York: Linden Press, 1984

Netter, Susan. *Paul Newman & Joanne Woodward*. New York: PaperJacks, 1989

Newquist, Roy. *Conversations with Joan Crawford*. Secaucus, N.J.: Citadel Press, 1980

Niven, David. *The Moon's a Balloon*. New York: G.P. Putnam's Sons, 1972

Oppenheimer, George. *The View from the Sixties*. New York: David McKay, 1966

Palmer, Lilli. *Change Lobsters—and Dance*. New York: Macmillan, 1975

Parish, James Robert, and Don E. Stanke. *The Swashbucklers*. New Rochelle, N.Y.: Arlington House, 1976

Parish, James Robert. *The Jeanette MacDonald Story*. New York: Mason/Charter, 1976

Parish, James Robert. *The Paramount Pretties*. New Rochelle, N.Y.: Arlington House, 1972

Parish, James Robert, with Gregory W. Mank and Don E. Stanke. *The Hollywood Beauties*. New Rochelle, N.Y.: Arlington House, 1978

Pasternak, Joe, with David Chandler. *Easy the Hard Way*. New York: G.P. Putnam's Sons, 1956

Pickford, Mary. *Sunshine and Shadow*. Garden City, N.Y.: Doubleday, 1955

Powell, Jane. *The Girl Next Door . . . And How She Grew*. New York: William Morrow, 1988

Pratley, Gerald. *The Cinema of Otto Preminger*. London-New York: A.S. Barnes, 1971

Preminger, Otto. *Preminger*. New York: Doubleday, 1977

Quirk, Lawrence J. *Norma: The Story of Norma Shearer*. New York: St. Martin's Press, 1988

Radner, Gilda. *It's Always Something*. New York: Simon and Schuster, 1989

Reagan, Ronald, with Richard G. Hubler. *Where's the Rest of Me?* New York: Duell, Sloan and Pearce, 1965

Reed, Rex. *Do You Sleep in the Nude?* New York: New American Library, 1963

Reed, Rex. *People Are Crazy Here*. New York: Dell, 1974

Resnick, Sylvia Safran. *Burt Reynolds*. New York: St. Martin's Press, 1983

Reynolds, Debbie, and David Patrick Columbia. *Debbie: My Life*. New York: William Morrow, 1988

Robinson, Edward G., with Leonard Spigelgass. *All My Yesterdays*. New York: Hawthorn, 1973

Rodgers, Richard. *Musical Stages*. New York: Random House, 1975

Rooney, Mickey. *I.E.* New York: G.P. Putnam's Sons, 1965

Rosenberg, Bernard, and Harry Silverstein. *The Real Tinsel*. New York: Macmillan, 1970
Ross, Lillian, and Helen Ross. *The Player*. New York: Simon and Schuster, 1961
Russell, Jane. *Jane Russell: My Paths & My Detours*. New York: Franklin Watts, 1985
Russell, Rosalind, and Chris Chase. *Life is a Banquet*. New York: Random House, 1977
Samuels, Charles. *The King*. New York: Coward-McCann, 1961
Schary, Dore. *Heyday*. Boston: Little, Brown, 1979
Server, Lee. *Screenwriter*. Pittstown, N.J.: Main Street Press, 1987
Silke, James R. *Here's Looking at You, Kid*. Boston: Little, Brown, 1976
Silvers, Phil, with Robert Saffron. *This Laugh is on Me*. Englewood Cliffs, N.J.: Prentice-Hall, 1973
Smith, Ella. *Starring Miss Barbara Stanwyck*. New York: Crown, 1974
Stack, Robert, with Mark Evans. *Straight Shooting*. New York: Macmillan, 1980
Steen, Mike. *Hollywood Speaks*. New York: G.P. Putnam's Sons, 1974
Streeback, Nancy. *The Films of Burt Reynolds*. Secaucus, N.J.: Citadel Press, 1982
Swanson, Gloria. *Swanson on Swanson*. New York: Pocket Books, 1980
Swindell, Larry. *Charles Boyer: The Reluctant Lover*. Garden City, N.Y.: Doubleday, 1983
Sylbert, Paul. *Final Cut*. New York: Seabury Press, 1974
Taraborrelli, J. Randy. *Cher*. New York: St. Martin's Press, 1986
Taraborrelli, J. Randy. *Diana*. New York: Doubleday, 1985
Taylor, Elizabeth. *Elizabeth Taylor*. New York: Harper & Row, 1964
Thomas, Bob. *Selznick*. New York: Doubleday, 1970
Thomas, Tony. *Harry Warren and the Hollywood Musical*. Secaucus, N.J.: Citadel Press, 1975
Thomas, Tony. *The Films of Gene Kelly*. Secaucus, N.J.: Citadel Press, 1974
Thompson, David, and Ian Christie, eds. *Scorsese on Scorsese*. London-Boston: Faber and Faber, 1989
Tierney, Gene, with Mickey Herskowitz. *Self-Portrait*. New York: Wyden Books, 1979
Truffaut, François. *Hitchcock*. New York: Simon and Schuster, 1983
Turner, Lana. *Lana: The Lady, The Legend, The Truth*. New York: E.P. Dutton, 1982
Vallee, Rudy, and Gil McKean. *My Time is Your Time*. New York: Ivan Obolensky, 1962
Vidor, King. *A Tree is a Tree*. New York: Harcourt, Brace, 1952
Von Sternberg, Josef. *Fun in a Chinese Laundry*. New York Macmillan, 1965
Wagner, Walter. *You Must Remember This*. New York: G.P. Putman's Sons, 1975
Wallis, Hal, and Charles Higham. *Starmaker*. New York: Macmillan, 1980
Warner, Jack L., with Dean Jennings. *My First Hundred Years in Hollywood*. New York: Random House, 1964
Warren, Doug. *Betty Grable: The Reluctant Movie Queen*. New York: St. Martin's Press, 1981
Wayne, Jane Ellen. *Stanwyck*. Toronto-New York: PaperJacks, 1987
West, Mae. *Goodness Had Nothing to Do with It*. New York: McFadden, 1970
Westmore, Frank, and Muriel Davidson. *The Westmores of Hollywood*. Philadelphia: Lippincott, 1976
Whitney, Steven. *Charles Bronson, Superstar*. New York: Dell, 1975
Wilk, Max. *They're Playing Our Song*. New York: Atheneum, 1973
Winters, Shelley. *Shelley, Also Known as Shirley*. New York: William Morrow, 1980
Winters, Shelley. *Shelley II: The Middle of My Century*. New York: Simon and Schuster, 1989
Wiseman, Thomas. *7 Deadly Sins of Hollywood*. London: Oldbourne Press, 1957
Woodward, Bob. *Wired*. New York: Pocket Books, 1985

Periodicals

After Dark
American Classic Screen
American Film
Aquarian, The
Asbury Park Press, The
Audience

Bijou

Cable Guide, The
Celebrity

Chicago Sun-Times
Christian Science Monitor, The
Cineaste
Cinema
Cinemacabre
Classic Images

Detroit Free Press
Drama-Logue

Exposure

Fame
Film Comment
Film Fan Monthly
Filmfax
Film Heritage
Filmograph
Films in Review
Focus on Film

Globe

Hollywood Reporter, The
Hollywood Studio Magazine
Horizons

Interview

Ladies' Home Journal
Los Angeles
Los Angeles Herald Examiner, The
Los Angeles Times

M
Manhattan, inc.
McCall's
Memories
Miami Herald, The
Modern Screen
Movie
Movie Collector's World
Movie Digest
Movieline

Newark Star-Ledger
Newsday
Newsweek
New York
New York Daily News

New York Herald Tribune
New York Journal-American
New York Morning Telegraph
New York Post
New York Sunday News
New York Times
New York World Journal Tribune

Parade
Paterson News, The
People
Photoplay
Playboy
Premiere

Quirk's Reviews

San Francisco Examiner
Saturday Evening Post
Screen Facts
Screen Stories
Show
Sight and Sound
Silver Screen
Soho Weekly News, The
Starlog
Sunday Compass, The
Sunday Star-Ledger, The

TV Guide

Us
USA Weekend

Vanity Fair
Viva

West Side TV Shopper
Women's Wear Daily

Television

Cinema Thirteen
Hollywood: The Golden Years

Pat Sajak Show, The
Tonight Show Starring Johnny Carson, The